A PROBLEM
OF EVIDENCE

Also by Joseph Bosco

Blood Will Tell
The Boys Who Would Be Cubs

A PROBLEM OF EVIDENCE

HOW THE PROSECUTION FREED O. J. SIMPSON

JOSEPH BOSCO

WILLIAM MORROW AND COMPANY, INC.

NEW YORK

Portions of this book appeared in different form in *Penthouse* magazine: "Notes from Camp OJ" in May 1995, and "Emperor Ito's New Clothes" in May 1996.

It is the policy of William Morrow and Company, Inc., and its imprints and affiliates, recognizing the importance of preserving what has been written, to print the books we publish on acid-free paper, and we exert our best efforts to that end.

Library of Congress Cataloging-in-Publication Data

Bosco, Joseph.
   A problem of evidence : how the prosecution freed O. J. Simpson /
by Joseph Bosco.
     p. cm.
   ISBN 0-688-14413-6
   1. Simpson, O. J., 1947– —Trials, litigation, etc. 2. Trials
(Murder)—California—Los Angeles. 3. Criminal investigation—
California—History. 4. Evidence, Criminal—California—History.
I. Title.
KF224.S485B67 1996
345.73'02523'0979494—dc20
[347.3052523'0979494]   96-24102
                                                      CIP

Printed in the United States of America

First Edition

2 3 4 5 6 7 8 9 10

BOOK DESIGN BY MM DESIGN 2000, INC.

This work is dedicated
in memorial to
Robin Clark
and in life and friendship to
Dominick Dunne, Joe McGinniss,
and
David Sheffield

CONTENTS

AUTHOR'S NOTE

W HEN YOU SPEND sixteen months in close quarters with a group of folks, you tend to dispense with last names after a while, and eventually it becomes habit. Consequently, in the pages to follow, if I sometimes refer to people as "Marcia," "Johnnie," "Bob," "Barry," "Chris," etc., it is in no way a sign of disrespect for that individual.

Throughout the work, whenever possible, I used my notes taken in court as opposed to the official transcript—that is what the jurors had to work from, their handwritten notes.

Also, the Simpson case being what it is, there are a lot of folks who will talk candidly only under the rule of confidentiality. Whenever it was journalistically sound, I honored such requests. And will forever do so.

AN INTRODUCTION

V INCENT BUGLIOSI IS so spitting mad at the verdicts in the Simpson trial he wrote a whole book by *himself*! He called it *Outrage*. No ghostwriter necessary for this one. The vitriol and righteous indignation poured forth with bountiful vengeance. Of course, according to Mr. Bugliosi, everyone involved with the case was double-digit IQ stupid— in particular the jurors—or, on the rarest of occasions, certainly not as smart as he was. An amazing notion, even for the self-absorbed Vincent Bugliosi, especially when you consider the fact that *he did not spend a single day inside that courtroom*. Mr. Prosecutor of the Century has written a raving one-note diatribe about stuff *he watched on television*. Yes, it is an outrage.

Me, I'm double-damn spitting mad, and *I sat in that courtroom every day for sixteen months*. Luck and fate put me in one of the handful of permanent seats at the Simpson trial. I can't match IQs with Mr. Bugliosi. And I haven't tried 106 felony cases. I'm just a guy who for the last few years has been writing extensively about murder, law enforcement, and the criminal justice system. I'm not a lawyer. I can't truly even accept the acknowledgment given to me as a true-crime writer, since I have in the past and will in the future write across a wide range of book-length journalism.

So what am I and why am I so spitting mad? First, I am, in this instance, Everyman. You could not be in that courtroom. But I, as *Everyman*, could. And if I can succeed in sometimes bringing you and others like you *inside* that courtroom, inside the O. J. Simpson case, with me, listening and watching in full dimension, then perhaps by the time we get to the end you will understand why I'm so mad at the likes of Vincent Bugliosi and—ironically for Vince—Marcia Clark (they truly are cut from the same cloth, as much as he is loath to breathe such a thought since she had the audacity to *lose*).

So what you have here is *Everyman* with an attitude. You are going to get "snapshots" of the crime, the trial, the event that are *mine*. And what I think about what I saw and heard is probably contrary to everything else you have read on the Simpson murder case, or come to conclude yourself. You are also going to meet and hear from some people you probably haven't heard much about before.

There is almost nothing in this book that can be considered politically correct under the prevailing "wisdom" on the case. At its essence, this was a messy, ugly, *nasty* crime, an aberration. Then, almost by definition, the people, events, and themes of the crime were aberrant. There are, as you will see but probably not like, very few good guys and gals at the center of this story. I will call the shots as I see them.

❖

WITH THE IRREVERSIBLE results of the Simpson trial there came a great rage within the belly of an overwhelming majority of the American population. It is a phenomenon that has been called "white rioting"—regular, upstanding white folks screaming about the lack of justice in America. It was a racial division that the civil rights movement of decades past teased us into believing was bygone history. There is, however, a significant minority of this nation that is outraged at the majority's outrage, the magnitude of which is unprecedented.

With Orenthal James Simpson being the most famous American since Aaron Burr to stand trial for murder, I suppose it should not have come as a surprise that the event became more an indictment of who we are as a society than it was a search for the truth of who butchered Nicole Brown Simpson and Ronald Goldman. But it is a very sad fact nonetheless.

We knew that racism as an individual evil had not been eradicated from all hearts and souls within the Republic, but institutionalized, ethnocentric, popularly sanctioned racism? Surely such ugly baggage was a thing gladly killed or at least dying. But it is not. And shame on us. All of us.

Black-white racism is the single most indelible undercurrent of the case. It is a fact that a majority of African Americans believe it is not only *possible* but it is *probable* that rogue elements of the criminal justice system were involved in a "framed" lynching of O. J. Simpson; it is also a fact that a majority of white Americans wanted O.J. not only to be found guilty but to be humiliated in the process.

Nowhere was this razor-sharp demarcation more visible than among the press corps covering the case. Almost without exception, the white journalists and commentators, from the getty-up, rushed to judgment, declaring the man's guilt even before the first piece of evidence was presented to the jury. Conversely, again almost without exception, the black journalists and commentators declared him most likely innocent *and* a victim of police misconduct of criminal proportions.

And why not? It is a simple matter of "life experience" according to race. It is a routine fact of African-American life that sooner of later a black male, no matter where he stands in the social order, by virtue of the color of his skin, is going to be hassled, harassed, or worse by a law enforcement officer. But it is an act of faith that, the social movements and civil disobedience of the sixties notwithstanding, most white folks today want and need to believe that the police are their legions against the barbarians at the gate, and police should be given even more power in the "battle to retake our streets."

The testimony of Carl Colby, the son of the late William

Colby, former director of the CIA and Nicole Brown Simpson's neighbor on Gretna Green, was a stunner. When the pristine, patrician Colby said he called 911 because the man in front of Nicole's house was of the wrong "description" to be in Brentwood at that hour of the night, but that it was soon "okay, because, it was O.J.," there was a chill that went through the entire courtroom, including the predominantly black jury. It brought instant, if disparate, recognition to each of us.

Now, the source of the almost rabid vehemence with which most white male journalists pronounced the guilt of O.J. may have more to do with the lack of life experience—namely, not only is O.J. black, but he was one of the greatest, most revered "jocks" that ever lived, and he was a fabulously wealthy man married to a movie-star beautiful wife significantly younger than he. There are precious few Caucasian males who will ever experience even a tad of that—especially journalists.

Me? Sometimes I just want to cry because, in my second life, baseball, I know what the example of an O. J. Simpson meant to many young black athletes in inner cities everywhere. No matter the not-guilty verdict, that shining light can be no more.

I also wanted to cry quietly in the courtroom (when I wasn't gaping slack-jawed in stunned incredulity) the day two very talented, very impressive black gentlemen, Johnnie Cochran and Christopher Darden, all too eloquently went at each other, hammer and tongs, over the impact the "n" word would have on the jury.

And I cringed and wanted to fade into the wall when, shortly thereafter, Andrea Ford, the fine reporter for the *Los Angeles Times*, a black woman of uncommon distinction, went face-to-face loudly with Thomas D. Elias, a veteran reporter and columnist for Scripps Howard, a Jewish gentleman proud of his liberalism, over whether the "n" word had a worse impact upon an African American than any of the pejorative terms for a Jew had upon him. Although Andrea with her salty wit won the moment, there were and are no winners in that argument. We all lose just knowing those words and hurts are still with us at the turning of the twenty-first century.

❖

THIS WHITE MALE journalist will confess to a predisposition to empathize with minorities. However, as an experienced crime writer I also plead a keen sympathy for the pain of the victims' family and friends. After all, almost everyone actually arrested in America, who is not just warrantlessly rousted or hassled, *is* guilty. So the outrage that I feel is, of necessity, ambivalent.

I was in that courtroom *every day* for sixteen months. So most of the intellectual baggage I brought with me was leached away through the total immersion process; I am not the same person who started the O. J. Simpson case in the summer of 1994. None of us is. Not the lawyers for both sides, not the judge, not the jury, not the permanent Simpson press corps.

Yet I think I know what I saw in that courtroom; I think I know what I heard; I know what I learned outside the courtroom from the sources that every investigative journalist must have; and I *know* I know what it *felt* like being inside that pressure-cooker of a little room for so very long.

It was amazing to me, each evening, to watch taped moments from the trial on television. It was amazing because, if the world seemed to be talking about a different trial, it was! Inside that room it *was* a different trial. But then everything was different inside that room. I have not seen or felt the like of it in my lifetime; I think I shan't see its match in what's left.

❖

I 'LL 'FESS UP and admit, no bones about it, how exciting it all was, being one of the few at the center of the biggest story going. I'm distrustful of any journalist who bitched about working the Simpson case, and I don't mean the away-from-home-blues and natural groanings of a reporter on the road. They were ensnared by it as much as anyone—no matter the reason they felt the need to deny it.

Yes, it is a glitzy, torrid, sensational story of bloody, evil doings among the rich, famous, and beautiful, but it is also much more. What major element of human misfortune or social conflict has *not* come within the parameters of this story?

Family, marriage, divorce, racism, interracial coupling, domestic violence, sex and sexism, infidelity, drugs, class, the validity of science, freedom of religion (the penitent/clergy privilege took up considerable court time), freedom of the press, crime and punishment, law and order, good cops and bad cops, good law and bad law (*Brady* as opposed to California's *Reciprocal Discovery* of Proposition 115 infamy), the true disparity between the haves and have-nots (so many mothers with young black sons in prison because they couldn't afford the brand of justice Mr. Simpson could), greed, envy, hypocrisy, disloyalty . . .

It was all there. Then, just when one thought there could be nothing left, along would come yet another cancer on the body politic. Along came Rosa Lopez and we would spend more than a week facing the shame of how we treat immigrants in the nation that is home to the Statue of Liberty.

However, since many of the folks who were in Department 103 (Ito's courtroom) every day with me are writing or have written a book on the subject, I am liberated from having to cover broad aspects of the trial that a journalist normally would. (Of course, I lost a lot of my best sources for the same reason: They are writing books!) Here I will endeavor to deal only with those matters I believe will add to the historical and literary record of the last Trial of the Twentieth Century. Primarily, I will deal with the pivotal "facts" of the case, the "facts" that are most in dispute, the facts, and the questions they pose, over which both sides in the gaping schism argue with an alarming disparity. In essence, this work is about understanding why the jury said, "Not Guilty."

Then, perhaps, the outrage, informed by truth and reason, may be more appropriately directed. Perhaps then we can begin the process of instilling a modicum of faith in what is the very essence of the Republic—the *rule of law*—in the minds and souls of citizens of all colors.

❖

BEFORE I REFLECT further upon the Trial of the Century, it is journalistically prudent that I qualify my full-time residency there. I was one of the lucky few chosen from among the many hundreds of journalists who applied and who would have all but killed to be included.

Why Judge Ito chose certain people and organizations for seats, what criteria he used, is known only to him, but what brought me to the trial was my relationship with Dr. Henry Lee, the preeminent forensic scientist in the world today. Over several years of working with Dr. Lee on an extremely complex, landmark "blood case" murder (for my last book, *Blood Will Tell*, Morrow, 1993), I gained invaluable experience in the forensics and strategies of investigating, prosecuting, and defending in such murder cases. Consequently, I was one of the few journalists already up to speed. Fortunately, my agent and an editor or two agreed. So, after a quick, inquisitory trip up to Henry Lee's Connecticut lab in July 1994 from my home in New Orleans, I went west and hoped like almighty hell I'd get a seat.

"You don't see, you don't remember, and it didn't happen. Those are the three things you say and you stick to it."

—MARK FUHRMAN, explaining to a
psychiatrist how cops deal with
Internal Affairs investigations of
police misconduct

A PROLOGUE

WITHIN THE LOS ANGELES District Attorney's Office, there is a procedure in place when a deputy district attorney is needed at a crime scene because of the complexity or peculiarity of any given case: The police are to call a central dispatch phone number. If it's after working hours, the number of the member of the DA's office on call that night is provided. In the early morning hours of June 13, 1994, LAPD Detective Philip Vannatter did not dial that number. Instead, he phoned a private residence, the home of Marcia Clark. The recently single mother of two young children picked up, listened to the details, and with a characteristic expletive and unique yelp-giggle, leaped upon the bare stage where an extravaganza would be played out unlike any the former actress and dancer had ever dreamed about.

1

"ALMOST TOO PERFECT"

THERE'S NOT MUCH that happens within the Los Angeles District Attorney's Office that Lucienne Coleman doesn't know about. She has been a prominent prosecutor and department head for seventeen years.

Ms. Coleman had been very close to Marcia Clark for most of the almost two decades they worked together at the DA's office. They are of the same age, and both began working around the same time. Lucienne and her husband used to go out socially with Marcia and her second ex-husband.

Lucienne and Marcia talked privately within hours of the murders of Nicole Brown Simpson and Ronald Goldman. Marcia was excited, explaining that while the blood hadn't been typed yet, the blood in the Bronco, the blood drops on Nicole's walkway, the drops in O.J.'s foyer, and the glove at Rockingham were "a trail right to O.J.!"

"Jeez, that's almost too perfect," Lucienne Coleman remembers thinking and saying out loud. "Do you think it could be a frame-up?"

At that, Marcia got loud and belligerent, "which was not unusual." Marcia was adamant: "He's guilty as hell. He's a wife beater! He's evil!"

"Oh, I didn't know that," Ms. Coleman said. "If he's a wife beater, then he probably did it."

It would be some days before Lucienne Coleman had reason to ask herself, "How did Marcia know that so soon? That file was over at the City Attorney's Office. Only Fuhrman could have been the source that quickly."

❖

IF YOU KNOW the case well enough to participate on most levels of relatively informed "civilian" debate on the Simpson case, you know that Pat McKenna, a private investigator in West Palm Beach, Florida, is as "inside" the O. J. Simpson murder case as it gets. The lawyer and former marine was a probation officer in Chicago and a public defender in Florida. Before the Simpson case, Pat was best known publicly for his successful private-detective work in the William Kennedy Smith rape case.

Pat McKenna looks, talks, and lives a life that comes damn close to rivaling the great PIs of fiction. If you spend much time with Pat, you can't help thinking that someone should do a TV series based on him. And cast it with an actor who looks a little something like Bruce Willis, but with the earthy, very salty wit, attitude, and talent of a James Garner in *The Rockford Files*.

Within the world of criminal justice, Pat McKenna was already becoming a legend before the Simpson murders. He and his mentor, John McNally, the legendary PI and former New York City cop who collared jewel thief Jack "Murph The Surf" Murphy, were the two private detectives the defense team went to immediately. He would spend the next year and a half living out of a suitcase in West Hollywood.

"I got hired on June fifteenth," Pat McKenna begins, "two days after the murders. I was totally convinced O.J. did it from what I'd seen on TV: He took a late night flight scooting out of town; a bloody ski mask was found on his property; bloody clothes were found in his washing machine. All the bullshit that was out there in the media then. After a while, the way it was covered, the spin that was put on it, it just snowballed anti-O.J."

Pat McKenna would change his mind soon, however. Oh, would he change his mind.

❖

"THE DA WAS *happy* about it," remembers Peter Bozanich, assistant district attorney, as regards Gil Garcetti in the hours and days after the murders.

"If O. J. Simpson killed his wife and this kid," continues Peter Bozanich, who until recently had been head of the elite Special Trials unit and assistant chief of Central Operations, a high totem working out of the downtown Criminal Courts Building, "that's just really an American tragedy and it's something we're not happy to see. But the DA saw it as an opportunity. Which kind of troubled me."

Peter Bozanich is today running the Compton office, a very unpleasant but busy place to be if you're law enforcement in Los Angeles County, because he, like Lucienne Coleman, began to question the ethics and the strategy of their office in the Simpson case, Peter just at a higher level than Lucienne.

"I'll never forget," he goes on. "I was out for lunch one day and I hear O. J. Simpson's wife is dead, and I think, 'Oh, man, O. J. Simpson's wife is dead!' And then I hear, 'O.J.'s *estranged* wife is dead.' Hmm. That kind of puts a different light on it. So it looks like, after a couple of days, a week, whatever it was, that he probably did it. And I ran into the DA and I asked if he understood who O. J. Simpson was. He said, 'Yeah, he's O. J. Simpson the football player.'

"I said, 'No, he's not a football player, this guy blocks out the sun! And if you had the prototypical defendant, somebody you *didn't* want as a defendant, this is *him*. Okay? He's probably the most universally admired man in America.' Politicians, a lotta people hate 'em. Sports figures, a lotta people hate 'em. But O.J. somehow transcended all that stuff.

"So, I said, 'If it's him, don't play it as if he's some Jack-the-Ripper type of murderer. Let it just run its course until the evidence comes in. If he did it, try to explain what he did, and why he did it. But don't use it as a bully pulpit for your domestic violence program.'

"Then, I see Garcetti on CNN. I just went, 'Oh, man, here we go. There's no going back from this.' It was real unfortunate to see. It was the fall of an American hero. I remember telling Gil, and I told Marcia, 'Do *not* call this guy a murderer. Call him the culprit or the perpetrator.'"

After a moment of long thought, the long, tall dapper Mr. Bozanich, who used to be Marcia Clark's direct supervisor, who has known her for many years, leaned forward on his desk and quietly, sadly said, "Marcia told me from the beginning that the case was 'a loser,' but it was 'going to make' her—and it did."

2

THE SPIN

I N THE DA'S OFFICE, in the days just after the murder, during the political process of assigning the case, it was decided that since Marcia Clark had worked the crime scene, already had hands-on participation in the case, and was a member of the Special Trials unit, she might as well stay on the case. This was not good enough to get her first chair, though, not yet. That spot went to Ms. Clark's colleague, and then constant companion, David Conn. But when the high-level decision to "dirty up" O.J. by releasing the tapes of Nicole's 1989 911 call, before O.J. was even charged, went belly up, Conn was removed by District Attorney Gil Garcetti as a sacrificial lamb. Somebody had to take the fallout over the unprecedented dismissal of a grand jury "tainted" by the media coverage of the tape. So Conn went back to Menendez II, Bill Hodgman came aboard O.J., but now Marcia Clark was first chair.

❖

I N WHAT WOULD later become a war of leaks and press-conference spin, it should be noted that the next major attempt at influencing the press and the jury pool also came from the prosecution. Only hours after a June 23, 1994, meeting between District Attorney Gil Garcetti and the city attorney, James Hahn, copies of Mark Fuhrman's 1989 report of the "1985 incident" were "released" under the guise of the Freedom of Information Act.

❖

W HILE RELEASE OF the tape was approved by the DA's Office, it was actually the City Attorney's Office that had physical possession of the original. And it was the City Attorney's Office that happily distributed copies to flocking reporters as if they were trinkets welcoming them to town.

The matter would, in fact, be litigated at length, more than once. Right in the midst of the early, fumbling days of trying to get a three-hundred-plus jury pool sorted out by number and questionnaire—on October 14, during a defense motion for sanctions against the State for news leaks—it was entered into the record by Robert Shapiro that 98 percent of the jury pool had heard the tape.

Hank Goldberg then made his appearance in open court for the prosecution. It was his first take-it-for-the-team assignment. And take it he did, arguing that releasing the 911 tape caused "no jeopardy to [an] ongoing investigation" and no "intentional polluting of the jury pool."

Not seeing a favorable response upon Judge Ito's countenance, Hank literally resorted to "They did it too!" and maintained that the news "coverage has helped the defense, not the prosecution."

Judge Ito looked over at Hahn, the Los Angeles city attorney, and then reminded Hank and the world that a "government agency did release the tape."

Hank quickly stated that there is no "agency relationship" between the District Attorney's Office and the City Attorney's Office.

Soon the city attorney was telling the court that the 911 tape was "public record" and not "directly related to the crime or the investigation," and that the "public had a right to hear" the tape. Hahn also argued that, anyway, there was no negligence because his people had not listened to the tape before releasing it.

Johnnie Cochran jumped up and said, "Judge, what about negligence in *not* listening to the tape? If they're too busy to listen, why should Mr. Simpson suffer?"

Since no one for a moment believed the tape wasn't listened to before being released, that argument was left dangling. When Johnnie sat down, Shapiro told him, "Good job."

Marcia Clark then stepped up to pinch-hit for Hank. None of this was relevant, she said, because there "was no harm done to the defendant."

"Can we say that?" Judge Ito asked Ms. Clark, before he added his statistic into the record, that "92 percent" of the jury pool said they "heard the tape" and that it had "made an impact" on them. Soon Ito shelved the matter, as always postponing as much as he could until he absolutely had to rule on something.

It should be noted that one Donna Jones, a city attorney directly involved with the release of the tapes, is the wife of an LAPD commander.

❖❖

O F COURSE, THE grand-jury dismissal itself, basically unheard of in these parts, or anywhere else with a grand-jury system for that matter, is extremely interesting—the truth about it, that is. What very few folks know is that the District Attorney's Office, in the words of one who was in that grand-jury room, had a "runaway grand jury on its hands"; it would only "*consider* indicting on manslaughter." The grand jury also kept asking troublesome questions about how the suspect could do all that he was supposed to by himself in the short amount of time.

Peter Bozanich tells a story about those grand-jury days: "You remember Jill Shively? She said she saw O.J. in the Bronco driving away from the crime scene. The prosecution said she wouldn't be called because she had sold her story to *Hard Copy*?

"That's not true; that's not what happened. What actually happened was the day that Shively testified before the grand jury and said she saw Simpson there, I was out to dinner with my wife [Pam Ferrero, prosecutor in the Menendez trials] and we came home and there were a couple of messages on the answer machine. There was a lunatic, or what sounded like a lunatic, on the answer machine saying, 'Pam! Pam! You've gotta call me, that bitch, that goddamn bitch!' and everything else. I'm going, 'What the hell is that?' And the message ended, and there was a second message, from the same guy. So I asked my wife, 'Who in the hell is that?' She said, 'Brian Patrick Clarke.' I said, 'Who's that?' She said, 'He was my former brother-in-law.' My wife's ex-husband's sister was married to this guy. This guy is an actor. He's a soap opera actor. He's on television a lot.

"So she gets on the phone and calls Brian, and Brian says, 'Jill is not a jogger'—he had seen her on *Hard Copy*—'she's two hundred pounds. She couldn't find her way to Brentwood. She's a liar. She's a felony probationer. She's got lawsuits going every place and she is not telling the truth. She has sued me; I've sued her, I've recovered . . . ' and blah-blah-blah. This guy Brian is a real good-looking guy, and she's a slob.

"The phone call's over and my wife tells me this. I say, 'Well, I'd better tell Bill [Hodgman].' So I went in the next day and went to Hodgman and Marcia, and I said, 'Your star witness is a piece of shit. You'd better check her out. She's on some felony probation in Santa Monica.'

"They checked her out. And they went to the grand jury that day and said, 'Never mind.' That's when the grand jury apparently went south. So all that stuff about not using her because she sold her story is not true—she did sell her story, but that was an excuse. They just put on a witness who was probably as bad as Gerchas [Mary Ann Gerchas, who Johnnie Cochran promised in his opening statement would testify for the defense that she saw four men running away from the crime scene]. That was the P.R. of this case. It was that kind of thing which I think caused the case to go south early."

After a pause, Peter Bozanich continues on the grand jury. "Terry White told Garcetti, 'You got about eleven to eleven. You're *not* going to get the indictment.'

"Then the grand jury was disbanded. And a couple of days later I ran into Vannatter up on the eighteenth floor [on the smoking 'porch']. It was Friday. I asked him what he was doing there; he said he was filing. I said, 'Filing what?' He said, 'I'm filing O.J.' I said, 'You're *filing* the case?' I was very surprised. So I walked down to Marcia's office, and there she was, filing the case. I was really taken aback.

"I said, 'Why was it filed? It's not as if the guy's going to go anyplace. There's no place he can go. Plus, you probably want him gone. You know, you don't want *him* as a defendant.'

"And Bill said, 'Gil wanted it filed because Shapiro was getting too much TV and he wanted to catch up on the airtime for the weekend.'

"So I know the reasons that the public got for the grand jury being disbanded, and Shively being pulled back, and the case filed when it was—all that stuff was lies. Every bit of it."

❖

O N THE IMPORTANT search and seizure question of O.J. being a suspect at the time Fuhrman jumped the wall, there has been much said and litigated. Even Judge Ito, in a pretrial hearing on the matter, said that Detective Vannatter had displayed a "reckless disregard" for the truth in his testimony and in the affidavits filed on June 13 in order to secure search warrants. Of course, Ito didn't have the political balls to throw out the evidence accruing from the first search warrant at Rockingham.

While few people really believe the cops did not consider Simpson a suspect when they went to Rockingham, perhaps just how official and bold-faced was the lying to get around the Bill of Rights and warrantless searches is enlightening:

There is an Administrative Log kept at Detective Headquarters downtown. In this log there is a notation that at 2:58 A.M., June 13, "O. J. Simpson" was the "suspect" in a "double homicide at 875 South Bundy." This was *hours* before any cops even went to Rockingham. This log was repeatedly asked for by the defense, but it was never turned over. It apparently "got lost."

There was also a draft of a press release that was written within the first two hours of the discovery of the bodies. This draft was never released, but it did contain the statement that "O. J. Simpson" was "under investigation" for the murders.

A fact that has been almost entirely overlooked and unexplained is the presence of an additional police unit, besides the two unmarked cars Vannatter, Lange, Fuhrman, and Phillips traveled in, outside the Rockingham gates before entry was gained. It was a black-and-white occupied by two uniformed LAPD patrolmen.

The four detectives have testified repeatedly that the reason they went to O.J.'s house was to make notification of "next of kin." Four detectives were not too many because Mr. Simpson might need help in dealing with the terrible news they had to deliver. So why the need for the black-and-white? That is something they would routinely do only if there was to be some "door knocking," a canvassing of neighboring houses in the early stages of a criminal investigation. It is also of interest that these two patrolmen, at the Bundy crime scene, had been observed "playing with the bloody Akita" whose barking caused the bodies to be discovered.

Perhaps most telling, however, is that on the afternoon of the thirteenth, only shortly after O.J. had gone downtown and given his statement to Lange and Vannatter, Marcia Clark excitedly told her friend Lucienne Coleman this: After conferring with the two detectives she wanted to "file the case" against O.J. that very day.

Gil Garcetti vetoed it for P.R. reasons.

3

JURY PICKING

I N RETROSPECT, ONE of the outrages about the case started as shock. It was shocking to sit in Department 103 during the long voir dire process in the fall of 1994 and learn that—even with the popularity of *LA Law*, *Matlock*, Court TV, etc., on the tube; Grisham, Turow, etc., at the bookstores and the cineplexes; not to mention high school civics classes—the overwhelming majority of potential jurors had not a clue about some of the most basic concepts of our constitutional liberties and responsibilities: That the accused is innocent until proven guilty; that the burden of proof is on the State alone; and that the accused is guaranteed the right of not testifying with absolutely no prejudice accruing from his silence.

It was scary to see this. However, what was even scarier, and more outrageous, was watching so many well-educated, well-heeled high and white folks of the Republic say or do *anything* to get out of serving on that jury. They were the same type of people who are now self-righteously attacking the citizens on the final Simpson jury.

❖

I T MUST ALWAYS be remembered that Marcia Clark picked that jury personally and even fired the DA's jury consultant because he told her that her theory was flat wrong, that African-American females as a whole do *not* view spousal abuse from the same cultural perspective as do white women.

Of course, Marcia is also the one who said that perhaps the potential jurors should take polygraph tests. This was said at a testy moment way back during those strange days of voir dire. The statement was widely reported at a time when sequestration was still months away. Potential jurors were under instructions to avoid all news of the case, but who's to say that some of Ms. Clark's attitude wasn't responsible for the hostility, defiance, and suspicion that Chris Darden said he saw in the jury panel when he joined the prosecution in the final weeks of voir dire?

❖

T O PROTECT THE identity of the potential jurors, the permanent Simpson press corps had to listen to voir dire in the officially dubbed "Judge Ito Memorial Listening Room"—we even posted a sign—on the twelfth floor of the Criminal Courts Building, in the midst of the thrown-together media maze that was Camp OJ Central. That is, if one wasn't among the pool reporters for that day. Four rotating journalists were allowed each day into the courtroom. At every court break, these reporters would go to the first-floor pool camera and serve as the eyes of their comrades getting only an audio feed of voir dire upstairs as they gathered around a big table. We had a wide view of downtown LA through the plate-glass windows, and we were "protected" by the sheriff's deputy standing in the hall just outside the door.

Only certain colored press passes allowed one to enjoy the serious-silly camaraderie that was the hallmark of the Judge Ito Memorial Listening Room. His Honor even came up and adjudicated the best poster-graffiti that collected on the walls, most of it poking rather barbed fun at his tryst with media stardom.

❖

D R. MARK GOULSTON, a prominent psychiatrist in private practice in Santa Monica and an assistant clinical professor of psychiatry at UCLA, is a neighbor of Gil Garcetti, the DA. While Dr. Goulston has no background in the criminal justice trenches, he has a long-standing reputation as an intuitive, in-sightful analyst.

During a conversation with Garcetti at a time when the prosecution and defense were working on the jury questionnaire, Dr. Goulston remembers saying, "Ask them if they ever changed their mind about the way they felt about someone. And what made them change their mind. That's what you're asking people to do.

"In the first place, if they have never changed their minds about a drunken, abusive dad or mom, they're not going to change their mind about O. J. Simpson. And if they did change their mind, if they changed it for logical reasons, then have a *convincing* case. If they changed it for emotional reasons, have a *compelling* case."

It was this type of counsel that caused Gil Garcetti to ask Dr. Goulston if he would advise the prosecution team from time to time—pro bono, of course. Mark Goulston agreed; he was not immune to the draw of the Simpson case. Garcetti had Marcia Clark and Bill Hodgman meet with Dr. Goulston at length on several occasions in the doctor's office. They were impressed enough to encourage him to send along any and all advice. Before the trial was over, he would send almost four hundred faxes. He would also sit in court at times to get a read on key witnesses and the prosecutors' performances.

Since Marcia had fired their jury consultant, Dr. Goulston

was all the prosecution had as far as professional advice about the what, why, and how of reaching people. If they had followed more of his suggestions, they might have been better served.

❖

THE BONDING OF lawyer and jury begins in voir dire. To one panel of prospective jurors, Johnnie Cochran said, "Don't be mad at us if you're sequestered. We argued against it." He was effortlessly congenial, positive, caring, and effective.

"This case is about human beings," he went on. "You will hear the prosecutors call him the defendant—he is O. J. Simpson; he is part of 'the People.' " Johnnie then nodded toward the prosecution table where sat the folks who represented the People of California.

On that same day in late October 1994, to the same panel of prospective jurors, Marcia Clark made a snide comment about the Simi Valley jury of the first Rodney King trial. This occasioned a mini-hearing upon the defense motion for sanctions against the prosecution for "criticizing" another jury. Judge Ito agreed. The sanction was to give Ms. Clark a warning, then bring the panel of prospective jurors back in and explain to them why they should disregard Marcia's comment.

❖

ON WEDNESDAY, OCTOBER 26, a prospective juror said she'd heard on the news Marcia Clark's remark about jurors lying to get on the panel and that they should have to take polygraph tests.

❖

ONE PROSPECTIVE JUROR, a forty-year-old Hispanic male, made no bones about how he felt. At one point Ito asked him if he was answering questions in such a fashion as to ensure his being dismissed. The man answered, "I am honestly biased toward Mr. Simpson. I believe he is guilty."

❖

THE FIRST TIME a prospective juror indicated that she had seen some of Judge Ito's five-part interview on KCBS-TV, Ito replied, with a straight face, "Well, it's sweeps week."

Soon another prospective juror told Ito that a co-worker had said to him: "Why doesn't the judge restrict himself like he restricts you?" He then said, "Sorry, Judge," when he saw Ito's pained expression.

❖

DURING HIS PERSONAL voir dire session, a fifty-four-year-old white male prospective juror, a retired probation officer with a degree in sociology, said, "O.J. is probably guilty." He was excused for cause.

A seventy-two-year-old white female used the phrase "gone pecan" in assessment of the defendant and actually laughed out loud at Johnnie Cochran's phrase, "cloaked in presumption of innocence."

In excusing her for cause, Judge Ito said, "I'll grant your wish."

❖

ON WEDNESDAY, NOVEMBER 30, after a round of television appearances by Denise Brown, Johnnie Cochran argued in open court that "an orchestrated effort" by the Brown and Goldman families was "impinging on our client's right to a fair trial—she [Denise Brown] is now an advocate."

Marcia Clark, in turn, defended Denise and slammed the defense as hypocrites. She assured the court she had told the families not to talk but that she "can't stop them." Ms. Clark also said that the publicity in the case so far "is a creature of their own making," and that if the defense really was "sincere, they'd be coming in here asking for a gag order!"

Bob Shapiro then took the podium to recite press events from the first week after the murders, reminding the court that DA Gil Garcetti had gone on national TV saying O.J. was guilty, even suggesting he would probably plead some kind of "abuse excuse." Bob reminded the court that Marcia Clark had also gone on TV that first week and said that O. J. Simpson was "the sole murderer."

Only minutes later, the first prospective alternate juror to undergo voir dire for the day, an Asian female, was in the box admitting to the judge that she had seen some television since her last appearance. She said she had seen Denise Brown say, "He did it!"

The juror was immediately bounced for cause, and Johnnie Cochran turned around and smiled broadly to the four media representatives in the courtroom that day.

The third prospective alternate juror that morning also saw Denise Brown's vitriol on TV and was bounced for cause. He was a white male.

The following morning, a twenty-six-year-old Asian male, the first prospective alternate juror of the day, said he heard Ms. Brown on television. "She said he killed her." He was excused for cause.

Then the third prospective alternate of the day, a middle-aged Creole from Mobile, Alabama, said he'd also heard Denise Brown's verdict. He was excused for cause.

Minutes later, a forty-year-old white male admitted he'd

heard Fred Goldman on the radio saying O.J. killed his son. He was excused for cause

❖

POTENTIAL JUROR NUMBER 992 said she didn't believe limo driver Allan Park's testimony during the televised preliminary hearing. She also said she believed the police were improper in their entry into Simpson's estate, and that they had already decided O.J. was their only suspect. She said she believed Fuhrman was "aggravated," that he was "perturbed about him being on trial" instead of O.J.

She was excused for cause.

❖

ONE MORNING MARCIA lost her patience with a long-winded prospective juror, a black male in his thirties: "I have a lot of questions to ask, so please stay with me."

She then asked, "Do you know who Ronald Goldman is?"

The man gave it some thought and answered: "No, I don't know a Ronald Goldman."

He was given a call-back.

❖

AN ELDERLY WHITE male who had served on three criminal juries, one as the foreman, when asked if the defendant should be required to "prove his innocence," promptly replied, "Definitely."

Another man, when asked, "What must Mr. Simpson do in this case," answered, "He must prove himself innocent."

❖

EVERYONE HAD A good laugh when Bill Hodgman asked before an assembled panel of prospective jurors, "Who has been to the Supreme Court Building in Washington D.C.?" and the only people in the courtroom to raise their hands were Judge Ito, Bob Shapiro, O.J., and me.

❖

PERHAPS THE MOST attractive juror never got her moment of stardom; she was one of the two alternates still sitting when the trial ended. Some of us in the press called her "Goldilocks" for her very long, beautifully cascading blond hair.

I remember the day, almost eleven months before the verdict when she sat through her individual voir dire, alone in the jury box with the lawyers, Judge Ito, and the four rotating members of the media in an otherwise empty Department 103. She was twenty-three when the trial began. That day she said she had a dog, a Doberman named Villain.

Judge Ito perked up and said, "Clever name for a Doberman." He told her he named his Dobie.

It took some beats before Judge Ito had to explain—to almost everybody—that the name came from the old TV show *Dobie Gillis*.

❖

IF FOR NO other reason, the Simpson case was important because, surely, at least some few hundred out of the thirty million or so Americans who watched the trial every day on television learned something about one of the most basic ele-

ments of a democracy—its criminal justice system. And that's a
start.

I hope some of them learned this: Under an advocacy system
a criminal trial is *not* about the search for absolute truth. Only
in a totalitarian torture system can absolute truth be the goal.
In this country, we love liberty so much we make it very hard
for the State to take it away from any one of us. We demand
that twelve citizens unanimously determine that the State has
proven *in the courtroom* that the *facts* it presents against the
defendant's presumed innocence are material to each element
of the crime and true beyond a reasonable doubt. Getting any
twelve Americans to agree on what time it is can be tricky—
and indeed was in the Simpson case.

But guess what? It happens many times every day in America. It is news when a jury returns a verdict of not guilty; it is
the exception, overwhelmingly. That is why we have more of
our citizens in jail, the vast majority deservedly so, than any
other nation on earth. The system, as developed through eight
hundred years of English common law and now two centuries
under the United States Constitution, works! It does break
down occasionally, but then so does a Mercedes-Benz automobile—one doesn't scrap a 450 SL every time it needs a me-
chanic.

Everyone who is screaming for major design changes in the
American criminal justice system because of the Simpson trial
needs to hang out for a while where it operates routinely—the
local courthouse, the jail, and the police station. Then perhaps
meaningful refinements can be made to a damn good engine a
bit overtaxed by an increasingly complex and fragmented environment it must operate in.

Now, if one is seeking absolute, moral truth, stay away from
our justice system altogether, please. There are any number of
fine religions in the world that will accommodate that compulsion.

4

BUNKER ARROGANCE

BESIDES THE ALREADY stated reasons for Marcia Clark's being on the Simpson case, she had one much more important qualification: She was unelectable. As a twice-divorced female with a quirky life history, she could never run for Garcetti's job. She could get as famous and rich as fate would allow, but she would never be elected District Attorney for the County of Los Angeles.

❖

THERE HAS BEEN much hue and cry about how the prosecution—any prosecution, anywhere—could lose a case with so much evidence, even given that, with the jury that was impaneled, the most the State could have played for was a split, a hung jury.

There are some few delusional folks who have mused that Gil Garcetti wanted to lose the case. Those folks must be smoking their socks. There is nothing in this world Mr. Garcetti wanted or needed more than a win in the Simpson case.

Garcetti's controversial decision to file the case downtown, with its disproportionate number of African Americans in the jury pool, was probably correct and certainly defensible. The Santa Monica Courthouse's already overburdened space wasn't sufficient to handle what became Camp OJ with its small city of media and its immense technical baggage. Plus, if he had filed the case in Santa Monica, even though it is the district the case normally would have gone to, he would have been vulnerable to severe criticism by minority leaders still sensitive from the Simi Valley verdict in the first Rodney King trial. Since high-profile cases are routinely tried downtown, to do otherwise with the Simpson case would have been a direct slap at the black community. For that decision, the Los Angeles District Attorney's Office should take no more brickbats from the plethora of second-guess artists. Logistically and politically, there was no other good choice. (However, it must be noted that when Peter Bozanich asked Bill Hodgman why it wasn't filed in Santa Monica, he candidly answered his old friend, "Nobody even thought about it at the time.")

The real problem lies deeper in the core of the DA's Office: bunker arrogance. It is an arrogance born of the same kind of myopia that plagued the prosecution's investigation and presentation of the case. If one hunkers down only with like-minded souls and shuts off from view all things contrary to why the group went underground to begin with, one develops an intellectual blindness that can be fatal to rational thought.

This Achilles' heel, however, seems to be a *haint* of the office and not of a specific occupant of its master suite. Gil Garcetti is not the first DA to eliminate his political competition by banishing the best trial prosecutors to Torrance or Compton or Beverly Hills. Ira Reiner and Bob Philobosian, Garcetti's direct predecessors, began the process. Consequently, by the time the Simpson case came around, most of the litigators who constituted the elite Special Trials unit were second-string players. If one adds up murder cases tried, Clark and Darden combined don't match the total of any one of a number of old pros and true-life "top guns" in the world's largest, most competitive, most freaky criminal-justice system.

So the false arrogance that compels some folks to surround themselves with mediocrity is there. But what of the arrogance even more stupid than that: We're Los Angeles Fucking County, for christsakes. We're *Dragnet, Adam 12, Mod Squad, T.J. Hooker,* and *S.W.A.T.*! We're supposed to win!

How dumb is that? Well, this is from the folks who've *lost* every high-profile case they've had in more than a decade, starting with the *Twilight Zone* murder case, through McMartin Pre-school, Menendez I, Rodney King, and now O.J.

To truly understand this arrogance we must know something of the history of Los Angeles law enforcement. One of the great ironies of the Trial of the Century was that the FBI tried to ride to the aid of the LAPD and the LA District Attorney's Office. For more than two decades, these giant entities have been in a virtual state of siege warfare. At different times the FBI and the Justice Department have appeared prepared to dismantle or take over the nation's largest crime and corruption factory.

One needs only to read Joe Domanick's highly acclaimed book, *LAPD: To Protect and to Serve,* a twentieth-century history of the Los Angeles Police Department, to wonder why anyone would find it preposterous, or just out of the ordinary, for an LAPD officer to plant or manufacture evidence in any kind of case, high profile or misdemeanor nobody.

The Los Angeles Police Department, while often the cinematic model for the world, is always rated at the bottom in national police studies. Its Scientific Investigation Division (SID) isn't even accredited by the lax quasi-official law enforcement professional association in that field. In a study done by the FBI, and reported in a national network TV documentary, the LAPD's crime lab was ranked dead last (Dr. Henry Lee's in Connecticut was first). This was in 1985! Judging from reports inside the department, and from its own public record, it is a certainty that things have only gotten worse. Its budget situation surely hasn't improved.

Pat McKenna, a combat veteran of Vietnam and longtime veteran of high- and low-profile cases over the years, says this about the LAPD's work on the Simpson case: "These stumble-bum motherfuckers never stuck around the crime scene to interview people, eye-witnesses and ear-witnesses—they took off for Rockingham. The lead detectives. This was the most fucked-up way to conduct a homicide investigation as you'll ever see in your life. And, I mean, I hang out with homicide cops. And I do homicide cases all the time. And you know something, this is the worst I've ever seen!"

Peter Bozanich sums it up well, with typical irony: "Everybody has been critical of the police department on this case. I've been working with the LA Police Department for twenty-five years—this is by far the best work they've ever done! This is the *best* they've ever done; this is their *crowning* achievement."

Given that bit of history, one would not think Los Angeles law enforcement a candidate for smug overconfidence. Yet there is some method to this seeming madness: By sheer brute force, they win some 95 percent of felony cases; indeed, they seem to lose only the big ones. It is when presented with a case that has cause to be defended by high-powered defense attorneys with ample resources that the roaring monolith spits, sputters, and chokes itself into defeat.

While it became a self-serving hymn of faith that poor little Marcia and Chris were outmanned by a nefarious gang of silk-stocking guns for hire, the truth is that the Los Angeles District Attorney's Office has some 925 deputy district attorneys with the kind of open-ended financing behind them that is available only to very big government in a cause where the taxpayers are in solid support. While only about a dozen were ever seen in court, some twenty-five deputy DAs worked in some fashion on the Simpson case. They had the logistical support of dozens of investigators and hundreds of police officers; they also had the support of the California Department of Justice and, in this case, the FBI. Also, large private firms donated goods and services to the prosecution effort. It is complete myth that O. J. Simpson outspent the State and therefore bought injustice.

Yes, Mr. Simpson was able to afford a defense that is not available to the vast majority of criminal defendants in America. And so did the defendants in the aforementioned string of high-profile cases the Los Angeles DA's Office has also lost. The problem, here, is really twofold:

The dark-blue monolith of Los Angeles law enforcement cheats and bungles so often on the way to ninety-five convictions out of every hundred defendants it prosecutes, its members can't break the habit even when the case is obviously going to be high-profile. And what happens in high-profile cases? The defendants are represented by counsel who have the talent and resources to put the State's evidence under the bright light of total scrutiny. As it should be. Would any high, white, and well-heeled citizen of the Republic *not* wish for the same if he or a member of his family was charged with a crime?

The other problem also has to do with talent. Since all of the best trial lawyers in the DA's Office are excluded for political reasons from working cases where they will receive too much favorable public attention, the top guns of the Los Angeles criminal-defense bar are almost always going up against second-stringers. Can anyone who really followed the Simpson case say, in total truth, that Marcia Clark and Chris Darden were as accomplished litigators as Johnnie Cochran, Bob Shapiro, or Barry Scheck?

Larry Longo, one of a number of real, seasoned pros in the Los Angeles District Attorney's Office, says he's tried cases with Johnnie, when Cochran was an assistant DA, and against him.

He has beaten Johnnie, one of the few trial lawyers who has. But Longo's a threat, so he's running the Beverly Hills office, sitting "embarrassed" as he "watched the massacre downtown."

"This was a punching bag that punched back!" exclaims Peter Bozanich, one of *the* most experienced and respected prosecutors in the Los Angeles District Attorney's Office.

"These were very good lawyers, very good preparation on the opposing side. I've known Johnnie since the early seventies when he was a young attorney down here in Compton and all the way through the time when he was the assistant DA, and then again when he was a private attorney. I've always found him to be a straight shooter. A *very* good lawyer—I mean, he'd get your dander up in the course of a trial because he did such a good job. But I've always liked him and appreciated him as a defense attorney. I can't think of a single incidence when I had any contact with him, over a period of twenty-five years, that he ever did anything dishonest with me. Plus, he just amuses the heck out of me." Peter laughs. It is the reaction of many who actually get to know Johnnie Cochran.

"I think in the end," Bozanich continues, "the jury found us to be wanting so many times they could no longer trust the evidence. I mean, a three-hour acquittal is not a reasonable-doubt case. It's *'Get this thing out of here!'*

"This was a debacle. It couldn't have gone any worse. Could not have gone any worse. And it still amazes me that the country holds the jury responsible for what I think was a reasonable verdict given what the prosecution looked like. It's real unfortunate to blame minorities . . . but it was a successful P.R. campaign. 'Poor Marcia. Poor Chris.' This was all about P.R. from the beginning." Peter Bozanich shakes his head.

Yes, it was total, humiliating defeat. Not a soul did the prosecution convince enough even to hang the jury—and it must never be overlooked that there were three *non*–African Americans on the jury, two of them white upper-middle-class females, perfect prosecution jurors.

❖

"I SAID TO THEM early on—this is how naive I am about the whole system—'If you really want justice, find another country that has the same democracy and try him there,' " recounts Mark Goulston, the psychiatrist neighbor of Garcetti and the author of *Get Out of Your Own Way: Overcoming Self-Defeating Behavior*, as he looks back at his involvement in the case.

"Because familiarity—there's no way: You're asking people to convict their son! That's what familiarity does. It's almost impossible. Familiarity is just so overpowering. And with O.J., the thing that I noticed is how O.J., I mean, how he's regal. He's regally handsome. And he'd look at the jurors—there would be times when he would push Shapiro aside so that he could look at them. And I'm sure the jurors, like voyeurs, are thinking, 'O.J. is looking at little nothing me!' And that's a powerful affirmation.

"Later, I remember I sent Chris Darden a fax, and he used some of it: What you're really going to have to do is, you're going to have to convince the jury that they don't know O. J. Simpson. 'You don't know the real O. J. Simpson. You think you know him, but let me ask you, how well did you know your dad or grandpa when they died? We think we know people. We really don't know people, even at close range. So don't kid yourselves. How many of you found out that your kids do drugs? Which means you really don't know them. So let's not get rolled away here, because this is more than familiarity, this is idealization. So don't go, Oh, I know O.J., he couldn't have done this. Shit, you don't even know your kids, if they're doing drugs.' "

5

ITO WEPT

THERE IS ANOTHER rather significant source of arrogance for the dark monolith: the highly politicized system of appointing and maintaining judges predisposed to law and order in Los Angeles County, or all of California for that matter. For instance, Superior Court judges in Los Angeles are appointed by the governor for an initial six-year term, after which they must stand for reelection, but as at-large candidates county-wide. There is no district or constituency in this very large county that a nonincumbent can build a base upon and raise enough money to see him through a successful campaign. Of course, with the stranglehold the Republican party has had on California since the end of Jerry Brown and his father, the appointees have mostly come from the ranks of the DA's Office. They are, almost to a person, former prosecutors, the few exceptions being former city attorneys or federal prosecutors. Then, with the at-large reelection system being a formidable barrier, incumbents almost always stand unopposed; a real election for judge is a rare thing in the land that brought us Nixon and Reagan.

❖❖

I WAS AN ITO watcher from the beginning. Oh, I'd swivel my head in O.J.'s direction often enough, as would the rest of the folks who sat in Department 103 (constantly craning to watch O.J.'s every move was the sure sign of a newcomer to the courtroom). Of course, when the jury was in the box, one *had* to watch them, or else have nothing to say to the obligatory TV cameras and reporters at breaks, lunch, or the end of the day.

But, I must confess, from that first day back in the summer of '94, my eyes were drawn most magnetically to that elfin, moonpie face of Judge Lance A. Ito: those eyes of piercing obsidian, that nervous, ready mouth, perpetually on the brink of mirth, mischief, question, tedium, or tantrum, surrounded by a devilish black beard. That is the face I see first and foremost in my mind's eye whenever I reflect, even briefly, upon any of the countless unforgettable moments of the Trial of the Century.

And it is also Ito's voice, not Johnnie's, Marcia's, Bob's, Chris's, or Barry's, that can still bring me up short no matter what, actually prickle my spine, tense my neck and shoulders, knot my stomach, and compel me to relive the moment viscerally whenever I chance to encounter it on some TV news retrospective.

No question about it, I was an unabashed Lance A. Ito fan and watcher—he would watch back!—from the getty-up. Which is why much of what follows disturbs me so. There is also a sense of disloyalty I feel. Thousands of journalists from around the world applied to attend the O. J. Simpson trial, and I was one of but a handful picked by His Honor to have what he himself called a "regular" seat. My daily, permanent seat at the Trial of the Century, seat B-13, His Honor *gave* me. (He personally administered all seating at his trial.) And he didn't know me from Adam! Am I to be an ingrate of the first order and bite that hand? Sadly, yes.

It also troubles me that His Honor has declined to speak with me since the trial. Jerrianne Hayslett, the judge's ever-faithful, tireless keeper of the gate, said he is declining all interview requests, that I should not take it personally. So I won't; I trust he will do the same.

❖

THE HONORABLE LANCE A. ITO came by the opportunity to have himself named Judge of the Trial of the Century honestly—as in being an almost flagrantly archetypal product of the Los Angeles judge mold.

A brilliant legal technician with an affinity for cowboy justice and putting away bad guys, Ito, as a prosecutor in the DA's Office, was known to sit at his desk during slow moments and twirl a loaded revolver, practicing his quick draw. That is, when he wasn't actually riding shotgun with police task forces bursting through dangerous doors in the heavy-artillery battles against gang violence in Los Angeles. Ito headed a special DA's unit working full-time to stem the appalling body count in the war between Bloods and Crips.

His feelings about law and order are indeed deep in his heart and soul. Some say that the time Ito the prosecutor was playing with a gun in his office and fired a round into the ceiling is most telling: On the other side of that ceiling was the public defenders' office.

Donald Wager, a highly respected Los Angeles attorney who has been close to most of the principal players in the Simpson murder case throughout his career, has this to say about Ito's judicial philosophy: "He's married to a cop . . . the cops consider themselves one family. That's everything, I mean, you're in it. That's the best clue you've got as to where he stands."

To this observer, the reports that Judge Ito and his wife, LAPD Captain Peggy York, cried in his chambers after the verdict ends any discussion of exactly where Lance Ito stands ideologically in the criminal justice wars.

So why did the defense team, particularly Johnnie Cochran, who as a trailblazing young black trial lawyer had once been Ito's supervisor at the District Attorney's Office, so readily accept him, specifically expressing for the record that the defense waived any conflict of interest? Because, looking at the shopping list—downtown judges with access to courtrooms on the ninth floor, the security floor—they knew they wouldn't get any better. Ito is as liberal as it gets among Superior Court judges in Los Angeles County, and at least he's a minority.

It was also important to the defense that Ito has a personality that lends itself to giving lawyers wide latitude in trying their cases. Ito, by nature, is a consensus builder—everybody get along to go along. His record is clearly not that of an obstructionist trial court jurist. While Cochran knew—and Bob Shapiro and the others would learn—that Ito was likely to rule against the defense on every major issue, he also knew that Ito would at least let the defense put on its case. Which, in this instance, was far more than a semantic or subtle distinction.

There would be no abuse excuse here. No the-devil-made-me-do-it, I'm sorry, I promise never to do it again. Uh-uh. Here was a classic, in your face, "I didn't do it. Now you prove I did. While I prove I was framed." That's cowboy justice John Wayne or Perry Mason style. Yes, Johnnie Cochran knew exactly what he was getting when he stood and said His Honor would be acceptable to the defense.

He would get to talk his talk to a jury, something Johnnie Cochran does about as well as any man alive.

❖

I T IS PROBLEMATICAL at best when a judge from the California system personally goes after and gets a case he wants to try. While it is one of the better kept secrets of the Simpson trial, according to many, that is precisely what happened here. Lance Ito, using his position as assistant supervising judge, preempted the case from an unhappy Judge Paul Flynn, who had been considered, even by Ito, the best-qualified judge to hear the Simpson murder trial.

"Ito stood up by the sidebar one morning and asked me about the Simpson case," a prominent criminal-defense attorney in Los Angeles remembers. "He said, 'Who do you think's gonna get it?' I said, 'I hear it's Flynn.' He said, 'Me too. And he should get it. He's the best choice.' Then he says, 'I know one thing, I don't want it!' *Right!*"

It was at the last minute, after all this, that Ito allegedly went to his boss and close friend, Supervising Superior Court Judge Cecil J. Mills and said, " 'I want it.' And, just like that, he got it."

There may, however, be more here than meets the eye. Donald Wager says the problem was that Judge Flynn is a member of the Los Angeles Country Club—which didn't admit a black member until 1991. When Wager kidded Ito about grabbing the case because of wanting to be a star, Ito took great umbrage, said he was "forced into" taking it, and would tell Wager "the true story one day." As of this point, that day has not come.

❖

"I TO LOST CONTROL of his courtroom and never got it back, no matter how many faces he'd try on," says a former colleague of His Honor. This opinion was shared by legal talking-heads in Los Angeles and around the nation as the reason the Trial of the Century degenerated into a grossly overlong sideshow aberration of justice on display.

"Maybe he was too nice a person" is how Donald Wager begins his assessment. "And in being too nice, he wanted the public to hear every word that anybody had to say. So that nobody would ever be able to complain he wouldn't let lawyers be heard—that he cut them off, made rash decisions without hearing arguments, all of that stuff. But he let them argue *ad nauseam*. I'm not so sure the camera didn't make that even more important to him. A lot of things seemed to take a long time.

"The problem is," Wager continues, "I don't know if any judge who wound up with that case, and that jury, [wouldn't have been] doomed. And I think the poor man *is* doomed. If he had any appellate ambitions, I'm sure they're doomed now.

"But, you know, he did silly shit. I don't know what he was doing with all that stuff—he should've known to clear the deck. 'Get the goddamn flowers out of here. Get the hourglasses out of here. Let's play ball!' Yet he survived this better than most. And who knows, he ain't done yet. He still could end up on the Court of Appeals. Somebody could feel good about him, 'Hey, let's put him up.' "

To this courtroom observer, Ito was like a substitute teacher who wants to be liked so much he lets the class walk all over him. Then, when he realizes people are making fun *of* him, not laughing *with* him as he so fervently desires, his efforts toward ascendancy come across as petulant, erratic, opportunistically mean-spirited, spiteful braggadocio.

But perhaps the Ito trait that the trial brought out most glaringly to those who were in Department 103 every day was an unseemly, surprising petty paranoia of the Captain Queeg variety. His incessant concern about *everything* that was happening in the unusually well-behaved gallery was astounding. It reached the point that the line "Who ate the strawberries?" from *The Caine Mutiny* was frequently repeated out in the hall during breaks or in media central on the twelfth floor.

Two examples illustrate best how far beyond the pale of priorities Judge Ito went:

The day Ito stopped the Trial of the Century, with a beleaguered, sequestered jury close to the breaking point, over a bag of Skittles candy, demonstrates just how Ionesco-like this legal theater of the absurd got at times. Kimberly Maroe, a Los Angeles television reporter, got the shock of her life one morning when the jury was hastily sent out by the judge and she was publicly summoned into his chambers—"for eating." When she got into his inner sanctum, mortified, he told her to sit down and watch a TV monitor. Soon, from a camera she didn't know existed, she saw a videotaped zoom of her in her seat holding a bag. For some moments, that was all she saw. But when she looked quizzically at the judge, he said, "Wait a second," and then she saw herself casually put a small piece of candy from the bag into her mouth, but then stillness again, and again she looked at Ito who snapped, "You're going to chew, you'll see. In just a second . . . there! See, you chewed!"

Not long thereafter, Ms. Maroe had to watch herself eating candy again, but this time before the whole world! Judge Ito kept a sequestered jury cooling its heels still further while he showed everyone that an important barrier had been breached. That barrier had been his response to this reporter's suggestion that the no-eating ban not include Life Savers or other hard candy as long as one did not chew. "Suck, don't chew" was another much bandied-about quip after His Honor, through Jerrianne Hayslett, had agreed to the compromise. Criminy, we had to do something to keep awake!

But Kimberly chewed. And Ito had it on videotape as proof! Everybody learned what a few of us had already found out. Not only was there a roving TV camera inside a black bubble in the ceiling of the courtroom through which Judge Ito, using a joystick and a second TV monitor under his bench (the other carried the Court TV live feed), kept all of us under personal surveillance, but there were other cameras *and* microphones in similar black bubbles in the ceiling of the ninth-floor hallway outside Department 103. Everything we did, every word we uttered during breaks, was taped and monitored by deputy sheriffs in a hidden room down the hall.

The second incident occurred when two reporters were banished from the courtroom forever because a bored alternate juror decided to amuse herself. She sent Ito a note saying that Kristin Jeannette-Myers, of Court TV fame, and Gale Holland, a reporter for *USA Today*, were talking so much that they were "distracting" her. Without so much as even a question asked, both were immediately banned from the courtroom.

But just before Judge Ito leaped to that measure, he could not resist the opportunity to rub our noses in his limitless power and to scare hell out of us all to boot. Before a scheduled break, His Honor announced that two members of the press would be banned for talking, but without saying who. I know at least six of us who felt our gullets jump into our throats, because all of us had whispered to each other during that very court session. Which ones were going to get the ax and lose their livelihood?

When next we returned to court and the guilty parties received their sentence, there was great relief among the rest of us—but also anger. Kristin and Gale had sat behind me, and I can swear, at least during the session in question, they had barely talked at all!

But since Ito felt he could fib at will to his jury about progress in the case while they were kept idle beyond endurance, one can only assume he felt justified in granting their most trivial wish as long as it did not undercut *his* priorities.

One such priority arose the day he called an unscheduled break, invited all counsel into his chambers, and then proceeded to spend forty-five minutes proudly running and rerunning a tape of the "Dancing Itos" from *The Tonight Show*. A number of the attorneys involved on both sides thought it a bit improper.

The transition of Ito, from fledgling to full-blown superstar, happened fast, right before our eyes. He also became the star-fucker to end all starfuckers: Emperor Ito, as he became known among the press corps, would hold court with the rich and famous in chambers while the lawyers, the press, the world, but most important, a jury near a collective breakdown, twiddled their thumbs. The list was long and impressive, from Larry King's unbelievable obsequiousness to Anita Hill's hard-edged rudeness; from Stephen Bochco's sweet actress wife, Barbara, to a gracious and genuinely curious Barbara Walters, and the stunning, brilliant Diane Sawyer; from a laid-back James Woods to a preachy Richard Dreyfus; from the Chief Justice of the Supreme Court of Peru to Geraldo . . .

And as always, whether it was a comedy routine he wanted to share, or the celebrity-of-the-day getting the full in-chambers Ito treatment, time seemingly of no importance, His Honor would say, "Don't worry about it, *they* can wait, *I'm the Judge.* It's my courtroom."

Yes, it was his show. More's the pity it couldn't have closed out of town.

6

ELEVATORS, GIGGLES, AND A BROKEN NECK

I T IS WIDELY proffered that the Simpson trial was the most open, scrutinized, public trial in American history. But was it? Much like what happened with the Persian Gulf War, what Americans saw in their living rooms was very controlled images. In fact, day by day, week by week, month by month, the First Amendment rights of a free press—and of the people who depend on that press to tell them what's happening—were consistently eroded and trashed. We in the media did nothing to stop this, so hungry were we to hold on to our coveted seats at the Trial of the Century.

While Judge Ito's disparagement of the press may have been just his wry sense of humor, from the day in early autumn 1994 when he publicly declared us jackals—as in, "Let the jackals in"—he endorsed an open season on journalists. The sheriff's deputies who controlled his courtroom took this to heart with glee.

There were sessions that were closed only because the deputies decided to lock us out in the hall. They did this knowing full well that by the time we got somebody to see they were breaking the law, the session would be over and the point moot to journalists with a daily deadline. This is exactly what happened the day of the dramatic first appearance in court of the bloodstained leather glove and blue watch cap during a hearing on pretrial motions, the day that Judge Ito announced he was going into chambers with the lawyers yet again, but "court will remain open for ten minutes while the defendant views the evidence." Surely, here would be one of the most poignant images of the case to that date—O.J. examining those notorious banes of his existence. But the deputy ordered: "Exit the court, quietly!" And everybody meekly obeyed. Except for Joe McGinniss, Dominick Dunne, and yours truly. When Joe tried to remind the deputy of what the judge had just ruled, the deputy got right in Joe's face and barked, "I said, clear the courtroom!"

Being dumber than Joe and Dominick, after first giving ground to the threat of physical force, I elbowed myself back in and, for a fleeting moment, saw what all America had the right to see but never would. Court TV, you see, had to leave the court too.

But even that was topped by a deputy taking Joe McGinniss's notebook out of his hands and reading the opened pages before handing it back without explanation. What better example of the arrogance with which the deputies rubbed our face into the First Amendment as if they had a mandate from on high—which, in fact, they did, from their boss, the judge.

"In chambers" sessions were numerous to the point that the term "star chamber" became a frequent journalistic aside.

There was also the matter of Judge Ito's audio and video kill switches. It can be argued that the more graphic crime-scene photos should not be broadcast across the land, but there is no good argument for denying the closed-circuit feed up to the twelfth-floor press room. The majority of journalists, who seldom got inside the courtroom, were left trying to report on the significance of something they were not allowed to see.

❖❖

THE ARROGANCE OF officers of the court almost reached the point of reckless endangerment. It was at the lunch break, and everybody was out in the hall of the ninth floor of the Criminal Courts Building, between the X-ray security checkpoint and the vending machines, waiting for the exceedingly slow—and often malfunctioning—elevators. About half the folks in the bustling crowd were in a hurry to get work done during the lunch break, the other half in a hurry to get a real lunch.

I found myself directly in front of one of the six elevators when the doors opened. Marcia Clark and Chris Darden were aboard—how they got an elevator that quickly, and obviously going in the wrong direction, is beyond me, except those elevators were quirky as the dickens. As is my custom, I stepped back and let the ladies in our group go first. Cynthia McFadden, the legal correspondent for ABC Television, was just about to cross into the elevator when a ranking uniformed sheriff's officer stopped her with the heel of his hand—like an old-fashioned stiff-arm in football, except this officer kept jabbing it into Cynthia's shoulder and shouting, "No press, no press!"

Many was the time when one of us in the regular Simpson press corps rode the elevator with Marcia, Chris, or any other members of the prosecution team, even Garcetti on occasion. This officer had suddenly decided to reinvent the rules and then to enforce them physically.

But we've got ourselves a problem here. The crowd behind can't see what's going on so it's pressing forward against me, Janet Gilmore of the *Los Angeles Daily News*, and Joe and Dominick. Because of us, Cynthia can't go anywhere, no matter how hard the officer is pushing her back. Then the doors start trying to close.

Standing in the back of this mostly empty elevator is Marcia Clark smirking. Cynthia is frightened of the doors slamming into her. And I'm pissed.

"No press on this elevator!" the uniform is shouting.

"By whose order?" I'm screaming at Marcia. "By whose order, Marcia?"

Marcia doesn't say a word.

Thankfully, those behind us caught on to the fuss and hollering and stepped back. Cynthia was able to pull back just enough for the doors to shut. Cynthia would later tell me that ever since she'd witnessed a serious elevator-door accident in New York, incidents like this terrified her.

But the greatest injury to any of us was that the incident was officially denied by the Sheriff's Office, even after ABC executives back in New York demanded an explanation. "It didn't happen. Period." We were liars, or crazy, was the message, because it did not happen.

And they got away with it.

❖

WITH PRESS BASHING so popular, it is interesting to note that at the other Trial of the Century, the trial of Bruno Hauptmann for the kidnapping and murder of the Charles Lindbergh baby, there were over five hundred reporters—print, radio, and newsreel—in attendance, with the country hanging on their every update or extra edition. Want to know who paid for Hauptmann's defense? William Randolph Hearst, media baron of the first half of the twentieth century, the manipulative, ruthless model for *Citizen Kane*.

To those longing for the good old days of press responsibility and sensitivity, I say, "Thank you, but no!" I'll take today's "manipulation" by the liberal media over then anytime, anywhere.

❖

I'LL NEVER FORGET the night a representative of one of the biggest supermarket tabloids called and sweetly let me know her publication "paid very well for good stories." Luckily I'd already had a scotch or two, because I only cursed and did not scream for the whole apartment building to hear. This was a first for me: Never had a fellow reporter offered me money for a story I was working. I was, in my naïveté, more hurt than anything else. Having spent the past year struggling to stay out of jail *because* of my journalistic ethics—I wouldn't turn my *Blood Will Tell* research tapes over to a Louisiana state court— I could not believe anyone could even think I'd be receptive to such an offer.

Many harsh words were said, even after the instant apology. I stewed for days until I learned that all of the other journalists working elbow to elbow in the print pressroom of Camp OJ Central had, at one time or another, been approached in much the same fashion. But the real kick in the gut came when one reporter added, "And you'd be surprised how many took 'em up on it, too."

❖

GERRY SPENCE OF Wyoming, the winningest criminal-defense attorney in America, has the distinction, in my opinion, of generating the two best lines spoken at Camp OJ. One of them came on his first day there, when he and Robert Shapiro greeted each other warmly inside the court-room. Now, actually touching any of the principals, let alone talking with them, in the courtroom, was absolutely forbid-den. Folks have probably lost limbs for less. So the statu-esque female deputy known as "Big Girl" jumped in and threatened to pull Spence's pass if he didn't immediately cease and sit down.

Bob Shapiro tried to explain, "He's okay. I mean, this is *Gerry Spence*, one of the most celebrated criminal attorneys in America."

Big Girl would have none of it, and barked in both men's faces, "I don't believe that for a minute."

Mr. Spence then drawled, "Suck my dick," and proceeded magisterially to his assigned seat for the day. *And she didn't throw him out!* That made him a hero to us, forget how many cases he'd won.

Spence's other great line was simply "People will always use as much power as they are given."

❖

SOMETHING THAT WAS truly amazing to me was how the residents of Brentwood meekly allowed 250 police officers to keep them inside their houses and off their streets during the visit of the jury to the crime scene and to O.J.'s house. Nor were they allowed to display their personal sentiments regarding the case. A very complex expedition was brought off almost without a hitch, so cowed were the rich and famous by the uncharted phenomenon that was the Simpson murder trial.

However, when the legal-beagle types began calling for Judge Ito to control his court, they didn't mean the gallery or the people of Los Angeles—they meant the *lawyers*. On both sides. Get hold of the proceedings was their point, not the press or the public.

The bullying tactics were not lost on Bob Shapiro, who asked me one day, "Why don't the daily press people report what's going on?"

"They're afraid of losing their seats," I answered.

"You're kidding," he said, incredulous.

I wasn't, not when chewing gum or dozing off was enough to get a grown-up journalist thrown out of the Simpson trial.

❖

"HER GIGGLING IS driving me and that jury crazy," Gerry Spence said. He was referring to what another scribe called Marcia's constant "preening," while noting the ritual mating habit common to a number of species, the "arching and offering of the neck."

"But mainly it's that constant flirting with Johnnie," another reporter said.

"She flirts with all of 'em, the judge and the camera too," added someone else.

With little thought, I offered, "She flirts with the *air!*"

"I like that," Mr. Spence said. "I'm going to use it tonight on TV."

❖

ANOTHER GREAT LINE of the trial was from the mouth of Dale Cochran, the very proper, beautiful, and gracious wife of Johnnie Cochran, after another session of watching her husband being pawed, caressed, and cooed at by Marcia Clark:

"If she doesn't keep her hands off my husband, I'm going to give her the ultimate sanction."

❖

AND CERTAINLY ANOTHER great line was by Dean Uelmen: "Locking the barn door after the Bronco has gotten out."

❖

A S AN AUTHOR I feel some obligation to address the impact book publishers had on the trial—and we must remember, the trial started on September 26, 1994, when the first panel of potential jurors started voir dire, which is when jeopardy attaches, *not* with opening statements in late January. The impact was enormous and unprecedented.

Faye Resnick's book, *Nicole Brown Simpson: The Private Diary of a Life Interrupted,* stopped the trial for two days when Judge Ito panicked, shut down his courtroom in the middle of voir dire, and made Ms. Resnick rich while he huffed and puffed that his jury pool was being tainted by irresponsible publishers. The book also gave the prosecution its case bible: They culled not only almost their entire nonexpert witness list from it but also their "case theory," which was presented at times verbatim in their moving papers and even their opening statement.

In fact, one of Judge Ito's better lines came when he made an impromptu visit to the twelfth-floor pressrooms and was asked his opinion of the prosecution's voluminous, salacious brief on the admissibility of domestic violence evidence at trial. "It reads like Resnick's book," said the judge.

Ms. Resnick's book also gave the defense a potentially rich vein from which to mine reasonable doubt, highlighting the seemingly shady, turbulent life that apparently shadowed Faye and some of her associates. Come to think of it, by writing the book, Ms. Resnick pretty much guaranteed she wouldn't be called as a prosecution witness.

While Sheila Weller's *Raging Heart,* a Brown family organ, and O.J.'s ridiculously self-serving *I Want To Tell You* caused headaches and delays in court, their impact on the trial itself was minimal at best. The ethics of the publishing industry are perhaps worthy of vigorous debate, but the right to write and publish freely is worth dying for and will get no ounce of admonition from this quarter.

It must be noted, however, that even with the Resnick book

debacle, not one potential juror was lost because of it; yet we lost at least six good jury candidates because of Judge Ito's five-part interview with KCBS TV (and of course more than six because of Denise Brown's interviews). While that was a source of sincere chagrin for His Honor, it perhaps proved once again the power of television as opposed to the printed word, which was once so mighty.

❖

IN EARLY DECEMBER Roosevelt Greer was the witness in a hearing on the privilege of clergy not to testify about things said between a penitent and his pastor. During the lunch break, Johnnie Cochran saw a black woman reading the Bible in the cafeteria. "Give me a scripture," he said to her. "I need a good scripture right now."

The woman read from the page she had open, "Oh, Lord, rebuke me not."

Johnnie said, "I'll take that one. Rebuke the prosecution!"

❖

ONE OF THE things I'm invariably asked about the trial is the relationship among "the Authors." While we made a pact not to write about our private doings together, I would be remiss if I didn't at least touch upon an incredible phenomenon I will be forever grateful to have been a part of.

Four book authors were granted "regular" seats at the Trial of the Century: Joe McGinniss, Dominick Dunne, Jeffrey Toobin, and myself. That combination alone is one of the oddest of the many extremes that became the rule, not the exception, of the unprecedented spectacle of the O.J. trial; it is hard to recall another event covered simultaneously by four nationally recognized writers for the purposes of writing a book.

Jeffrey is significantly younger than Joe, Dominick, or me; he has young children at home back east, so he was not able to attend the trial every day the way we did for the duration. A fine mind and an excellent word stylist, Jeffrey is already an important young American writer—would that we could have gotten to know him better as a person.

So from the first day together, Joe, Dominick, and I became known as "the Authors." Because of the super-celebrity status of Mr. Dunne, and Joe's standing in the publishing world, the three of us were noticed, watched, and often hailed in the hallway, the cafeteria, the few surrounding downtown restaurants we could get in and out of in keeping with the ever-changing court lunch schedule, and the streets and avenues around the Los Angeles Criminal Courts Building.

For whatever reason, these two giants of contemporary American publishing chose to invite me warmly in as a full partner in what turned out to be one of the damnedest three musketeer sagas of any similar literary grouping. For longer than some marriages, the three of us met early each morning over coffee in the hallway outside the print pressroom as we waited for the seat badges to be handed out, worked together all day in that tiny, tension-racked courtroom, ate lunch together every day, underwent some very bizarre circumstances, and then checked on each other by phone at night.

For me, it never ceased to be a treat and an education to experience one of the more sociologically revealing and nationally relevant events of our lives with the likes of such men and unique talents as Joe McGinniss and Dominick Dunne. Between them, they have sold more books than any several dozen of us other full-time authors put together; the television miniseries created from their works have been major broadcast events. For good reason, I will say. Each has a style and persona as different as day is from night, but each is a genius at that style, that persona.

Joe is as good a reporter—almost a recorder—of fluid, live events as it gets. His ability to observe and take accurate notes of what he sees and hears is uncanny. In the rush of a big moment, Joe could be counted on to have taken notes to rival Ms. Janet Moxham, one of the court stenographers. I, and any number of others, came to rely on Joe's getting it right. But as great a skill as that is, Joe's talent is his almost immediate insight, his ability to comprehend the *meaning* of what happened and its place in past and future happenings of the larger event. He is, of course, a master wordsmith, responsible for as clean and revelatory prose as there is in our times.

It is unfortunate that Joe's career has been so racked with negative controversy, because this much I know: If Joe ever publicly told his side of things, the controversy would soon evaporate. But Joe chooses to look only forward in his writing, and will not allow his friends to write it for him.

To me, Joe McGinniss, the man and journalist, more than passes muster at the highest bar. He is a friend. He is a rock. In good times and in bad. Joe McGinniss is there; and you want him there. (And that's the name of that tune, Ms. Janet Malcolm.)

While the Authors managed to be present at most of the stories within the story that will be the stuff of working media folklore for some time, those kinds of stories may be the better for never being written down; let them grow and ripen in the oral tradition. But I will tell a couple of anecdotes.

The first one only because it's never been told, one of the very, very few "crimes" of the Trial of the Century never reported on. The second one because it has been reported on extensively but seldom accurately.

Back in the winter of '95, during the early days of the prosecution's case in chief, I was living in an apartment in Los Feliz, one of LA's more quaintly pleasant neighborhoods. Joe was living in the InterContinental Hotel—yes, where the jury was se-

questered. We knew it almost from the start, as did most of the
legitimate Simpson press corps, which to their credit never reported or abused the knowledge.

Now Joe hated living downtown, and who can blame him?
After eight o'clock it's a ghost town. Yet during happy hours
some of the watering holes and restaurants do a lively, fun business. One February evening, fairly well into the evening actually, one of those happy hours when suddenly, lo and behold,
it's nigh on midnight, Joe and I were making our exit out of a
place called Steppes, a neat, trendy bistro on the first floor of a
gleaming bank skyscraper with this plazalike space in the middle
that had walkways and sculptures and planters and such. And
it's those planters that did it. They were full of azaleas, a flower
fixed in the heart and gut of anyone from deepest Dixie. I had
been in Los Angeles six months and I was homesick for New
Orleans and the Mississippi Gulf Coast. And Joe knew this.

So I'd stopped in our journey out to the street, admiring and
clucking over these azaleas, all in their own individual pots inside this gigantic cement planter. I believe I made some remark
about how one of those azalea plants would look nice back at
my apartment.

"Take one, please," Joe said, as if we were in his backyard.

"You know," I said. "I think I might do just that."

"Absolutely." Joe was very positive about this.

"You really reckon I should?" I asked, looking around sur-
reptitiously.

"That's what they're there for. Why else would they have
them all potted up to go like that?" Joe answered, a sop to my
scotch-rocks reasoning of the moment.

"For true? Hell, yes, b'lieve I will." So we start walking for
the street again except now I'm carrying this potted azalea.
We're pretty close to the exit when we hear someone barking
serious noises behind us. It was an armed female security guard,
and she's acting very much like a real cop apprehending a real

criminal. I'm steadily explaining that I was just borrowing it like I thought it was meant for, that I wouldn't steal anything, that in fact I was liberating it by giving it a wanted home.

I swear, she started radioing for backup. I was stunned. Of course, Joe sized things up immediately and just said, "Put it down. Don't say another word. And walk fast."

"Joe," I remember muttering all the way, "she was gonna arrest me. I mean, she was really gonna arrest me! Can you imagine that? For azaleas!" I then knew for sure that the white-wine, white-fish, brown-rice Southern California establishment took its law and order the way its ultra-conformist individuals took their cholesterol and testosterone levels, not to mention their melatonin supply, and that's damn *seriously*.

The second anecdote is the story of how I broke my neck. (The story of a different incident, about how during the early weeks of the trial I broke my collarbone in a barroom brawl in an altercation over racial issues in the case, which was how it was cryptically reported in the national press, will get no further facts added here; that also is a story best left to the process of oral history and its intrinsic revisionism.)

For the summer of '95, Joe had rented the noted composer Leslie Bricusse's house in Beverly Hills so he could have his family with him, since the Trial of the Century was looking like it might go into its second year. Needless to say, it was an incredible house, furnished with literally everything, including two Oscars, and it would host some of the most fun and also most somber moments inside the world of the O. J. Simpson trial.

Not long after we got Joe moved in, one Sunday evening in mid-July, Joe, his lovely wife, Nancy, their two teenage sons, and I had a quiet barbecue around the pool. Great steaks with all the trimmings, and, I swear, only one bottle of wine between us. After the meal, the five of us got in the Jacuzzi, which is immediately adjacent to the pool, separated by a tiled wall.

Soon, Joe and Nancy's fine young sons got into the pool

proper and were horsing around. They called for their dad to join them, and Joe did. Then they were calling for me to come on in, too, and I, not thinking a whit, immediately clambered up on the tile lip and did a dead-man roll headfirst into what turned out to the shallow end of the swimming pool. Perhaps I'd also pushed off a little too much with the balls of my feet. It didn't matter, I had done the single dumbest thing one can do around any body of water, go headfirst where you have never been before; and I was raised around the water—the Gulf of Mexico was my front yard growing up in Ocean Springs, Mississippi. But in a fraction of a second, all that was irrelevant and the top of my head thudded loudly into the cement floor of the pool. What I will always remember is a sick, black dread exploding deep within me. I knew something very bad had happened.

I never lost consciousness, but I was stunned. I know that, almost immediately, Joe and Nancy had me secure and were pulling me out of the pool. I remember shivering and then Nancy had a blanket around me. I had a racking headache and my neck was hurting like hell—but I took a quick inventory and apparently all of me was working. There was no feeling of paralysis. I began to relax. Nancy and Joe did not. They wanted to take me to an emergency room, they were insisting on it.

However, with the headache leveling off and the pain in my neck becoming more intense but more localized, it occurred to me that I had once experienced an almost identical set of pains—back in my football days when I jammed my neck in a headfirst spear (which was still legal and actually encouraged in those days), wrenching soft tissue in the neck that hurt like all get-out for a few days but didn't keep me out of a single game.

"I've just wrenched my neck, y'all," I said to Joe and Nancy. They insisted that I go to the hospital. But, to me, it was totally unnecessary and I'd already ruined everybody's evening; I'd better just drive on home, I said.

Absolutely not. No way Nancy and Joe were going to let me drive home. They insisted I sleep there in the poolside guesthouse. To this I acquiesced. My neck was barking a blue streak, and the thought of lying down wasn't bad at all.

I slept fitfully, awakened by pain with almost every move of my head and neck, but still it was a familiar pain, nothing to worry about.

Early in the morning, with me still functioning at all levels, just in a lot of pain, Joe and Nancy were convinced enough to let me drive home in time to dress and get to the courthouse. Which I did. I was hurting like three kinds of hell but otherwise fine. Dominick, Joe, and I had our usual banter and coffee in the hall, but of course, Joe and now Dominick were saying that I should still go see a doctor. I'm not so sure. Soon we're in court and I work a full day in my seat in the courtroom and the hallway outside—and the neck is about to kill me. Everyone is telling me to go see a doctor.

When court shut down a little before five that afternoon, just to keep my associates happy, I promised to drive myself to a hospital and get it checked out.

St. Joseph's Hospital in Burbank isn't the closest hospital to where I lived in Los Feliz, but it's where I went for my broken collarbone, so why not? I knew the way. I drive across town and into the valley, just past Warner Brothers. I walk into the emergency room and tell a lady behind the desk how I managed to hurt my neck. Her eyes pop, she squeals, and the next thing I know I'm surrounded by doctors, nurses, and technicians, strapped to a long flat board, my head duct-taped down with sandbags on either side of my neck, and I am scared to death by the way these folks are talking and acting! One doctor actually screamed at me, "Haven't ya heard of Christopher Reeve!" Exactly what I needed to hear.

What I remember most, though, was after being wheeled in and out of the X-ray room, the ER doctor leaned over me and said, "It's what I thought. You have a fracture of the C-1 vertebra, and it is unstable."

I've got a broken neck! Soon there was talk of surgery that very night. A lot of commotion. I remember asking someone to please call Judge Ito's office to leave a message explaining that I might be late to court the next day. That person told me I'd be lucky just to walk out of the hospital. Not to worry myself with thoughts of covering the Trial of the Century.

Then, suddenly, with me still taped, strapped, and sandbagged to this board on top of a gurney, everybody left. I was totally alone in this cold, sterile room for the longest time. Just me and fear. I suspect most humans think pretty much the same sort of things at a time like that, so no need to note them here. But, I mean, along the way in life you learn that it does not get much worse than breaking your neck. Of course, I'm quietly lying there imagining the worst.

Then I hear people arguing in the room. Quickly I realize that a neurosurgeon—he turned out to be Dr. Joel White—was reading the riot act to the ER doctor for telling a patient his C-1 break was unstable when he didn't know that for sure.

Dr. White has a very magisterial bearing and he snaps commands—even to patients—and soon I was in a CAT-scan tube. There was a reassuring quality to this new doctor's arrogance. He probably really knew what he was doing. Very few folks in such positions stay there by being *falsely* arrogant.

After spending quite a bit of time looking at film and probing and prodding all parts of me, this hotshot doctor announced that while the C-1 vertebra was indeed "sheared clean through," the break was *not* unstable. That basically I was lottery-winning lucky and not only would I be walking out of the hospital, I would be walking out that night, after he put me in this neck harness.

This is how he explained it to me: The ER doctor was wrong to have said what he did; while the situation was serious, *his* medical opinion was that the break was stable; yes, I likely should have been paralyzed from the chin down, or more likely dead, since the break was above the breathing line; but I was not, as the impact had been so in line with the angle of my spine that the effect of the concussion had been straight and when the bone broke it did not turn or twist in to the spinal cord. It was, in other words, dumb blind luck. I was okay.

I was to return to Dr. White the next afternoon and be fitted into a permanent harness. I fully planned on it, honest. But court was compelling that day and I couldn't bring myself to leave until it was done, too late to go to the doctor's office. So I go home and soon the phone rings. It's Linda, my wife, back in New Orleans, whom I hadn't wanted to worry so hadn't called yet. But the doctor's office had called her because I hadn't shown up for my appointment—she was learning about it for the first time, from a doctor she'd never heard of before.

The next day I got permission from the judge to miss a session without its being marked against my attendance record and got fitted into this hideous contraption that would become my identity for months to come.

Yes, I was very, very lucky, having been very, very stupid.

❖

DOMINICK DUNNE IS a marvel, an absolutely unique individual. He is America's best chronicler of the tragic foibles of the rich, famous, and beautiful; no one understands the world he writes about better than Dominick. Also, no one enjoys it more. Perhaps because his own celebrity life has been so cruelly touched by tragedy, which he has shone through, he has the confidence to enjoy living his dreams without apology or qualification. The next best thing to spending time with Dominick is hearing him tell about his latest time spent with the rich, the famous, the beautiful . . .

Never was there a morning that couldn't be enlivened by Dominick's tale of whom he had dinner with the night before, what happened, and who said what about whom. For this small town Mississippi boy, it was head spinning. I couldn't get enough of it. A storyteller always appreciates an attentive audience. Consequently I was the happy sounding board for many of the morsels America ate up in Dominick's *Vanity Fair* pieces on the trial and the TV talk shows. And for many that were *not* for public dissemination, ever.

Dominick Dunne is one of the most kind, generous, and gentle of souls. No matter the sometimes scathing judgments in his articles, Dominick Dunne the person does not have a mean bone in his body. I am quite blessed to call him friend.

Dominick tells his own stories so well, I won't compete with him here. I will, however, tell a story that Dominick would never tell, because I think folks should know.

When Dominick's son was missing for several days in the Arizona desert in late summer of 1995, the news was withheld. Joe McGinniss, myself, and very few others knew the truth but, at Dominick's request, were not giving information to the press as to his absence from the courthouse. Why? Because that same weekend in August the Simpson press corps was rocked to its core by the death of one of its most beloved members, Robin Clark, killed in an automobile accident.

Dominick did not want his anxiety and grief to interfere with the mourning for Robin. Eventually, the authorities convinced Dominick that it would help the search for his son if they announced the disappearance. Only then, several days after Robin's death, did Dominick oblige. Of course, the good news was that Dominick's son walked out of the desert alive, and for that we all rejoiced.

❖

ONE OF THE things people want to know about the Authors during the trial was what we did with tips and scoops and such that came our way individually. In other words, was there competition and deception among us?

In truth, not even once. We decided early on if we were going to have frank and open discussions about what was happening around us in the biggest story going, which we wanted to do, which we needed to do, then we couldn't really censor ourselves. So we shared. We did have a gentleman's agreement to try to keep track of who came up with what and if it was to be proprietary or not. Over so long a time, I'm sure some minor revelations became murky as to their exact time and source and might get overlapped in one or the other's work, but no thefts were intended. Honest, guys.

❖

THERE WAS A good deal of controversy in the daily mainstream press, both print and electronic, about four book authors getting those coveted "regular" seats. I don't want to open old wounds that I believe have all healed over, but there are just a couple of points that need to be made for the record.

First, Dominick and Jeffrey were given their seats based as much on their magazine employment as on their books-to-be, Dominick for *Vanity Fair*, and Jeffrey for *The New Yorker*. Joe and I were the only freelance writers given seats by Judge Ito, permanent or otherwise. So we were the interlopers; if historians of the established press ever want to revisit this issue, holler at us.

The second matter is the location of the Authors' seats; they were very good seats. This only fueled the controversy. Not only were we getting seats that entire prestigious news organizations weren't, but they were choice seats to boot.

What we were asked not to say then, I can now. Judge Ito

believed that putting a book author next to family members would be preferable to a journalist with the pressures of a daily story to file. That's the skinny of that; Ito rules.

❖

JANUARY 11, 1995, was the first time Bob Shapiro sat to the left of O.J. and Johnnie to his right. The transition of power had been completed. What Bob Shapiro had planned and set in motion months before continued to play out; it had been understood from the moment Johnnie Cochran came aboard that the reins would shift.

It was also the first day all four Authors were in court together. (I had been there since July '94.)

❖

USING A FLASH camera in the courtroom, of course, was strictly forbidden. And rightly so. Flashing cameras would be at least as disruptive as ringing cellular phones or beeping beepers, which the Court routinely confiscated at the first offense. Banishment was the penalty for repeat offenders.

One day Annie Liebowitz was given special dispensation to join the chosen press photographers in the back row of the gallery. As a test, she squeezed off a flash shot; I'd just happened to be stargazing myself, at the renowned photographer.

Ito immediately, harshly demanded to know who the culprit was. When Ms. Liebowitz said she did it, the judge just smiled!

7

TIME...

FOR THE PROSECUTION to try selling damaged goods—in the form of one Mark Fuhrman—to a jury was an act of immoral stupidity. The prosecution would have had a better case to argue by losing the so-called evidence that Fuhrman represented. But aside from this fundamental blunder, the two worst, and totally unnecessary, decisions the prosecution made were to immediately, and forevermore, lock itself into a strict time line, and to stick unbudgingly to a case theory of a lone killer acting without assistance of any kind.

It is common sense that very few watches or clocks of private parties will display exactly the same time at any given moment. Yet blind adherence to such an exact time line, anchored to when a neighbor said he first heard a dog's "plaintive wail," might have cost the State the closest thing to an eyewitness the Simpson case has.

Robert Heidstra was not a witness who came forward of his own whimsy. The wiry, fidgety little man with the heavy French accent was found by the LAPD in the days just following the murders as they canvassed the South Bundy neighborhood. Mr. Heidstra told police that while walking his dog on the easement behind Nicole's condo on the night of the murders he heard the slamming of a metal gate, a loudly barking dog, a young man's voice yelling, "Hey! Hey! Hey!," and then an "older black man's voice" hollering back in harsh, angry words he could not distinguish. Shortly thereafter, he said he saw a "white car or truck, like a Jeep or Bronco," speed out of the alley.

There was only one problem with this otherwise credible witness who seemed to have heard and seen an abbreviated version of what the evidence suggested did in fact occur: He said it was almost 10:40 P.M. when he first heard the gate slamming, the barking, and the voices. That was *five minutes too late* for the prosecution's theory that O.J. *had* to have been done with the murders and gone by 10:35 P.M. So Marcia Clark blew Heidstra off completely, pushing him into the defense camp, which then used him to effectively muddle the time line further.

But why? It is so much easier, and more sensible, to argue to a jury the circumstantial inferences of a *sequence* of events within a given span of time than it is to argue their precise time. Particularly when one's only fairly hard limit is at the back end, 11:45 P.M., when the plane left for Chicago with O. J. Simpson aboard. Before that, everything is flexible, even with the exactness of the 10:03 call made to Paula Barbieri's number from the cell phone that O.J. kept in the Bronco. Jurors, being *Homo sapiens*, understand this species's peculiar problems with *other* folks' version of exactly when something happened.

❖❖

S INCE WE KNOW that many of the jurors had a problem with the prosecution's time line, let's look at what the defense offered the jury toward mitigating what the State chose to prove beyond a reasonable doubt. The State, by law, needed only to prove "opportunity" to commit the crime, not exactly when the crime happened, but it recklessly shot for the moon, and a precise crater on the moon at that.

The defense put on Danny Mandel and Ellen Aaronson. The two were credible witnesses whom the prosecution went after hard, even though they had gone to the police and the DA's Office first with their story. Here were a couple of honest kids with no ax to grind. They might have been mistaken about exactly what time they walked past 875 S. Bundy on the evening of June 12—"10:30 P.M."—returning from a blind-date dinner they'd shared at Mezzaluna, where Nicole's party had eaten only a short while earlier. But because they were attacked so harshly, they were needlessly harmful to the prosecution's all-or-nothing time-line credibility.

Ms. Aaronson testified she called police on June 14 because she was hearing news reports that were "different from what I know."

She even said she saw a couple walking a dog when the police and prosecution finally got around to interviewing her. Her sworn testimony was the same as the statement she gave Vannatter and Lange—with Marcia present—in September. What she and Mandel told the jury they did *not* see at 10:30 P.M. was any bloody paw prints on the sidewalk in front of 875 S. Bundy. Neither did they hear a barking dog, nor see a bloody one.

The defense put on Francesca Harmon, a convention manager for a hotel. She testified she left a dinner party just around the block from Nicole's condo at 10:15 and drove past 875 S. Bundy at 10:20—she was "certain"—the night of the murders and saw and heard nothing.

The defense put on Denise Pilnak, also a credible witness. With her home on the 900 block of S. Bundy, seventy-five yards from Nicole's condo, she testified she was on her front porch with a friend who was leaving after using Ms. Pilnak's computer "between 10:21 and 10:25." She remembered the neighborhood was "absolutely quiet" at that time. The moment her friend left,

Denise Pilnak called her mother; the phone bill documents that phone call being made at 10:25.

It wasn't until "10:33–10:35," when she was in the bathroom, that she heard a dog start barking. Ms. Pilnak said she heard one continuous barking for a very long time.

Ms. Pilnak was acquainted with Pablo Fenjves, the screenwriter who had set the time line in stone for the prosecution by saying without a doubt he heard a dog's "plaintive wail" begin at "10:15." The day after the preliminary hearing in early July, Denise Pilnak talked to Pablo; they disagreed then on the time of the barking. In fact, she had seen Mr. Fenjves the morning before her trial testimony, and they still disagreed, honestly.

But Marcia Clark, spitting venom, attacked the woman. This was no defense groupie; Denise Pilnak was wearing a popular trial lapel pin showing support for the LAPD.

The prosecution also attacked the credibility of Judy Telender, the friend who left Denise Pilnak's house at 10:25. She corroborated Pilnak's testimony and went a bit further. She testified she got into her car and drove right past 875 S. Bundy and saw or heard nothing. After the preliminary hearing, Ms. Telender called the DA's office to say there was no dog barking when she was there. No DA or cop ever called her back.

Marcia Clark went so far as to suggest collusion on the part of these two women, whose profiles would not suggest a tendency to favor the defense of a man accused of two brutal murders. Indeed, both were on record as saying they believed O.J. was guilty.

The defense then put on Robert Heidstra. After a needlessly mean cross-examination by Chris Darden, the jury was left with the implication that soon after the crime Heidstra told someone that "it was O.J." He certainly also gave Chris all he wanted on a "white Jeep or Bronco-like" vehicle speeding away.

He should have been a prosecution witness—and still could have been one in effect, except the more Chris tried to tear away at his credibility, the more he became identified with the defense in the jurors' minds, no matter what he said.

By such tactics with the defense's time-line witnesses, the prosecution only diminished itself. If the State was so sure of its physical case against O.J., why was it so afraid of a few arbitrary minutes? I believe a jury can smell a running-scared lawyer the way our ancestors surely must have once smelled scared edible critters.

❖

"WHY DID THEY attack and belittle and humiliate the ten or twelve people that came forward on Bundy the day following the murder with what they saw and heard?" Pat Mc-Kenna asks rhetorically as he recalls his work investigating the time line.

"They took 'em all into the fold and told 'em all they were honest and truthful and thanked 'em for coming forward *until* they found out it all was 10:40 to 10:45. Then, whenever a witness would come forward on Bundy, they would muscle 'em around, trying to move 'em fifteen minutes backward, or acting disgusted with people like Denise Pilnak, who would say 'But wait, look, here it was different, blah blah blah,' and they'd get pissed off at her. People that were trying to give them honest information, if it didn't fit, if it wouldn't make sense to make O.J. the killer if this information was true, they tried to shove it aside.

"So they go to the wailing-dog theory. I mean, Fenjves's the only guy on the block that *didn't* look at a clock. Everybody else somehow made reference to time they saw."

❖

I N ALL, THE defense put on five solid time-line witnesses, plus the wild card Heidstra, to the State's four: Fenjves, Eva Stein (a neighbor of Nicole's; she testified she also was awakened by a barking dog at 10:15), Mark Storfer (another neighbor; he said he heard a dog barking at 10:20 as he was putting his son to bed), and Steven Schwab (also a neighbor of Nicole's; he testified he started walking his dog at 10:30 and moments thereafter encountered the bloody Akita).

Of course, the prosecution anchored its time line to two other witnesses, Kato Kaelin and the limo driver, Allan Park. With Kato's beginning time (O.J. and he returning from McDonald's "about 9:35") and ending time (hearing the three thumps on the wall "about 10:40") being uniquely beneficial and problematic to both sides, you could say it was six witnesses for the State, six for the defense. A wash. With Heidstra left over to tantalize everybody with what might have been.

By law, all such ties must go to the defendant. So on the element of opportunity to commit the crime, the State, by overreaching the capacity of its evidence, lost another major element of its case.

❖

W HAT ABOUT THE theory of one killer acting totally without accomplices? Every day, somewhere in America, talented but unknown prosecutors with complex, multiple-crime scenes and only one forensically identified suspect are making successful arguments to a jury that include some version of the following: "While you may hear evidence suggesting the possibility that this defendant had help from some of his friends, that's not your problem. That's for another jury on another day. Because, if he did, the State's going to put them away too. . . ." Works like snake oil.

The complexity of the crime scene and the post-crime flee-concealment-flee time line begs for accomplices after the fact at the very least, whoever the killer(s) may be. We now know that a number of the jurors had a problem with O.J. doing everything himself in the time allowed. Big mistake to let that happen.

❖

NO MATTER HOW controversial and sensitive the issue is in American society, it must be said that not only was domestic violence as a prosecutorial tool in the Trial of the Century used badly but in the end, as an issue in the murder case, it was also irrelevant. The documented incidents of violence the State chose to present to the jury occurred almost five years previously, plus the method and level of violence were different in the extreme. Never has there been the suggestion that O.J. used an object other than his person in any prior act of violence on a human being. No evidence suggests an escalating factor in the incidents of domestic violence that were documented. Indeed, we know from police reports, a 911 tape, and Kato's statements as an eyewitness that during the 1993 incident at Nicole's Gretna Green house, O.J. tore up some French doors as he ranted and raved about his ex-wife's promiscuity but never came close enough to Nicole, who was talking to a police 911 dispatcher, to touch her. He didn't even attempt to take the phone from her hand or say something mitigating to the dispatcher or hang the phone up.

The evidence further indicates that after the 1989 incident of documented, relatively severe physical abuse, when O.J. pled no contest and was sentenced, physical acts of violence ceased totally. This may have been due, one would think, to O.J.'s agreeing to the nullification of their prenuptial agreement if he ever struck Nicole again, a very expensive consequence. Set against studies of domestic violence that strongly indicate that chronic batterers cannot stop so easily of their own free will, O.J. does not appear to fit the empirical model.

Indeed, that was what Dr. Lenore Walker, who pioneered the legal defense of Battered Wife Syndome—it was she who coined the phrase—was prepared to testify to after some forty hours of interviews with O.J. after his arrest. (Feminists were furious, declaring Dr. Walker a "traitor" for even taking the assignment.) She was not put on the stand once it became obvious to the defense that the State had not been effective with the domestic-violence aspect of their case.

Also, while Ito ruled it inadmissible, there is an interesting letter Nicole wrote to O.J. in March 1993, a little over a year before the murders. In the letter, she pleaded for a reconciliation of their marriage and asked to be let back into his life. Exactly who, then, was obsessed with whom? In the sixteen hours of tapes Kato made with his erstwhile biographer, Marc Eliot, Kato himself speaks often of being confused by the extremely contradictory behavior of Nicole toward her ex-husband. While she enjoyed her newfound freedom, she couldn't reconcile herself to *not* having O.J. in her life intimately and socially.

Whatever. Regardless of the endless debate between the causal ratio of battering to murder, in this case and especially for this jury, it was a nonissue.

The defense need not have bothered to contest the matter. Since the jury didn't buy the causal motive of domestic violence, another major element of the prosecution's case went the way of reasonable doubt. (It must be noted that here again the prosecution chose an increased burden of proof that wasn't necessary: Motive is not an element of the crime—corpus delicti—the State must prove; intent is, and there is a very big difference between the two.)

❖

W HEN THE OUTTAKES of O.J.'s exercise video were played
for the jury, *none* of them caught the bad joke O.J. ad-
libbed on tape about punching a spouse. Not a note was taken.
Not a glance or twitch. Then, when Richard Walsh, the trainer
from the exercise video, took the stand, and the tape was played
again, the jurors still did not react. Only after Chris Darden
came right out and read the reprehensible comment from a transcript of the tape did most of the jurors finally get it—well, at
least a number of them scribbled in their notebooks at that
moment, the only barometer we had to indicate cognition by
the jury.

❖

T HE PROSECUTION SPENT a good deal of time with what were
called demeanor witnesses. These were primarily Brown
family members and friends who testified about O. J. Simpson's
behavior at his daughter's dance recital the afternoon before the
murders, with Kato and Allan Park to fill in some of the blanks.

For the jury, there were a couple of problems right off the
bat. One, and perhaps the most damaging, is the video of O.J.
outside the hall after the recital. Denise Brown and Candace
Garvey could say all they wanted about how sullen and fore-
boding O.J.'s manner was inside the hall, trying to paint word
pictures in the jurors' minds, but with the video, no painting is
necessary.

I don't know what it looked like on the TV screens around
America, but in that little courtroom, on that big screen, what
the jurors saw was the familiar, congenial, nice O.J, smiling,
hugging, and kissing the very people who were coming up to
the stand denouncing him. The jury also saw O.J. grimace in

pain, slightly but unquestionably, when Justin jumps into his arms and wants to be lifted up high. Like it or not, it's there. O.J.'s arthritis is a factor; it is real. How probative it is or is not to culpability is an open debate. But it is a legitimate debate.

Also, the prosecution's demeanor witnesses could testify only to Simpson's manner and visible "state-of-mind" clues several hours before the murders. It is common sense that social demeanor *before* a murder would most likely be less probative than demeanor immediately *after* such violent, messy butcheries as were the murders of Ron and Nicole. There are fewer physiological indices of "prior guilty knowledge" to be controlled before the explosive, aberrant behavior than immediately afterward, when glandular activity should be all but seismic in a nonpsychopathic perpetrator. Of course, if the perp is psychopathic, in the manner of a Jeffrey McDonald, then interpreting demeanor in the normal sense becomes highly dubious from the outset.

Problem number two is having Kato as a witness for the State. No explanation necessary.

❖

SO WHAT DID the jury get from the defense to offset the naturally subjective demeanor testimony of family and friends of Nicole?

Wayne Stanfield, the pilot of American Airlines Flight 688, testified that after a flight attendant came into the cockpit and said O. J. Simpson was aboard, he went into the cabin to meet him. He got his autograph. There was nothing unusual about O.J., he said; O.J. was relaxed and alert. When asked if he had seen a cut or bandage on Simpson's hands, the pilot replied, "My only impression was that his hands were much larger than I expected." He had seen no wound or dressing. A very strong demeanor-and-fact witness for the defense.

Michael Gladden and Michael Norris, two couriers who chatted with O.J. at Los Angeles International Airport before his flight to Chicago, appeared to be solid, objective witnesses to what they saw and heard. Again O.J. signed autographs and made small talk. Neither saw any cuts to O.J.'s hands, but both were similarly impressed by how "big his hands were."

Howard Bingham, a noted sports photographer, whose most recent book is a photographic study of Muhammed Ali, *The Champ*, was also on Flight 688 to Chicago. He had known O.J. professionally for years. "He seemed like the same old O.J.," he told the jury.

Mr. Bingham, incidentally, made such an impression on Judge Ito that the judge requested a signed copy of Bingham's book on Ali, and one for every member of the jury. In exchange, Emperor Ito offered Bingham the privilege of lunching with the judge and the jury! Reportedly, Mr. Bingham was taken aback by the manner and tone of the request but felt obliged to fulfill it. What folks don't realize, however, is that above the twenty or so complimentary copies most authors get by contract, the rest cost money.

Stephen Vallerie, also on Flight 688, testified that O.J. "looked absolutely normal." He said he noticed O.J.'s hands because he was looking for a championship ring. He did not see any injury to Simpson's hands.

❖

"AND OF COURSE we take a captain and we take the stewardesses and we take the passengers that never saw him bleeding, but again the prosecution tries to make fun of all those people," Pat McKenna says. "I thought those people were tremendous witnesses.

"I mean, we traced this guy from the moment he stepped off the plane till he got back on the plane. Then I came back to California. I spoke with all the American Airlines employees. I spoke to everybody. *He is not cut.* He is not cut. And people are paying attention to his hands."

❖

ACCORDING TO DETECTIVE Ron Phillips, who called Simpson in Chicago to notify him of his former wife's murder, O.J.'s first words were, "Oh, my God, Nicole is killed. Oh, my God, she's dead," Phillips testified that Simpson was "very upset."

The prosecution elicited from Phillips testimony that O.J. asked no questions about the circumstances of the murders, the implication being O.J.'s response to such terrible news was inappropriate.

On cross-examination, however, Phillips conceded that O.J. did ask him, "What do you mean, she's been killed?"

Phillips "never had a chance" to answer because, he said, Simpson became so distraught, "repeating himself and talking to himself over and over and over." Most important, under cross-examination, Phillips admitted he would not have given any details of Nicole's death to O.J. even if he had inquired further, "because it was a homicide investigation."

❖

WHEN MARC PARTRIDGE, a Los Angeles attorney who sat next to O.J. on American Airlines Flight 1691 back to LA, told the jury that O.J. was "such a nice man to sign [an autograph] in all his grief," Simpson started crying at the defense table. Now, in the courtroom the jury saw something apart from what the television viewer saw. O.J.'s actions and reactions always appeared so different, amazingly different, in person in that courtroom than when I later saw the day's coverage on television. Why? I don't understand it, and I have no explanation. Perhaps if Marshall McLuhan were still with us, he could shed some light on the transformation that magically occurs from lens of the eye to lens of the camera. In the lens of my eye, O.J. in the courtroom was not disingenuous.

Mr. Partridge told the jury O.J. was very upset and didn't seem to be acting. "No, I thought he was very sincere."

Marcia Clark attacked him mercilessly, so much so that Judge Ito snapped at her: "Counsel, these questions aren't necessary."

I kept writing in my notebook, WHAT A BITCH!, and wondered how many of the jurors were writing something similar in their notebooks, because they too were suddenly scribbling away. How many times throughout the trial had they had the same urge? If you don't like the message, destroy the messenger.

❖

SOME MORE MEMORABLE lines of the Trial of the Century:
Chris Darden: "We have enough evidence to convict Christ."

Lucienne Coleman: "Maybe you should be trying him then."

Dr. Mark Goulston faxed this to Chris Darden at a time when Johnnie's baiting of Chris was at a peak:

"You know, if I could think as fast as Johnnie Cochran talks, I'd be a hell of a lawyer. In fact, if Johnnie Cochran could think as fast as he talks, he'd be a hell of a lawyer."

Chris never used the line.

8

ODDITIES AND SUCH

OR A CASE so publicly investigated and litigated, there remain a large number of significant forensic mysteries and perplexing oddities. Indeed, some go right toward the heart of the case: What really happened in Brentwood that late night of June 12, 1994.

At 10:30 P.M., June 12, 1994, almost two hours before the bodies of Nicole and Ron were discovered, an anonymous female called the LAPD and inquired about a "double homicide on the Westside." There was nothing to report at that time, and a double homicide on the Westside is about as rare as hen's teeth. Indeed, there was only one double homicide in that pricey section of Los Angeles on that night—Ron Goldman and Nicole Brown Simpson. So who the hell made that call at almost precisely the time when the murders are believed to have happened? And why? Could it have been a coincidental prank?

The set of keys that Ron obviously had in his hand when he was confronted by the killer(s)—the bloody keys that are in the crime-scene photos only inches away from the watch cap, the Bundy glove, and the envelope—were given back to Andrea Scott, whose car Ron had borrowed that night, still bloody, the blood untested, according to the prosecution. Through more than one source, I have reason to believe the State *did* type the blood, but then chose to deny it. It would be of some interest to know whose blood that was, or what mixture.

The easy assumption is that the blood would have to be Ron's, an assumption likely to be wrong. If Ron did not use them in any way to defend himself, as the prosecution avows, because there are no corresponding wounds on O.J., then how did they get bloody? If the keys were dropped immediately after he was attacked, as the prosecution says, then, since Ron had no initial wounds with bleeding that could have logically found its way to his fingers all but instantly, the blood would have to come from either O.J. or Nicole, the only other persons bleeding at the crime scene, according to the State. It is difficult to picture a scenario whereby the blood on the keys could be Nicole's; the only other choice would be O.J.'s, but if that were so, the prosecution would have surely used the keys as evidence.

How did Ron Goldman get inside the gate? The mechanism to open the gate from inside Nicole's condo was broken; she had to come down the steps and halfway to the sidewalk to manually let visitors in after they buzzed. But if Nicole came out and let Goldman in, and had walked back to the steps and landing outside her front door where she first started bleeding, then the killer had to have attacked while Ron and Nicole were together. Which means they were simultaneously aware that one or both of them were being assaulted, taking away the element of surprise for the second victim. That "Hey! Hey! Hey!" Mr. Heidstra heard, however, isn't quite the response of someone who sees a companion suddenly descended upon by an attacker with a slashing knife, particularly if the villain soon turns on him.

O.J.'s taped statement to the police about the gate buzzer goes this way:

> *Vannatter: Was she [Nicole] very security-conscious? Did she*
> *keep that house locked up?*
> *Simpson: Very.*
> *Vannatter: The intercom didn't work apparently, right?*
> *Simpson: I thought it worked.*
> *Vannatter: Oh, okay. Does the electronic buzzer work?*
> *Simpson: The electronic buzzer works to let people in.*

Obviously, by this time, Detective Vannatter knew about the problem with the gate-security mechanism, that the intercom worked but the remote gate opener didn't. O.J. apparently did not. Unless, of course, he's lying straight out, but artfully—he didn't fall for the detective's true-false interrogation gambit.

Was Ron Goldman a total accident? Or was he a secondary but still intended victim? There is circumstantial evidence to suggest that O.J. took special notice of Nicole's budding relationship with the younger man. He seemed to be particularly upset that out of the group of young men Nicole would hold court with at Starbucks, Ron was the only one she let drive the Ferrari O.J. had bought her in better times.

There is circumstantial evidence to suggest certain friends were keeping track of Nicole's activities and whereabouts for O.J. It is not hard to imagine that a waiter or bartender could have been told, "There's fifty bucks in it for you if you let me know when Goldman's going over to Nicole's." He or she would not think the tip would entail being party to a murder; hospitality workers in LA are used to being offered rewards for tips on the rich and famous.

Of course, since it's difficult to imagine O.J. planning to slaughter one person with a blade, it is doubly difficult to believe that he planned to butcher two. But if it is true that he killed Nicole with premeditation, and not instant, on-scene premeditation—otherwise, according to the prosecution's case theory, why go over and lie in wait with a knife, wearing attire suited for concealment at night?—then that means he must have lain in wait other nights, working the scenario out. But then why go through with it when Ron is added to the mix? Why not let it be another dry run, and come back again?

No, if O.J. went over to kill Nicole, then he was at least prepared, if not planning, to slice up whoever else showed up—remember, with the broken gate lock, Nicole and Ron almost had to have been together when the attack began. The gate lock makes it difficult to believe the most logical theory, that Ron literally walked in on the murder of Nicole and had to be killed because he was a witness. Surely, if O.J. was planning to kill only Nicole, that tall heavy gate being closed would add to the concealment factor. And just as surely, O.J., if he was the killer, did not have Nicole come out to the gate to let him in before he did the deed dressed as he allegedly was (leaving the gate open in the process). The killer, O.J. or not, almost certainly came by way of the back gate, coming from the alley behind the condo, not out front from well-traveled Bundy.

All of that, however, must fit with the fact that Keith Zlomsowitch, then the manager of Mezzaluna Restaurant, has said that the morning after O.J. had seen Nicole giving him a blowjob on the living-room sofa of her house on Gretna Green, O.J. had not been threatening toward the younger, smaller man. He said O.J. shook his hand and said his beef wasn't with him but rather with Nicole for allowing it to happen where it could be seen, especially with the kids in the house. So O.J. screamed bloody hell at his wife for giving head in a bay window, but was totally civil with the guy involved, even though this conversation wasn't in public, but around Nicole's pool.

"I think that's one of the big reasons why they didn't wanna put Zlomsowitch on," Pat McKenna says. "Because he would've had to say how O.J. shook his hand and said, 'You understand, man, I'm a proud guy, these are my kids.' Meaning, 'Hey, if you're gonna fuck my wife, don't do it with my kids here.' O.J. used to tell me this when he was in jail," Pat says.

Yet O.J. then butchers Nicole and another young man at the mere suggestion of intimacy? You've got to wonder. Of course, inconsistent behavior is not something foreign to the species.

❖

PHIL VANNATTER AND Tom Lange, two of LAPD's most experienced homicide detectives, supposedly took no extemporaneous notes at the crime scenes and during the early days of the investigation. In distinguished careers of more than two decades apiece, neither detective had ever neglected this aspect of basic homicide investigation before. It is also contrary to the norm throughout law enforcement. This reporter, furthermore, has personally never experienced nor heard of a murder investigation wherein the homicide case officer in charge did not make notes of his initial observations at the crime scene.

Pat McKenna's theory about Vannatter and Lange not taking notes, never considering any suspect other than O.J., is this: "You know what happened when they arrived on the scene and said they were taking over? Fuhrman must've made a fucking impassioned speech to these guys. 'Look, I know it's Simpson. Here's what happened in '85. Here's what happened in '89, and blah blah blah.' And they probably said 'Well, jeez, maybe Fuhrman knows.'"

Of course, during the trial much was said about Detective Vannatter leaving downtown headquarters with O. J. Simpson's whole blood sample but, instead of walking a few hundred yards and booking it into evidence at Parker Technical Center, driving twenty-two miles to the Rockingham scene where he says he handed it over to criminalist Dennis Fung. (Barry Scheck's cross-examination of Fung brought out *ad nauseam* that we have to take Vannatter, Fung, and Andrea Mazzola's word that the transfer of the blood vial actually took place; on news video, the gray envelope was *not* in the hands of Fung or Mazzola when they twice brought evidence out to their van before leaving Rockingham.) Such a thing, all agreed, was totally contrary to LAPD's written rules and procedures, to say nothing about simple logic.

Still, even privately, Vannatter's only answer to why, in his twenty-five years as a cop, working many big cases, this was the first time he had ever done anything like this is "I don't know. I just don't know, all right!"

Forget the baloney being peddled by Vannatter's high-visibility apologist, Vincent Bugliosi, that since Vannatter didn't know the reference number to book it under, it would've messed up Dennis Fung's numbering system. If that was reasonable, why has nothing like this ever happened before? Everyone from the police chief on down has said that it was against procedure and precedent.

Why did Mark Fuhrman, when he picked up Kato's shoes while questioning him and searching his room, say the soles "looked similar" to the shoe prints back at Bundy except they "were too small"? He said this about shoe imprints that FBI Special Agent William Bodziak went to extraordinary lengths to identify, imprints that were not represented within the FBI's enormous computerized data bank of worldwide shoe imprints, imprints that were finally traced to a pricey Italian shoemaker who had made only a few hundred pairs of that model, of which three hundred were shipped to America. Nearly every pair was accounted for and traced—none to O.J.

After this worldwide shoe search turned up what the FBI believed was a match, the prosecution showed a pair of the rare Bruno Magli shoes to Denise Brown and asked her if she recognized them as being shoes her sister's husband wore. Conveniently, Denise said yes, but that is as close a link between O. J. Simpson and the Bruno Magli shoe imprints as the State has ever been able to draw.

A second, identical knitted dark-blue watch cap was found inside the Bundy Street residence, but does it mean something? Anything?

Why are there unidentifiable bloody fingerprints on the envelope containing Juditha Brown's glasses that Ron was bringing to Nicole? Even odder, why are there also unidentifiable bloody fingerprints on the glasses *inside* the torn envelope? If O.J. took the time to find out what was inside the envelope, he had the time and reason to notice that he'd dropped one or both of his gloves. It certainly wouldn't have been hard for him to find the glove if indeed it was O.J. who opened the envelope and handled the eyeglasses with his bloody bare fingers; the envelope was found only inches away from the Bundy glove.

Just what in the hell did bang into Kato's air conditioner anyway? Three times. If it was O.J., where is the bruise or cut on him; window air-conditioning units have sharp metal corners and edges. And what did he do, back up and run into it twice more? Again without blemish to his person?

Or did anything really go thump at all? Can Kato be lying about almost everything? But what is he lying about and why? For all we know, the banging could have been a signal from O.J. saying he was back and needed help. But why would he tell the police about the thumps? Nothing about the banging on Kato's wall makes sense, one way or the other.

❖

"I THINK IF O.J. bumped into it the first time," says Pat Mc-Kenna, who has thought at length about the three thumps on the air conditioner, "then I think he's going to know where it is. I don't think he'd be going to bump into it a second time, and then a third time—he's not trying to score from the one-yard line, you know," Pat laughs.

"Who knows what Kato heard?" he continues. "I think there was something that obviously shook the picture. I think it's unrelated to anything to do with Bundy. I think it could have been a number of things. Shirley [Baker, O.J.'s sister] tells me when they stayed in that room, if even a squirrel landed on the air conditioner, from the fence or a tree or something, the wall would shake.

"We did a number of experiments out there. It's important to understand the structure—it was added on to the house, that whole section there. The construction is not what you'd expect. The integrity of that wall is nothing. I mean, if you bump into it, I mean just push it with your hand, you'll shake the shit out of the place.

"There's another thing, too; we never did establish whether Kato had the air conditioner on. I had a billion guys call me that own air-conditioning companies, or work on air conditioners, and they told me, especially with window or wall units, 'It's the condenser. Sometimes it shuts down and when it gears back up it shudders the whole thing.' I mean, it could have been just a mechanical thing in the air-conditioning unit.

"But we always felt whatever it was was unrelated to anything. It just didn't fit in. I mean, according to their theory, he has been able to hide a murder weapon, and bloody clothes, and everything else in the world, and yet he was clumsy enough . . . I mean, I don't know how he had the stealth to hide the shit. Because they've looked all over LA, they had the Boy Scouts, they had everybody with mine detectors, everything was out there, and no one's ever found anything. Yet he was dumb and clumsy enough to bump not once, not twice, but three times into the wall, thereby dropping one glove. And where was this glove, was he cradling it? I guess they're saying he was cradling everything, but dropped the glove.

"If you buy that theory, then it falls flat from there forward, because then he really doesn't have time to get rid of anything. We always felt it was preposterous.

"From the moment we started to think Fuhrman put the glove there, it made all the bumping have nothing to do with nothing. I swear, if Kato never heard a bump, that glove would've been found in the Bronco. Fuhrman never would've taken it from the Bronco, because that's where I think he puts it first.

"He hears about the three thumps, he goes back in. Phillips is on the phone with O.J. in Chicago. Lange is talking to Arnelle. Vannatter is standing there. Fuhrman conveniently deposits Kato with Vannatter at the bar and says, 'Talk to this guy.' Phoom. That's when he goes out—in his own testimony—he then goes outside to start looking around. Fuhrman's gone fifteen to twenty minutes. That's plenty of time to walk out, get the glove out of the Bronco, and carry it up to where the three thumps were. Then, of course, he brings each cop back one at a time to see this amazing discovery."

❖

WHY IS THERE a crucial blood drop on the back gate of the Bundy scene in photographs taken weeks after the murder that does *not* appear in photos taken the morning after the crime? Why does that blood drop have a much more concentrated level of DNA than samples collected the morning of the murders when they were fresh and far less exposed to the elements? Why did this stain have the highest level of EDTA, a blood preservative added to whole-blood samples?

"Photograph may distort but it not lie," Dr. Henry Lee reminds us.

Pat McKenna's thoughts on these blood drops at Bundy are, as always, both interesting and unabashedly dogmatic. "Everybody's saying, 'You guys think Vannater went over and dropped blood next to the shoe prints.' We never said that; all we're saying is we're not sure they did the right collection process of those Bundy drops. These are all degraded here. And this one's a little bit better. Maybe they were all too degraded. Maybe they really were O.J.'s blood, but maybe he dropped it, you know, walking along with a kid's bike or something that he might have fixed three months earlier, it was so degraded. One was even a completely different color. It was brown and so dry they had to use solution to pick it up with the swatch. However, why is some of it real good O.J. and some of it too degraded? In other words, if, according to their theory, it's coming off of his finger, they've all gotta be the same. One can't be all degraded, one can't be good. . . .

"And then you go to the blood on the back gate, which is hysterical to me. I mean, okay, so now you say, 'Wait, if it's O.J.'s blood on the back gate, why is that so good quality?' Of course, it's also got EDTA in it. How come that doesn't match the so-called blood that's dripping from his finger? And since he's gotta open the gate—obviously, one glove he's carrying back to Rockingham, but he must have it somewhere because he doesn't have it on his hand because his hand's cut—but his fingerprints aren't on the gate.

"It just doesn't make sense," Pat McKenna says. "If there's this, then there should be that. I mean, if that was him going out the back gate. . . ."

❖

WHY DOES AN athlete, a real jock, wear dark sweats or a workout suit to a murder, but then also wear dress socks and ugly, weird-looking Italian designer hush-puppy–type dress shoes? Not cool at all. A real athlete would wear gym socks and a tried-and-true pair of sneakers; he wouldn't be able to help himself. A sign of a dweeb "uncool"—that is too much to risk.

Being a former jock of the same age as O.J., I am speaking of that which we understand.

Why does O.J.'s family, those closest to him, such as his mother, Eunice, and his sisters, Carmelita and Shirley, and his brother-in-law, Benny, believe that Ron Shipp was involved in Nicole's murder? When Shipp said to O.J. from the witness stand, "I will not have the blood of Nicole on Ron Shipp," Carmelita told me later out in the hall that she immediately "thought of Macbeth."

❖

T HROW INTO THIS bubbling caldron of sex and lies the fact that a psychiatrist who treated Ron Shipp, and also treated both O.J. and Nicole, has privately said that Shipp had a "fatal attraction" for Nicole.

And that it was Mark Fuhrman who answered the phone at Rockingham when Ron Shipp first heard the news and called O.J.'s at ten o'clock the morning of the thirteenth. That phone call was not logged in on any report, as according to procedure, but we know it happened because of phone records and adroit cross-examination by the defense.

"O.J.'s take on Shipp always was 'Hey, he's a nobody, don't even worry about him,'" remembers Pat McKenna. "'[Shipp] was a hanger-on, he'd bring cops by to try to just be next to me.' O.J. said, 'I treated the guy okay because there are a lot of guys like that. I understand why the guy's just sucking up to me. He wants to be a star.'

"[Shipp's] 'fatal attraction' for Nicole," McKenna continues, "we knew that. That's why he'd be hanging around there, too. But I just can't make the leap that he's the murderer, and O.J. didn't either. A drunk and a liar, yes."

❖

O N THE STAND, Ron Shipp, the former Simpson sycophant, testified that O.J. told him, "I dreamed about killing her, Shipp," when they were alone in the master bedroom upstairs at Rockingham on the evening of the thirteenth. However, certain family members and friends who were there that day note that while something of the sort *was* said to Shipp, it was said by a visitor to the house that day. It was *not* O.J. Was Shipp deliberately lying, or was it that in his intoxicated condition, when someone said to him, "Man, I dreamed O.J. killed her," Shipp just jumbled it all together?

❖

W HAT, IF ANYTHING, should be made of a used pregnancy test found in Nicole's trash? Of course, it was one of the supermarket tabloids on a trash run that found it; the LAPD never considered searching Nicole's garbage or really anything else in or around the Bundy condo, other than the death scene itself. Does it mean anything that the front door to Nicole's black Jeep Cherokee was left ajar only a few feet from the stair banister upon which the still melting Ben & Jerry's ice cream was found? Or that loose change was found on the garage floor by the Jeep?

How is it possible for criminalists with the experience of Greg Matheson, Collin Yamauchi, and Dennis Fung, as well as pathologist Michael Baden to miss seeing a bloodstain the size of a half-dollar on the socks?

While much of the serological evidence was sent directly to either the California Department of Justice's Crime Lab or to Cellmark for processing and testing, the Bundy blood-trail drops, the Rockingham glove, the socks, and O.J.'s reference sample—the most questionable evidentiary elements of the case—were processed by the LAPD SID. What are we to make of that?

❖

For a man compulsively obsessed with his ex-wife, O. J. Simpson had a strange way of displaying it the day of the murders. Here is a man almost fifty years old ringing up three young models—Paula Barbieri, Gretchen Stockdale, and *Playboy* "Playmate of the Month" Traci Adell—in one day in a manner suggesting romance and great sex in the immediate future. These are women the likes of which the rest of us only get to look at in pictures. Then, minutes after a phone call to one of the three swimsuit playthings, this man who has never attacked anyone with a weapon in his life becomes clinically depressed enough over yet another final breakup of his marriage to suddenly carve up his ex and her boy-toy suitor? And then be cool O.J. again only minutes later? We know there are certain mental illnesses that would account for such extreme dissociative thought processes, but they are rare and usually manifest themselves before the subject reaches his mid-thirties.

❖

There is, however, steroid psychosis, a well-documented syndrome occasioning hyper-violent, superhuman, psychotic rage with the assailant having little or no memory of the carnage afterward. O.J. took a lot of cortisone for his arthritis and old football injuries. Cortisone, in its many pharmaceutical forms, is a steroid. Dr. Robert Huizenga, whom Bob Shapiro brought into the case within two days of the murders, and who testified as to O.J.'s physical condition at trial, is an expert in the field of steroid psychosis—he has written a book about its tragic impact on professional athletes—but he wasn't asked a question about it while on the stand, not even by the prosecution. A number of doctors involved with this case or with O.J. prior to the murders privately agree that steroid psychosis presents the most plausible explanation if in fact O.J. is the killer. But no one—not the police, the prosecution, or the defense—wanted to open that door for even a quick look-see. Even when the prosecution was alerted to this explanation of how and why it could be possible for O.J. Simpson to be mentally and physically capable of being the lone butcher of two human beings, they ignored it. Why?

It is understandable that the defense would not bring it up. Yet it was Bob Shapiro's choice that Dr. Huizenga examine and treat O.J. as soon as Bob took over the case on June 15, 1994. Bob not only discarded O.J.'s regular doctor for his arthritic condition, but he also replaced O.J.'s—and Nicole's—regular psychiatrist. If, that early on, things had looked hopeless for a not-guilty verdict, then Shapiro already had the players he needed to go the route of a diminished-capacity defense. And probably a pretty good one, at least sentencing-wise, since steroid psychosis has been so well documented and recognized (on *60 Minutes*, for example) as a medical and forensic phenomenon.

The civil attorneys for the Goldman may have stumbled onto this. They have subpoenaed all of O.J.'s principal doctors from before the murders, and they have subpoenaed Dr. Ron Fischman, a very close friend of O.J.'s who was also featured prominently in the videotape after the dance recital. It has long been alleged by Simpson insiders that Dr. Fischman was O.J.'s supplier of legal prescription drugs in the large quantities he needed or wanted.

9

CONSPIRACIES, GRAND AND OTHERWISE

IN THE COURTROOM and the pressroom, when the subject was whodunit if O.J. didn't, much was heard, derisively, about drug lords, "Colombian neckties," the murky world that Faye Resnick inhabited, spurned lovers, and even enemies of Ron Goldman. However, whenever I found myself in the company of civilians—real folks away from Camp OJ—there was another theory or question that always came up, usually first and quite often to the exclusion of all others: "What about O.J.'s kid, the grown son, Jason? Why wasn't he a suspect? Where was he the night of June twelfth?"

With so many asking, it's obviously a question worth answering—as much as one can, of course. The facts in then twenty-five-year-old Jason Simpson's history are intriguing indeed.

Jason, O.J.'s son from his first marriage, was a heralded high school running back up in the Bay Area with apparently great potential, but he bombed in college ball. O.J. said at the time that his son was more interested in rock 'n' roll and hanging out than playing ball. There are people who wonder if attempting to fill his daddy's cleats was too big a task for Jason. There is little wonder about the fact that O.J. was disappointed with his son, and that Jason knew it.

Also, public statements notwithstanding, the relationship between Jason and Nicole was strained at times.

On December 22, 1992, Jason was arrested and charged with felony assault. While court records indicate that at one point he was charged with assault with a deadly weapon, some probing reveals that Jason most likely punched or kicked his boss, Paul Goldberg, the manager of the Revival Café, after being fired, and that he only "brandished" a cook's knife during the episode. In the end Jason was allowed to plead guilty to disturbing the peace, a misdemeanor, that carried a sentence of two years' probation and ten days' community service. When contacted, Mr. Goldberg adamantly refused to discuss any aspect of the assault.

When Jason's case went to court, O. J. Simpson allowed his son to be represented by a public defender. Yet, the day after the murders of Nicole Brown Simpson and Ronald Goldman, a real top-gun criminal-defense attorney in the African-American community, specializing in death-penalty murder cases, *was retained for Jason by* O.J. Carl Jones confirms without hesitation that he was retained to "protect Jason's interests in the investigation" of the double homicide.

Most recently, Jason pleaded no contest to driving with a suspended license and misdemeanor hit-and-run. That was February 3, 1995; he was placed on three years' probation and fined $700.

It must be noted that the manager of the restaurant where Jason now cooks says the young chef was working at the time of the murders. This seemingly was an iron-clad alibi.

❖

ONCE AND FOR all, perhaps, we can be done with the constant buzzing about Robert Kardashian and the infamous
luggage bag. Millions upon millions of people believe that Kardashian pulled a fast one and skipped away from Rockingham
with that piece of luggage and the bloody clothes and knife.

What I want to know is where were all those folks when
the video showing Robert Kardashian trying to bring the bag
up the driveway of Rockingham in order to leave it was played
in court? The jury saw it. In the video, clearly, Kardashian was
turned back by the very large Los Angeles police officer Don
Thompson, whose orders were to keep everybody and everything
civilian out of the crime scene. Christ, he was trying to return
the bag. It's a video-fact.

But what I really don't understand is why anybody would
believe that a murderer who had successfully secreted bloody
evidence out of Los Angeles and into Chicago would then bring
it back into the spotlight of the media world?

❖

O.J. NEVER TOOK the stand, of course. Other than his official
statement given to Lange and Vannatter on the day after
the murders, everything else O.J. has said about his activities
the night of June 12 has been after the verdicts. It has been for
mass-media public consumption, which can legitimately be
viewed as self-serving and designed for image repair. But what
of the millions of words O.J. said to Pat McKenna, the dyed-in-
the-Irish-wool cynic, who for a year and a half had to keep
grilling his client so that any door the prosecution opened the
defense would be prepared for? It seems to me that such information, as recounted by McKenna from conversations with O.J.,
can be viewed in almost the same light as would any cross-
examination by Marcia Clark, had there been one.

Pat McKenna on the luggage, the limo, and the airport:

"When Park rings the buzzer—this was always the signal from Dale Saint John [the owner of Town and Country limo service and O.J.'s regular driver]—O.J. figures it's Dale at the gate, because that's who's always driving him. What Dale always did is, once he rang the buzzer, he knew he was notifying O.J. I interviewed Dale, and this is what he told us early in the case. God knows what he'd say now, but this was July of '94 when his memory was fresh and not polluted by everything. 'I'd ring the buzzer, that lets O.J. know I'm there, then I'd let myself in the gate,' which anybody can do, it's not a secure compound there. You can just push the button and let yourself in. You can even push that gate open with your hand.

"Then Saint John would drive up and load the clubs and shit in. He'd always load the car. Now, the clubs are down on the little two benches that sit by his front door. There's one bag there, too, the Louis Vuitton bag: it's gonna be checked luggage. What he's still got upstairs is his suit bag and his leather over-the-shoulder thing.

"So O.J.'s assuming Dale's already come in, so he starts to get ready. He comes down—O.J. always said, early on, 'I was waving to the guy.' You know, Park said there was a dark figure going into the house? That's O.J. in a bathrobe!

"O.J. thought it was Dale out there, and he thought the guy heard him, he said, 'Hey, Dale. Come on in.' He went back into the house. O.J. never until the last minute decided what clothes he was going to wear at the golf tournament for Hertz. He is either wearing all black or yellow, you know, because of the Hertz colors. So he was undecided what he was going to wear.

"When he decides on the all-black outfit, he realizes his black golf shoes are in the Bentley. Remember he'd played golf that morning and had driven the Bentley. He goes out to get them and he figures it's Dale—he's still in his robe, he's not even dressed yet. He gets his shoes out of the car and goes back into the house. He puts his shoes—which is actually this so-called 'other bag' that they all thought was missing, which never was 'missing' and they knew it—he puts his shoes and some tees and some balls in that little black bag, which he just throws there. He puts it down on the ground. He doesn't put it in the golf bag yet, because he's going back inside. Then it goes into the trunk of the car.

"Now, when he gets to the airport, Park goes to get the cart from the skycap to put the clubs and shit on. O.J. is now in the trunk. He puts his black leather bag on the trash can. He takes the black bag with his shoes and everything in it and puts it within the golf bag, because it's getting checked. See, the golf bag is within another bag made especially for traveling, the kind that's not just for your clubs—it's a big bag with handles on it. So he just opens it up to drop in the shoes and shit; it doesn't really go inside a golf bag, it goes inside the bag that is *holding* the golf bag. That's what people never understood.

"He wasn't stuffing anything in a trash can like Chris Darden wanted everybody in the world to believe. I went out and interviewed those people. They said, 'Are you crazy? That guy didn't hide anything in the trash can.' I talked to the head of Airport Security, the woman who runs the whole airport, and she said, 'We checked every trash bag, not only in the airport; we went to the dump, we went everywhere.'

"Plus they have all those surveillance cameras from the airport, they've got him all the way through. Why didn't they bring all that out? You know why? O.J. ain't hiding nothing! He's strolling into the airport. And walking onto the plane. We didn't get 'em all. But the security lady told me they had 'em all. They've got him coming through the magnometer, everything, all the way through. It's on the video. He didn't hide anything."

❖

A C. COWLINGS? "A little help from my friends"? Mr. Cowl-
ings would fall on a grenade for his hero and best friend.
I don't believe there are any limits to what A.C. would do for
O.J.

That does not, of course, indicate he did anything unlawful;
Chris Darden admits openly in his book that he could not get
an indictment of Cowlings from the grand jury.

❖

I T IS TIME again to answer one of the most persistent questions
of the Simpson case, one that has an answer but an answer
that no one seems to hear. Or remember. The pundits who were
not in Department 103 every day (particularly that loudmouth
Vincent Bugliosi, who did paid, continuing commentary on the
trial he didn't attend for *Hard Copy*) always harp on why the
prosecution didn't introduce any aspects of the "slow speed
chase" of June 17, 1994, before the jury. So let me go through
the paces:

As regards the Bronco, it was not introduced into evidence
that almost $9,000 in cash was in the car (the money was ac-
tually found in A.C.'s pocket, but it belonged to O.J.). Nor was
it introduced that O.J. had his passport with him. Or that a
dime-store fake beard was in the car. Or that when originally
spotted, the Bronco was heading south toward Mexico. Nor was
the so-called "suicide note" discussed. Nor even the fact that
O.J. was considered a fleeing armed fugitive at the time. Why
were these aspects not brought before the jury?

The answer is that, very early on, a tacit understanding was
reached by both sides that each would voluntarily stay away
from the Bronco chase and the events of June 17 in front of the
jury. Why? Because it was a wash, hurting both sides, with perhaps the prosecution having more to lose.

If the prosecution had introduced any of the seemingly incriminating evidence, they would have to live with the defense's cell-phone records, which prove that many of the calls O.J. placed while in that Bronco were indeed made from the area of Nicole's grave site. (For some time O.J. and A.C. were parked in an orange grove across from the cemetery because there was a press horde waiting for him at Nicole's grave.) The defense would also introduce tapes the police made of O.J.'s cell-phone calls; most of them with a dramatic O.J. Simpson telling everybody that he was being framed. The jury would have heard him talk with his mother over and over, something that would be far more poignant than inculpatory.

The defense also would have put folks on the stand to testify that compulsive O.J. never went anywhere without his passport, that O.J. and Nicole always carried very large sums of money ($10,000 was the average for O.J.). The reason the cash was with him in the Bronco, Simpson insiders say, is that he wanted his children Jason and Arnelle—both of whom were often in need of financial assistance from Pop—to have immediate cash available upon his suicide or arrest; indeed, that is why he gave the sum to A.C. to hold.

Yet the defense didn't want to fool with the chase either, because in the state of California the act of flight from prosecution may be considered by a jury as an indicator of guilt or guilty knowlege. Why even take the chance?

Bob Blasier, who came into the defense's case after the tacit understanding, forgot this and once almost opened the door, but the prosecution and Blasier's colleagues quickly called for a sidebar and got it. Nothing more was ever said about the Chase of the Century in front of the jury.

Was it a good idea by the prosecution? Hindsight and the words of at least one juror suggest it was not. But then they were woefully short on good ideas period. And while I agree that the Dream Team was nowhere near being a collection of the best criminal-defense attorneys money could buy—most of the really best private trial lawyers work in relative anonymity in court districts all over America—in this instance, as in so many others during the Trial of the Century, the Dream Team were far and away better courtroom strategists and technicians than Marcia & Company. They may have bluffed, and the State blinked.

❖

IN TRUTH, AT the heart of most of history's grand conspiracy theories is a random run of uncanny coincidences that only in retrospect begin to resemble an overall scheme. Since he who turns to theories of conspiracy usually does so in frustration when seemingly significant pieces of a crime puzzle do not fit the officially accepted theory, he is often operating under the spell of wishful thinking. He is susceptible to most anything and everything in hindsight that appears remotely connected. The Simpson case, like the John Kennedy and Dr. Martin Luther King assassinations, is fertile ground for just such phenomena.

But then, as history also amply demonstrates, many great crimes *were* conspiracies, grand or small. Now, one might think I'm referring to the notion of a broad police conspiracy to frame O. J. Simpson: If, as much of the evidence suggests, certain rogue members of the LAPD did tamper with evidence, it was an endeavor overtly of only one or perhaps two police officers. But I'm not referring here to a police conspiracy.

No, I'm referring to a number of uncanny coincidences surrounding the Simpson case—of which the public knows very little—that when placed together have at least that tantalizing, beckoning aroma of CONSPIRACY irresistible to those so inclined.

First, there is the Brett Cantor story. It was of sufficient interest that Judge Ito ruled in a pretrial motion that the LAPD and prosecution must turn over the Cantor "murder book" to the Simpson defense, that it was "discoverable under Brady."

In his mid-twenties, Cantor was a budding promoter and producer of underground music, which is to say any music that is an alternative to the current trend in rock. A busy and ambitious young man, he was an executive with Chrysalis Records, acquiring and producing up-and-coming new bands. He also worked as a promoter of nightclubs, organizing special nights by using what is called an "A list" of hip people and celebrities whom he could induce to show up as VIP guests, instantly establishing the newest "in" spot in town. Cantor also was part owner of the Dragonfly (10 percent), one of the hottest "in" spots in the summer of 1993, and was there frequently.

Brett's father is Paul Cantor, a prominent entertainment manager. His clients have included Dionne Warwick (who was close enough to O.J. that she was among the family and friends who gathered at Rockingham the day after the murders) and B. J. Thomas. However, according to friends and family members, Brett struggled to break into the business, doing it without the contacts or help of his father.

Brett Cantor was murdered July 30, 1993, on the Westside. His throat was slashed, his head all but decapitated, and he also suffered multiple stab wounds throughout his torso. Although the LAPD case officers in charge, Detectives Rick Jackson and Rich Aldahl of the elite Robbery/Homicide Division (Vannatter and Lange's unit), both say they vigorously investigated the case, there has never been a prime suspect, and the case remains open. No murder weapon has been found.

Other than the fact that the murder was almost exactly a year before Ron's and Nicole's, and that there were similarities in the method of killing, what coincidence links it with the Simpson case? Primarily, only opportunity.

Separately, Ron Goldman and Nicole Brown Simpson frequented the Dragonfly in the spring and early summer of 1993 (there is no indication that Ron and Nicole were aware of each other at this time, a year before their murders). Employees of the club remember seeing Ron and Brett Cantor together. And they remember Nicole coming to the Dragonfly with her coterie of party-time girlfriends. It has been said that Ron Goldman realized he'd be a long time coming up with the money to open the restaurant he now dreamed of on a waiter's income—as with so many other handsome young men with Hollywood dreams, he was fast losing faith in his wannabe acting career. Consequently, it appears Ron was considering the nightclub-promotion business himself.

There are also some intriguing elements to the story *after* Cantor's murder. Tom Sturgiss, the head of Chrysalis Records and Chrysalis Music, for whom Brett had worked only six months, from November 1992 to the time of his death, put up a $25,000 reward for information leading to the arrest of the murderer(s). The phone number given out with the reward was a private number, not the police. Detectives Jackson and Aldahl say that in all the time since the murder, Sturgiss gave them only one called-in tip to investigate, which turned out to be nothing; there were not even the flakes who usually come out of the ground whenever a reward is on the line. There are some who have wondered why an employer would be so emotionally impacted by the death of a new employee.

Sturgiss must also have been fond of Brett's brother Cliff Cantor. Only days after the murder, Sturgiss hired Cliff to replace Brett at Chrysalis Records. Then Cliff, starting with Brett's 10 percent of Dragonfly, soon managed to buy full ownership of the club.

Tom Sturgiss is very defensive about any connection between Brett's murder and the Simpson murders. When I talked repeatedly about Brett's murder, he would get his back up first, loudly; then he would shut up. When he spoke about Brett alive, however, he spoke of him almost reverently.

Besides Cliff, Brett had another brother named Mark. When contacted, both brothers immediately became defensive and adamant in their insistence that there was no connection between Brett's murder and the Simpson and Goldman murders. They have said the same to at least a couple of other reporters. One would think that with so much time gone by and still not even a suspect in the murder of their brother, they would welcome any media spotlight on the crime. But not these brothers. To me, they claimed there was a prime suspect but that "he was out of the country" and the LAPD "couldn't get him extradited." Aldahl and Jackson have flatly denied this. They say there is no suspect in or out of the United States, and there never has been.

The Cantor brothers have ordered their spouses not to talk about the case with reporters. Tyger Cantor, Mark's wife, however, weakened somewhat on the phone one day and admitted that she believes "there is a connection," but that it's taboo to even discuss it with her husband and brother-in-law.

❖

THEN THERE IS the murder of Michael Nigg, also on the Westside, only days before the verdicts. Mr. Nigg was a waiter at Mezzaluna Restaurant, and according to other employees, Goldman and Nigg were friends or at least close acquaintances.

Michael Nigg was shot twice in the back of the head. Two men were seen running from the scene. Young Mr. Nigg drove a Mercedes. On a waiter's take-home? To some, he appeared to live beyond his visible means. There were and are no suspects in the case.

❖

BUTCH SUCHARSKI OWNED a popular sports bar in Buffalo, New York, during the years O.J. was starring for the Buffalo Bills. It is reported that O.J. was a regular patron of the bar. Allegedly, Mr. Sucharski's tavern was also popular for the cocaine distributed out of there. In time, Butch Sucharski was convicted on drug charges.

Some two weeks before the Simpson murders Sucharski visited Los Angeles. Then, almost two weeks after the murders of Ron and Nicole, Mr. Sucharski and two female companions were annihilated by machine guns in his Miramar, Florida, estate. Miramar—and other such exclusive enclaves in Dade County—have for some time been home to any number of prominent mob members. The murderers were quickly apprehended due to a high-tech video surveillance system Sucharski had installed in his home. They were Caribbean teenagers in the employ of cocaine dealers.

❖

"AND NO ONE'S solved the Cantor murder yet, have they?" Pat McKenna says with an Irish edge of indignation on his sarcasm. "Yeah, and they always say, 'If O.J. didn't kill Nicole, who did?' Well, if O.J. didn't kill Cantor, who did?

"Yeah, there're a lot of strange deaths around this case," Pat continues, "that, as an investigator, I think should at least be looked at for coincidences or similarities or something like that. And there *are* those coincidences and similarities. I mean, here's Nigg and Cantor knowing Goldman, all three of them are dead—that's a coincidence that should be looked at."

❖

W HILE COCAINE WAS not found present in either Nicole's
     blood sample or O.J.'s, it is beyond question that coke and
the commerce of coke permeated the world O.J. and Nicole
moved in. Very reliable anecdotal evidence of Nicole's increasingly "more intense" involvement with cocaine, and O.J.'s longtime on-again, off-again recreational use of the drug, abounds
throughout Southern California. Indeed, Dominick Dunne documented and then reported on a notorious Westside dope hus-
tler by the handle of J.R. and his tales of being O.J.'s drug
supplier.

Faye Resnick's cocaine use is public record, of course.
She had been staying at Nicole's condo, strung out in the
days immediately preceding her reentry into a substance-
abuse treatment facility, where she was the night of the
murders.

Based upon the experiences of Faye Resnick's former associates in San Francisco, where she had lived—and worn out her
welcome in her usual modus operandi, which is to say, get involved in a couple's life, then leave them in a shambles—and
some of her acquaintances in Los Angeles, where she moved
two years before the murders and lived with Christian Rei-
chardt, a wealthy party buddy of O.J.'s, Ms. Resnick moved in
a dangerous world. That world included knowledge of and access
to big-time cocaine distributors. We know that this was a significant part of the world Nicole ran with in her newfound freedom—people on the fringe, which is the really dangerous place
to be in the big-money narcotics business. These people are the
most expendable.

Accordingly, Pat McKenna poses this question about Faye
Resnick's going into a drug-treatment program just prior to the
murders: "Why does she go to a *secure* facility, this Daniel Free-

man treatment facility, as opposed to the Betty Ford like the two previous times, which is not secure?"

One individual known to be a major player in the drug business, one who appears to be the common denominator among a number of the people involved, is the real-life Mafia boss Joey Ippolito, who was arrested a year before the murders on narcotics charges. A. C. Cowlings worked for Ippolito as chauffeur and bodyguard, and was with him when Ippolito was arrested. Ippolito was tried, convicted, and sentenced to ten years in prison.

We know that A. C. Cowlings shares some incredible bond with O. J. Simpson; what one does, the other knows about. This would be confirmed in the interesting detail of one Samantha Hill. During an argument with her boyfriend on a train in Northern California, Ms. Hill grabbed her suitcase and tossed it out the door. In the suitcase, there were many pounds of cocaine—different accounts put the quantity anywhere from ten to fifty pounds. Ms. Hill and the cocaine were collected by the police when she returned and was walking down the tracks looking for her tossed cargo. In her electronic organizer police found the names and numbers of A. C. Cowlings and O. J. Simpson. Ms. Hill was also carrying a bottle of prescription drugs belonging to Cowlings.

Joey Ippolito was one of the few suppliers in Brentwood and Santa Monica who dealt in cocaine shipments of that quantity.

There is also the wild-side life of Denise Brown, Nicole's oldest sister and close companion. When barely out of her teens Denise became the paramour of Robert Evans, a man with one of the more unsavory life histories in Hollywood. Evans rose from the crap tables of Cuba before Castro, all the way up to be head of Paramount Pictures, where he became implicated in what would become known as the "Cotton Club murder." The victim was Roy Radin, who produced the movie The Cotton Club for Evans at Paramount.

Denise also had an affair with the popular singer/musician/ producer Rick James, who has led a tumultuous life on the edge, to say the least. She had an affair with A.C. himself. And, of course, the world saw her affair with Tony "The Animal" Fiato played out during the trial. While he appeared more punk than mobster when he took the stand in the Simpson trial, Fiato would not be in the Federal Witness Protection Program for the reason he is if he weren't a thoroughly bad apple.

There is also the matter of Keith Zlomsowitch, one of Nicole's more serious lovers during her and O.J.'s first breakup and divorce, the guy O.J. saw his wife blowing on the living-room sofa. He had transferred from Denver to manage the Mezzaluna Restaurant in Brentwood. According to several sources, the principal reason Zlomsowitch was never put on the stand to testify for the prosecution about incidents he witnessed of O.J. stalking Nicole is his alleged drug history. Not only could the defense have used this to discredit his testimony, it could also have accidentally opened doors *no one* wanted opened.

Again there is an abundance of anecdotal testament all over the Westside that cocaine might as well have been on the menu at Mezzaluna Restaurant at the time, so widely was it talked about as a place to score.

Pat McKenna on Mr. Zlomsowitch: "We heard he was going to be their next-to-last witness. Our information was that he was hanging out with sleazy people down in Florida. He was looking bad."

On Mezzaluna's reputation as a place to score coke: "Without a doubt." McKenna was the only detective from either side of the case to go up and down San Vincente Boulevard and its cross streets, interviewing people who worked in the shops in that area of Brentwood about this or any other aspect of the case.

"Zlomsowitch was also in a car when it got stopped by the cops and busted for drugs, but the driver got charged with it. She swears up and down it was Zlomsowitch's drugs."

Where there is cocaine, there is money; where there is a lot of cocaine, there is a lot of money. For the serious investor who doesn't run it up his nose, the chance to get financially healthy is definitely, temptingly, there in cocaine, and the risk to life and limb through violence is almost manageable. There are those who should know who wonder if O.J.'s recently declining yearly income might have caused him at least to explore this business.

For the impetuous amateur investor who is often his or her own most frequent customer, on credit, the potential reward is still huge, but so is the risk to life and limb. We know that Nicole really wanted a house on the beach in Malibu: She didn't want to be stuck in that condo in ordinary Brentwood, and the down-scale side of it at that. For Malibu she needed money. And if we are to believe Faye Resnick and Kato Kaelin, she wanted to go into business also, quite likely the restaurant business, which she was increasingly familiarizing herself with through the younger men she'd been dating.

The freelance journalist and author Alex Constantine (*Blood, Carnage and the Agent Provocateur*), a prime devotee of conspiracy theory research and a serious proponent of linking the Cantor, Nigg, and Sucharski murders with the Simpson case, sums up that school of thought this way:

"Nicole was moving in some interesting circles. I believe the reason she was murdered was because she was no longer chained to O. J. Simpson, knew too much, and she wasn't taking care of things the way she might have. I mean, suddenly, with the divorce, she was in this state of heady freedom. She was on the loose, and the gadflies around her were addicts with little sense of responsibility. Cash slipped through her fingers like wet soap."

So, just a rash of coincidences and bad associates? Almost certainly. But then . . . ?

10

BLOOD WON'T TELL

D R. IRWIN GOLDEN'S autopsies of both Ron and Nicole and his subsequent testimony during the preliminary hearing posed major problems for the State. That much is well known. What isn't as well known is to what lengths the State went to procure another law-enforcement pathologist who would come on board and mitigate the problems before a jury, and how unsuccessful the effort was.

Every major city in California was asked to loan its coroner to the prosecution; every single one turned the request down. No one was willing to risk its medical examiner's reputation by having him try to tidy up such shoddy work from the witness stand. The call went out nationally. Nothing. No law-enforcement pathologist of note anywhere agreed to help. Even more galling to Marcia & Company was that no private pathologist or forensic biologist of national stature would step forward either.

In the end, the prosecution was forced to put Dr. Lakshmanan Sathyavagiswaran, Dr. Golden's boss, the coroner for the county of Los Angeles, on the stand for a torturous nine days. Dr. Sathyavagiswaran, a gentleman of sterling personal and professional reputation, did his best to support his office and employees in what was only a lose-lose proposition. But he was an administrator who hadn't personally worked a murder in years. This was painfully apparent when the State also called upon him to reconstruct the crime scene, a highly specialized field he has little or no practical training or experience in. Which, of course, is why Dr. Henry Lee and Dr. Michael Baden, testifying for the defense, came after Dr. Sathyavagiswaran and had such impact on the jury. Both men stand at the top of the forensic-science world, in both expertise and credibility.

There is, at the core of the Simpson murder case crime scenes as presented, something very wrong forensically. It is no surprise that so few things fit even close to the surface. That eerie, unsettling certainty does not ipso facto mean that O. J. Simpson did *not* kill Ron and Nicole. It simply means that, as expected, the most appropriate words on the matter came from Dr. Henry Lee, when he said from the stand: "Something's wrong."

❖

THINGS STARTED GOING wrong early. The problems and peculiarities in the relationship between the LAPD and the Coroner's Office, as regards this case, started from the very beginning. We know that for a fact.

Let's go to the audiotape:

Detective Ron Phillips and Coroner's Investigator Paul Willis. First call 6:49 A.M., June 13.

> Phillips: *I got a homicide that we want to let you know about. It's going to be . . . the press is going to be crawling on us like ants when they find out what's going on.*
> Willis: *Okay . . . what . . .*

Phillips: We're kind . . . we're kind of not following procedure, but we are kind of asking a favor . . . and . . . you know . . . kind of work a little bit on this one.

Willis: Okay . . . um . . . you're at the scene now.

Phillips: Yeah.

Willis: Do we have names on these people?

Phillips: No, I don't.

Willis: Okay, and you say they're . . . in . . . uh, plain view.

Phillips: Well, you can see them, yeah, from the street here. They're, they're a little off the sidewalk here in front of the house, but the problem is . . . we're going to be a high-profile type deal. It's the . . . it's the ex-wife of a very, very prominent sportscast star or sports celebrity. So . . .

Willis: Can you give me the name?

Phillips: Well . . . I . . . you're not . . . you're not going to let this . . .

Willis: No . . . I'm an investigator . . .

Phillips: Okay . . . I'm going to have to trust you on this. It's O. J. Simpson's ex-wife.

Willis: Oh boy—okay . . . uh . . .

Phillips: And he is in Chicago.

Willis: He does not know anything about this?

Phillips: He knows now, and that's what's going to break this thing wide open.

Willis: Okay . . . uh . . . I'll . . . you want us rolling out now?

Phillips: Hold on a second . . . Tom [Detective Lange] . . . Tom . . . you want the coroner now? No. Hold on a second . . . how long? Okay, you're just getting the first call.

Willis: Is it . . . ?

Phillips: We'll give you a call back when we want them moved.

Willis: Okay, fine.

Phillips: It's probably gonna be about an hour and a half.
Willis: An hour to an hour and a half, okay. I won't give you
                 any numbers yet.
Phillips: Right.
Willis: Okay.
Phillips: What this is going to be, uh . . . it originally was ours,
                 but it's going to be taken over by RHD [the elite Rob-
                 bery/Homicide Division].
Willis: Okay . . .

The second call to the coroner was made by Phillips at
8:08 A.M. It was almost ten hours after the discovery of the
bodies before medical examiners of the Coroner's Office would
arrive at the Bundy crime scene.

Perhaps this needs little amplification. *This is a big case and
we're going to go a bit off the book, all right?* The professional
courtesy reply: *Sure.*

The battles between LAPD Homicide and the Coroner's
Office had been settled with legislation in Sacramento mandat-
ing that in the event of a murder case, the coroner be notified
immediately. Yet the law lacked any real teeth. Everybody saved
face. A truce. So recently the two parties had begun trying to
be mutually conciliatory. No doubt, that is what happened here.

Of course, Dr. Sathyavagiswaran probably wishes his investigator had been less so, because of an instant new axiom in law
enforcement: *If you're going to put your coroner on the stand for
nine days, don't keep his people away from the crime scene for ten
hours.*

❖

I F PROPERLY PROCESSED, preserved, and documented, a crime
scene can be the next best thing to an eyewitness. The full
range of forensic sciences is advanced to that point. Of course,

there is never going to be the perfect investigation of a crime scene because the investigators are human.

But 875 S. Bundy, being a small, contained crime scene where a lot of physical, bloody activity took place, cries out to tell its story. With the great multiplicity of different but pattern-distinct depositions of blood—a liquid whose physical properties under almost all conditions are well known—from at least three human sources easily identifiable, the scene would be almost as revealing as if on Betacam. That is, if it could be frozen in time (or were documented properly).

But the Bundy crime scene was officially shut down, the yellow tape was removed, and the area was opened to water hoses and the public shortly after three in the afternoon of the thirteenth. Barely twelve hours after the first homicide detectives arrived, and far less than that for the SID criminalists and coroner's investigators, and it's over. The curtain dropped on whatever tale the scene might have told.

Instead of a tale, what we have are questions. The following are only a few that were not really addressed by either side in court, primarily because they have no answers:

Why is Nicole lying beneath the large, descending pool of her own blood, which begins two risers *up* the steps from the walk where she came to lie and die? In other words, the gaping neck wound that killed her—the wound the prosecution took great pains to characterize as a "coup de grace" delivered after Nicole had been initially subjected to multiple "sharp force injuries" and then "incapacitated by blunt force trauma" so that the killer could turn and deal with Ron's death struggle—had to have been inflicted while her head, neck, and shoulders were some feet *above* and *over* from where her body was later found, with absolutely no blood patterns to suggest that she moved or was moved.

What is to be made of the two dark, dense striation blood-stains (linear, straight-edged bloodstains from some type of instrument or tooled object) on the second step, just to the right of the beginning arc of Nicole's descending blood pool? What activity, unlike any other suggested by the rest of the crime scene, caused these blood "stripes"?

The trail of blood drops across Nicole's back that are clearly visible in the crime-scene photographs—but were then lost forever when a blanket from inside her condo was placed over the body—are much closer together than the drops that accompany the Bruno Magli shoe imprints down the walk. (There is also what appears to be medium-velocity impact spatter and cast-off spatter patterns among and *over* these blood drops; we will never know because of the blanket.)

Whose blood was dripping steadily from a laterally moving source above and parallel to Nicole's back? If it was O.J.'s, from what wound? If this is from the finger cut on his left hand, the only place we know he was bleeding, the blood would more likely have been deposited in some form of a primary swipe or smear pattern in her neck and shoulder areas, according to the prosecution's theory of a lone assassin grabbing an incapacitated Nicole with his left hand and applying the coup de grace slit to her throat with his right. These drops of blood also do not appear to match the other blood trails the prosecution maintains were made by the killer, neither the trail leading up the driveway at Rockingham, nor the trail inside the foyer of O.J.'s house. If it's Ron Goldman's blood, how did it get dripped in such singular fashion when we know his blood was deposited widely from great quantities of medium-velocity impact spatter, cast-off spatter, satellite spatter, primary and secondary wipes, swipes, and smears—all of this several feet away from a position ninety degrees above Nicole, where the source of the quick blood *drop* trail on her back had to have been.

What are we to make of Nicole's blood being deposited on Ron's shoes in a pattern that indicates he was upright on his feet while she was bleeding from a spot *above* his shoes? Appar-

ently there are also direct deposits of blood on Ron's shoes that
are a mixture of his and Nicole's blood. In other words, were
they both on their feet, bleeding in some fashion at the same
time as these particular bloodstains would indicate? If so,
wouldn't that suggest more than one assailant dispatching the
victims more or less simultaneously?

What mystifies even more, however, is that in the photographs of Nicole's body, before the blanket was put over her,
there appears to be medium-velocity impact or cast-off blood
spatter on otherwise clean feet. This would suggest that she
stepped in no blood and was down on the ground with her soles
out while forceful bloody activity was going on above and a few
feet distant from her. So with physical evidence itself, there is
contradiction.

FBI Special Agent William Bodziak testified that at about
the midpoint of the Bruno Magli bloody shoe-imprint trail, there
was one right foot going west and one left foot going east, but
that he was at a loss to explain the phenomenon. He theorized
that it could have come with the killer turning and ducking
into the bushes along the north side of the walkway—which is
in fact what the trail appears to do—but the foot placement,
no matter the maneuver, is more than a little strange. Bodziak
was similarly confounded by two sets of identical bloody shoe
imprints paralleling each other down the walkway *away* from
the killing ground.

Also, the blood-drop trail on the left side of the first Bruno
Magli shoe-imprint trail does not follow those steps in toward
the garden bed. Nor does it accompany the identical shoe imprints that parallel the first trail away from the crime scene. In
fact, the Bundy blood-drop trail actually consists of only five
widely separated blood drops.

The shoe imprints are trying hard to tell us something, but
what? Without other evidence—evidence that wasn't preserved
or well documented—we know only that someone with blood

on the soles of his Bruno Magli shoes walked west down the walkway on the north side of Nicole's condo, away from the bodies and toward the easement behind 875 S. Bundy. We know that this person with the bloody soles turned and ducked into the bushes on the right, and then came back out—using one very acrobatic foot placement which makes no sense whatsoever—and continued away from the "killing cage" until the imprints fade away short of the back gate. Then we know that someone with blood on the soles of what appear to be the same Bruno Magli shoes repeats the trip away from the bodies and toward the back gate, paralleling the other imprint trail.

Different scenarios come to mind. They consist of mostly differing versions of something along the lines of this: A killer with bloody shoe soles is walking away from his victims, hears something that concerns him, and ducks into the foliage for concealment to watch and listen. When all is clear, he continues on his way. But then, after having reached the back gate and alley behind Nicole's condo, for whatever reason, he decides to return to the bloody cage and then leaves again, and again tracks blood with him on the soles of his Bruno Maglis.

Any scenario with those basic elements, which is governed by the evidence as collected and documented, has some immediate problems, however. We know it couldn't have been Goldman's arrival that prompted the turn into the bushes. Not only does that not fit with the evidence on the bodies and around them, but also the mere fact that the imprints come out of the bushes and continue to the rear, *not* the front where the killer could confront the intruder—namely Ronald Goldman— negates that. Of course, someone just out walking his dog and passing by could have been reason enough to cause the turn into the bushes out of caution.

But the real kicker is, if the killer is returning to the area of carnage to retrieve evidence that he suddenly realizes he's left behind, then why doesn't he pick up any of the several evidentiary items lying there bunched together smack dab in the middle of the crime scene? What other reason would prompt the killer to return to the bodies? I can't think of any logical explanation that is also supported by evidence physical or circumstantial. Yet those parallel shoe-imprint trails are there. Somebody made that trip away from the killing cage twice.

It doesn't make sense.

❖

OF COURSE, IF the killer was O.J. and he ducked into the foliage with his cut finger, there should have been concentric blood-drop patterns with satellite spatter on the garden bed. When you cut your finger, early on the bleeding is rapid, and if you're standing still, on the ground or floor or whatever is below the source of the blood drops, you're going to create a telltale grouping of bloodstains. But then, no one looked for any blood on the ground where those shoe imprints turned off the paved walkway.

❖

THE "HANG FUNG" comment by Bob Shapiro occasioned a lot of flak. This is what happened. One day while Dennis Fung was on the stand, a Chinese restaurant made Bob a present of a whole box of wrapped fortune cookies.

Just as we were going out into the hall for the afternoon break, Bob handed Joe McGinniss and Dominick Dunne each a fortune cookie. I was directly behind Shapiro as we came out of the double doors and stopped in a little huddle. Bob, trying to have fun, said that when they read their fortune out loud they were to end it with the phrase "in bed." Joe read his, I don't remember what it said per se, but with the added ending it was pretty suggestive and funny. It was during the ensuing repartee between Bob and Joe that I heard the words "from the Hang Fung restaurant" come off Bob's lips. Punning was one of the things the Authors did a lot of to pass the time. Bob would participate when he could. These conversations with the Authors were always considered "off the record."

However, a daily reporter overheard the "Hang Fung" phrase and immediately filed it on the wires. It became a big story. What was entirely missed, however, was Johnnie Cochran, during that same break, almost dancing up and down the hall singing, "We're having Fung . . . Oh, we're having Fung . . . ," which one would think even more politically incorrect—eating a minority after you've hanged him has got to be worse than just the hanging.

But, innocently intentioned or not, what Bob said was an ethnic slur. His prompt and complete apology to the Chinese community was proper and, I believe, sincere.

❖

So AS NOT to do disservice to a fine pathologist and administrator, let us dwell here mostly on those matters where Dr. Sathyavagiswaran was fully within his expertise and was able to give the jury sound, probative, consistent medical and scientific observations based upon a review of the available evidence and records.

The LA coroner told the jury that Nicole bled to death within a minute of the fatal throat slash. That gaping wound severed both the left and right carotid arteries, occasioning immediate, massive arterial gushing. She had been immobilized by a blunt-force trauma to the head prior to the throat slashing. At least one minute or more elapsed between the beginning of the assault and her death, judging from the condition of an abrasion to the right side of her face. The seven major sharp-force wounds to Nicole's head, face, and neck were more than likely caused by the same kind of blade, but a second, different-shaped blade making some of the wounds couldn't be ruled out. Her time of death was between 9:00 P.M. and midnight. She had eaten a vegetable and pasta meal at least an hour or two before, ingested with a small amount of alcohol, probably wine. She had been wearing a black dress, its skirt short, and a sun top and black panties. She was lying on her left side in a semi-fetal curl in an enormous pool of her own blood, which had all but completely drained her body and run in a thick stream almost to the sidewalk. She was a Caucasian female of above average health and condition.

And that's about it. Virtually all of Dr. Sathyavagiswaran's other testimony was in the form of crime-scene reconstruction for which he said he had little or no specialized training or experience. In days of highly speculative conceptualizing on Brian Kelberg's could-it-have-beens, it produced nothing of any further probative value for the jury to fit into the prosecution's case theory.

Of his review of the evidence and records from Ron Goldman's autopsy, the LA coroner told the jury:

That the two parallel linear wounds on Ron Goldman's neck in the area of his Adam's apple were superficial and unlike any other wound suffered by the victim. These wounds were consistent with what can be called control wounds. That is, wounds meant to still a struggling victim by mortal threat and intimidation, by drawing the knife blade across the neck just enough. In essence, it was an act of torture, suggesting some "playing" with the victim.

It is possible that not all of Ron's wounds were caused by the same blade. The major wound to Goldman's neck was a fatal wound in that it severed the jugular vein, but death from the bleeding of that wound alone could have taken fifteen to twenty minutes. At least three other fatal wounds would have killed him sooner. There were two chest wounds that penetrated the lungs deeply. The body's reaction to the jugular wound and the lung wounds would be a fairly rapid loss of blood pressure and compromised breathing, with death coming shortly thereafter. However, a stab to the lower back that entered the abdomen and cut the aorta, the largest blood vessel in the body, would have brought death within a minute and clinical shock with diminished capabilities sooner than that.

There was also a severe stab wound to Goldman's left thigh that the doctor believed occurred after the two fatal chest wounds and definitely before the severed aorta. He said that the aortic wound could have been delivered while Ron was down, but because of the corresponding knife holes in the shirt, it is more likely he was standing up when that most deadly of his wounds was received.

The extensive bloodstaining of the left jeans leg indicates that Goldman was upright for some period of time after the initial causation of blood flow.

The LA coroner also told the jury that in his expert opinion the large contusion on Ron Goldman's right knuckles was more likely the result of a glancing impact with a tree or fence.

❖

I T WAS DURING Dr. Sathyavagiswaran's testimony that the jury learned there were construction workers who were allowed to gawk at Nicole's body in the autopsy room. There was also a steady stream of identified and unidentified police officers who came to this unseemly viewing of the still shapely remains of Nicole, one of whom was almost surely Mark Fuhrman.

❖

W HILE CRIME SCENE photos of Nicole's and Ron's remains were on the screen and being testified about only feet away from the jury box, Marcia Clark giggled and flirted with Johnnie Cochran and Chris Darden. Several of the female jurors appeared to take note of this inappropriate behavior one day. A short while later, when Ron Goldman's chest wounds were the subject of testimony by Dr. Sathyavagiswaran and were projected on the screen, the alternate juror known as Goldilocks started crying quietly and then ran from the courtroom.

Not long thereafter, the Goldman family succumbed to the horrific photographs and testimony about Ron's last seconds and, for the first time, left the courtroom while it was in session. The tears had been dripping off Kimberly Goldman's delicate nose.

Marcia giggled and flirted on—after a couple of cursory postures of sympathy were duly displayed for the record.

❖

D R. MICHAEL BADEN, the former chief medical examiner for the city of New York, who along with Dr. Henry Lee consulted with the defense from June 15, 1994, onward, was the pathologist who testified during the defense's case in chief. Dr. Baden, simply put, is to pathology what Dr. Lee is to crime-scene reconstruction, the top of the world's pecking order.

Dr. Baden has worked on identifying remains of victims in the Bosnian war and the remains of the Romanovs of czarist Russia, and he has at different times been appointed by governmental commissions to work on the investigations of the John F. Kennedy and Dr. Martin Luther King assassinations. He recently testified for the prosecution in the second trial of Byron de La Beckwith for the assassination of Medgar Evers in Mississippi and helped win a conviction twenty-nine years after the fact. He worked the John Belushi homicide and the Ron Settles death for the Los Angeles District Attorney's Office. He has done over twenty thousand autopsies. He very seldom testifies for the defense because "they usually don't like my findings."

Michael Baden is a man of considerable presence. With his scientific bona fides and sense of humor, he is an abundantly effective witness. The following is, in summary, some of what Dr. Baden had to offer the Simpson jury.

He did not see blood on the socks in visual examination at SID on June 22, 1994. While working for the defense, he discovered the severity of the blunt-force trauma apparent on the back of Nicole's head and pointed it out to the LA coroner long after Nicole was buried. The blow, which had been missed by Dr. Golden, had caused damage to brain tissue.

Because the cluster pattern of wounds to Nicole came from different directions, Dr. Baden believed it likely Nicole struggled with her killer or killers. There were defensive wounds to Nicole's hands, which bled.

Nicole was most likely *not* unconscious before her throat was slit; the wound shows evidence of her moving during its causation. Probably she struggled for some time before that, evidenced by the amount of blood on the steps above her. The slash to her throat was the final injury, since she would have been rendered unconscious in seconds and incapable of moving down to the level where she was found.

Nicole's stab wounds, all of which came before the slit throat, had widely varying orientations—up, down, left, right, etc.

Of Ron Goldman, Dr. Baden was able to tell the jury that he put up quite a struggle. There were more than twenty-two stab wounds to Goldman, and many were cluster wounds coming from different directions.

He indicated that Ron was "upright long enough" for blood to flow all the way down his left side and into his shoe. There was no injury that would have prevented him from calling out.

Indeed, even after the large, terribly cavernous neck wound that sliced the jugular vein, Ron could have remained upright and struggling for several minutes; he could even have *survived* that wound with quick medical attention.

Dr. Baden estimated that it was within the medical range for there to have been, at the outside, as much as ten to fifteen minutes between the jugular wound and the trauma to the lungs and aorta. The trauma would have caused more internal bleeding than external, and would therefore be less critical as a source of blood flow down Ron's clothes and body than the neck wounds, further indication that Ron stayed on his feet well after the neck wound.

The cuts on O. J. Simpson's hands, which Dr. Baden examined shortly after the murders, would have ceased to bleed within six to eight minutes.

Dr. Baden's expert opinion was that Ron Goldman was not likely to have "punched a tree." The large contusion on Goldman's right knuckles was far more likely the result of a "forceful blow" solidly struck to the person of his assailant than from a glancing impact with a tree or fence.

❖

ONE OF THE most effective aspects of Dr. Baden's testimony was that Brian Kelberg—known by his colleagues and referred to ironically by the press as "The Genius"—let him tell O.J.'s story of how he cut his hand, thus eliminating an important reason for O.J. to testify. As Dr. Baden recounted this conversation, before his trip to Chicago, O.J. had cut his hand on some sharp part of the car-phone bracket in the Bronco; in his Chicago hotel room, O.J. cut his hand again, this time on a water glass he backhanded and shattered after getting the call from police with news of the murders. O.J. maintained that this was when he received the fairly deep, jagged, fishhook-shaped cut just above the middle knuckle of the middle finger of his left hand.

But still the prosecution chose not to introduce O.J.'s thirty-two-minute statement taken by Vannatter and Lange on June 13, in which he says he does not remember exactly when or how his hand was cut while in LA, just that he knew he cut it while "running around" to get packed for the Chicago trip. According to many, most particularly one Vincent Bugliosi, O.J.'s statement was dead-to-rights inculpatory.

Not surprisingly, Pat McKenna disagrees. "Here's what no one ever realizes: When O.J. is being talked to by Vannatter—before they go on tape—he's got the bandage on from the cut he got in Chicago, and they're talking about it. He tells him about *that*. This is all before his statement, okay. Then he starts talking about around the fingernails, where these little cuts are. He remembers nicking himself at the house, because he says he was getting a paper towel. He'd seen that his finger was bleeding and he was looking for a paper towel; Kato was looking for a flashlight because of the thumps on his wall. O.J. says that what Vannatter and Lange were pointing to was not the bandaged cut but the cuts here at the fingernails. He says, 'Yeah, I don't know where I did this. I think I did this at Rockingham.' He doesn't really remember, but he knows he did the one with the bandage in Chicago—because, shit, he was bleeding all over the place and he got a bandage from the front-desk girl.

"But then, when they go on tape, they only talk about the cut with the bandage, and he's assuming they're still talking about the little cuts. He's telling them, 'I think I did this at Rockingham.' So they pulled a Mutt and Jeff on him, and he didn't even realize it. He's trying to cooperate.

"I thought that statement was great. When you listen to the tape, and you know what's going on, you know that they think he's the guy, so they're trying to set traps for him—and this guy is trying to be as cooperative as possible."

Bugliosi and others have asserted that it is rare for people to cut themselves and that O.J.'s cuts are far too coincidental. McKenna's response: "Bugliosi's an asswipe. I've got a bandage on right now from cutting vegetables the other day. I mean, I'm forever nicking myself. This one bled for hours. Bugliosi's a big fucking blowhard."

❖

BRIAN KELBERG'S TENDENCY to shout at witnesses was on full display in his cross-examination of Dr. Baden. At one point, Judge Ito reminded Kelberg, "The jury is only about six feet away."

"Perhaps I should move over," Kelberg said.

"No, just move on," the judge said.

❖

IT SHOULD BE understood that the prosecution again chose a higher burden of proof than was necessary. How the victims died is not a prescribed element of any murder case. The State need prove only that the victims died by unlawful means at the hands or intent of another. Marcia & Company tried to prove exactly how Ron and Nicole were murdered. When it was obvious to the jury that the State didn't have a clue, beyond rank speculation, as to what actually happened at the murder scene, the prosecution lost more of its case to reasonable doubt.

11

THE QUESTIONS OF
DR. HENRY LEE

T IS PATENTLY absurd—and an insult to his memory—to say that the many contusions and abrasions on Ron Goldman's hands are the result of his beating up a tree or a chain-link fence rather than striking his assailant even once! Yet the State adamantly maintains that all of Ron Goldman's flailing about in his struggle for life landed only on an inanimate object. If Dr. Baden's expert testimony is scientifically consistent with the medical facts, the large contusion over the middle knuckle is not the result of a glancing motion, but rather of a closed-fist, direct-contact punch that found its target on a human.

An examination of the crime-scene photos would indicate that while the struggle between Ron and his assailant was not long in real time, it was fierce and protracted in physical scope, and extensive in fight time, when seconds are minutes and minutes seem mercilessly infinite. But where is the evidence of such a struggle that would have to be somewhere on O.J.'s body?

From the first day this question has confounded Dr. Henry Lee. It still does.

❖

T HE SINGLE MOST compelling suggestion that O. J. Simpson did not stab anyone is also the most rudimentary. In the opinion of Dr. Lee, it is beyond probability that a lone perpetrator of the murders of Nicole Brown Simpson and Ronald Goldman would not have extensive physical damage upon his own person if he'd been involved in the terribly violent, very physical act of murdering the victims in the fashion in which they were killed. In the some six thousand homicides he's investigated in his career, Dr. Lee has never seen a situation where there was this much evidence of violent struggle, with two full-grown victims, and so little evidence of trauma to the alleged lone perpetrator.

"Have to be some kind martial-art superhero do that," Henry says in his inimitable style.

Simply put, you bust someone in the chops, the victim might be eating through a straw thereafter, but your hand is also going to be sore as hell and undoubtedly bruised or abraded. According to Dr. Lee, the evidence as known suggests that an assailant, even if he was wearing protective clothing, could not inflict the dozens of stabs of the type found on the bodies of Ron and Nicole and not have more extensive personal trauma than cuts on the knuckle and fingernails of one hand.

The physical dimensions and topography of the Bundy crime scene also must be considered. It is much smaller than the image conveyed by photograph or TV screen; it also contains a great deal of shrubbery and heavy foliage of various types. This would almost certainly add to the argument that the murderer should have contusions or abrasions upon his person.

Even though O.J. was an especially gifted running back, he was never a power runner known for brute physical strength. He was also now a forty-seven-year-old man with more wear and tear on his body than most men of similar age and physical structure precisely because he was a great football star who played at such a high level of competition for so long. Today, his knees are basically arthritic mush—that is medical fact, no matter how many times the prosecution wants to show O.J.'s exercise video. For pride or money a real athlete plays in pain; ice will deal with the swelling later. Yet the prosecution maintains that O.J. all by himself did what is an improbability for the most gifted martial-art assassins of the world.

❖❖

FROM THE FIRST weeks of the case, it was obvious to insiders that the pivotal witness in the trial could very well be Dr. Henry C. Lee, the preeminent forensic scientist in the world today, and chief of the Connecticut State Police Forensic Science Laboratory. The fact that he was even working with the defense was a matter of surprise and controversy within the world of the forensic sciences.

On the face of it, there is nothing remarkable about an expert witness, even a highly regarded one, working in defense of a very wealthy, very prominent defendant. It happens somewhere in America almost every day. But not with Dr. Lee. More than a decade ago, he stopped doing any criminal defense work. He has since broken that self-imposed stricture only twice. The first time was the William Kennedy Smith rape case. His testimony proved to be the difference between freedom and prison for Mr. Smith. The second was the Simpson defense effort. (His expert fee in both cases was donated, the first to a task force investigating the serial murders of prostitutes in Connecticut, the second to two similar causes.)

As a government employee and a teacher of law enforcement personnel, Dr. Lee has limited himself to these cases primarily because defense work holds too great a potential for conflict of interest. This has been his decision even though his counterparts in most other states do augment their salaries by appearing as expert witnesses in criminal trials (almost always in states other than their own, of course) at no risk to their professional standing. Moreover, Dr. Lee's time is fully engaged in what law enforcement authorities throughout the world, let alone the state of Connecticut, sometimes desperately call upon him to do.

It was daunting that the Los Angeles District Attorney's Office would have to go up against Dr. Lee in this murder trial. Without a confession, eyewitness, or murder weapon, and considering the method and forensic circumstances, the Simpson case boiled down to a prototypical "blood case." Purely circumstantial blood cases where sufficient resources are available to the defendant are rare indeed; but when they do occur, they often result in new law and the revamping of crime-scene processing techniques.

The problem Marcia & Company had was thus twofold. Not only was it clear that Dr. Lee was the expert's expert, but also it was likely that any criminalist the State might use would have been a student of Dr. Lee in one fashion or another. Be it by seminar, college curriculum, or the dozen-plus forensic-science textbooks he has authored or co-authored, any recognized forensic scientist in the world has been, to some degree, educated by Dr. Henry Lee.

❖

DR. LEE'S AND Dr. Baden's presence early in the case is noteworthy. One would think their expertise critical only after an arrest, but Henry Lee and Michael Baden were brought to Los Angeles by Robert Shapiro almost immediately after the murders to interpret what evidence there was. If the news from them was bad, Bob Shapiro believed their stature would help convince O.J. that a plea bargain was the best course of action. That did not happen, of course. As forensic scientists, both men advised Bob that he had a legitimate reasonable-doubt case, even as they reserved the right to change their scientific opinion as incoming evidence dictated.

Both men also then offered their scientifically objective assistance to the State's investigation. They were refused. Impolitely.

❖

THERE REALLY ISN'T a better way to describe Dr. Lee's position in the criminal justice arena than as a pedestrian just-the-facts approach. How else do you qualify a man whose curriculum vitae runs over fifty pages and is weekly, if not daily, obsolete, but which at this moment includes some of the following:

He has investigated over six thousand homicides, as said earlier, yet has a Ph.D. in biochemistry and molecular biology from New York University. After "stepping too much blood and mess" as a young police officer in his native Taiwan, he came to America with his wife and children to "become scientist, but still step too much blood and mess, crazy, huh?" Along with his work at the Connecticut State Police Lab, he is a professor of forensics at the University of New Haven and lecturer at Yale and the People's University in Beijing. He is the only bad-guy catcher in the world to be the recipient of the Distinguished Criminalist Award from the American Academy of Forensic Science as well as the International Association of Forensic Science, the highest honor of both organizations. He is also a charter member of the International Homicide Detectives Association.

He once solved a murder case by finding and identifying the minute remains of a wife who was fed through an industrial-grade wood chipper by her insurance-hungry husband and then scattered over acres of Connecticut roadside. He worked the 1980 murder case of Scarsdale Diet Doctor Herman Tarnower and the 1985 shootout between Philadelphia police and the radical group MOVE. He has been involved with almost every major governmental commission or investigation concerning forensic matters of national and international interest and security in the past twenty years. He spent a good deal of the winter and spring of 1996 in the former Yugoslavia with Dr. Baden, attempting both to identify the remains in those monstrous mass graves and to determine who put them there.

He is the Grand Master of what those in the business call the scenario game. It is what being a criminalist is really all about. No one is more skillful at it than he. Or more honest.

He is an athletically trim and agile man of medium build and soft voice, with a perpetually quizzical nature and an infectious smile that more often than not is a full-blown grin. Rare indeed are the human beings who don't immediately like, trust, and admire him. Jurors and jurists alike have been known to name children after him. Of course, he can be one of the funniest men alive, when he needs to be, using his exaggerated accent and fractures of English syntax to their full measure.

❖

THE UNSINKABLE CREDIBILITY of Henry Lee as a witness in the Simpson case may have been best expressed by Judge Ito in his admonition to Hank Goldberg before he began his cross-examination:

"Frankly, if I were in your shoes, I would cross-examine [him] for about half an hour. . . ."

Surely Hank now wishes he'd been allowed that strategy by Marcia and Brian "The Genius" Kelberg.

"Poor Hank," Assistant DA Peter Bozanich remembers.

"Hank worked at one of my offices when I was downtown—Santa Monica was one of my offices—and he'd come to me every day [during the trial] and say, 'When can I go back to Santa Monica?' I said, 'Hank, I've got nothing to do with this. You work for those guys.'

"Whenever there was any 'heavy lifting' to do, [it was] 'Let's get Hank to do it.' And then of course the media is killing Hank."

❖

SINCE THE VERDICTS, a number of the jurors have volunteered that Dr. Lee's testimony was exactly as advertised—crucial and effective; a number have singled out Dr. Lee's testimony in defense of their verdict. Let's look at what new evidence Henry Lee was able to present to the Simpson jury:

Among the almost limitless variety of bloodstain patterns at the Bundy crime scene were the contact smears on Goldman's shoe sole—he had stepped in blood and then moved, probably to the back of the killing ground since what turned out to be blood was caked with dirt.

Definitely one shoe imprint in blood on the tiled walkway of Bundy was not from a Bruno Magli shoe.

Some bloody shoe imprints found on a piece of paper and another envelope near the murder scene also were not Bruno Magli. This piece of paper and envelope were recovered from the crime scene thirteen days after the murders; somehow the LAPD had neglected to pick them up.

There was a great deal of medium-velocity impact spatter and cast-off spatter on the fence and foliage at a level four to five feet above the ground from vertical sources with much movement. Most significant, at that height range many large direct-contact smear and swipe bloodstain patterns were found: "multiple contact with dynamic movement [from] an upright source."

The Defendant of the Century, O. J. Simpson, in court looking into the gallery.
Copyright © 1995 by Haywood Galbreath

Marcia Clark, first-chair prosecutor. *Copyright © 1995 by Haywood Galbreath*

Judge Lance Ito on the bench, watching testimony, with court-reporter transcription, on his laptop computer. *Copyright © 1995 by Haywood Galbreath*

For the defense, The Dream Team. *Copyright © 1995 by Haywood Galbreath*

Christopher Darden. *Copyright © 1995 by Haywood Galbreath*

Hank Goldberg and Marcia Clark, *foreground*, conferring during a sidebar. *Behind*, Barry Scheck leaning to make a point to a skeptical judge. *Copyright © 1995 by Haywood Galbreath*

Carl Douglas, Johnnie Cochran, and Barry Scheck. *Copyright © 1995 by Haywood Galbreath*

Robert Shapiro, looking on as O. J. Simpson writes on his legal pad. *Copyright © 1995 by Haywood Galbreath*

Dr. Michael Baden,
pathologist, on the stand.
*Copyright © 1995 by Haywood
Galbreath*

Barry Scheck.
*Copyright © 1995 by
Haywood Galbreath*

Johnnie and Marcia, "the happy couple." *Copyright © 1995 by Haywood Galbreath*

Dr. Jo-Ellan Dimitrius, jury consultant for the defense. *Copyright © 1995 by Haywood Galbreath*

Dr. Robin Cotton, director of Cellmark Laboratories, looking back at Peter Neufeld during cross-examination. *Copyright © 1995 by Haywood Galbreath*

"The coup de grace": Los Angeles County coroner Dr. Lakshaman Sathyavagiswaran demonstrating on Brian "The Genius" Kelberg the prosecution's theory of Nicole Simpson's final moment, using a ruler in place of a knife. Darden and Clark look on. *Copyright © 1995 by Haywood Galbreath*

Allan Park, limo driver, examining a piece of O.J.'s luggage. *Copyright © 1995 by Haywood Galbreath*

"*This* is a magnifying glass." Dr. Henry Lee, the leading forensic scientist in the United States, on the stand. *Copyright © 1995 by Haywood Galbreath*

Another sidebar. *From left,* for the defense Dean Uelmen, Bob Shapiro, and Johnnie Cochran; Judge Ito, drinking coffee; for the prosecution, Marcia Clark, Bill Hodgman, Cheri Lewis, and Chris Darden. See how they smile. *Copyright © 1995 by Haywood Galbreath*

Dr. Herbert MacDonell, demonstrating how bleed-through in a sock is impossible if someone is wearing it. *Copyright © 1995 by Haywood Galbreath*

LAPD criminalist Dennis Fung on the stand, holding large envelope with several chain-of-custody signatures and notations. *Copyright © 1995 by Haywood Galbreath*

LAPD detective Phil Vannatter on the stand, demonstrating the position of the bandage on O.J.'s finger. *Copyright © 1995 by Haywood Galbreath*

LAPD detective Tom Lange on the stand. *Copyright © 1995 by Haywood Galbreath*

The family of O. J. Simpson making a statement at the first-floor press-conference area. *From left,* sister Carmelita Durio, brother-in-law Benny Baker, mother Eunice Simpson (*in wheelchair*), daughter Arnelle Simpson, sister Shirley Baker, and son Jason Simpson. *Copyright © 1995 by Haywood Galbreath*

Suzanne "Bubbles"
Childs, P.R. chief for
the prosecution.
*Copyright © 1995 by
Haywood Galbreath*

Chris Darden receiving
congratulations from
Marcia Clark upon being
named prosecutor of the
year 1995 by the National
Black Prosecutors
Association. Los Angeles
District Attorney Gil
Garcetti applauds.
Copyright © by Globe Photos, Inc.

The family of Ronald Goldman, during an emotional moment. *From left,* Patti Goldman, Fred Goldman, Kimberly Goldman, and Victims' Family Assistance personnel.
Copyright © 1995 by Haywood Galbreath

Anita Hill attending the trial. Shortly after this photo was taken, Professor Hill was ushered into the judge's chambers for an audience with the "Emperor." *Copyright © 1995 by Haywood Galbreath*

LAPD homicide detective Ron Phillips, partner of Mark Fuhrman. *Copyright © 1995 by Haywood Galbreath*

Mark Fuhrman. *Copyright © 1995 by Haywood Galbreath*

The Simpson and Brown families in court. *Front row:* Benny Baker, Shirley Baker, Carmelita Durio; *second row:* Eunice Simpson, Denise Brown, Dominique Brown, Juditha Brown, Lou Brown, and Tanya Brown. *Copyright © 1995 by Haywood Galbreath*

Barbara Walters on her day in Department 103. *Copyright © 1995 by Haywood Galbreath*

Rosa Lopez, maid of O.J.'s Rockingham neighbor, during bilingual questioning. *Copyright © 1995 by Haywood Galbreath*

Denise Brown in court with her attorney, Gloria Allred. *Copyright © 1995 by Haywood Galbreath*

Author Joseph Bosco ("my most embarrassing moment: on the stand with a broken neck") with his attorney, Mike Sullivan. *Copyright © 1995 by Haywood Galbreath*

The badge of reporter Robin Clark, taped to the wall above his seat on the Monday morning after his death. *Copyright © 1995 by Haywood Galbreath*

Geraldo Rivera, another celebrity visitor to the court.
Copyright © 1995 by Haywood Galbreath

The cut on the toe of Goldman's boot was "a fresh cut," which was "consistent" with his kicking out and making contact with a knife; the position of the cut on the shoe suggested it was in the air. Goldman's beeper and keys were found in two different locations, suggesting he was in one place during part of the struggle and then in another.

Dr. Lee testified that when he held the socks up to just ordinary light, he saw bloodstains. Those bloodstains had gone undetected by LAPD criminalists for the first few weeks.

Three additional bloodstains were found in the foyer at Rockingham; the LAPD had not seen these either. The size and pattern of these stains were "consistent" with cast-off spatter from a superficial cut on the inside of a finger—what one might expect from a minor finger cut, say, if it was disregarded and in rapid motion.

The envelope that held Juditha Brown's glasses had some two hundred bloodstains. It was creased after being bloodied, accounting for one large "mirror image" bloodstain pattern. Therefore the envelope had been "manipulated while blood still wet."

There was blood spatter on the envelope and then more spatter on top of that, and there was a partial fingerprint in blood on the glass lens.

Dr. Lee testified that when the envelope was photographed, there was trace and fiber evidence visible; after the evidence was collected, this evidence was gone. Using a projection on the screen, he demonstrated how the envelope and surrounding evidence appeared to have been moved at different times in the process of photographing the crime scene.

An unidentified but unique repeating bloodstain pattern was found in a number of areas within the crime scene. These "parallel lines could be consistent with" a shoe imprint, but to any degree of scientific certainty Dr. Lee said he could not "come here to you today and say that" it was a shoe imprint. One thing

Dr. Lee did not tell the jury was that a clearly visible shoe print made in the walkway when the cement was wet during construction of the condo *was* a part of the crime scene.

The crime-scene evidence was "consistent with . . . a prolonged struggle." And the assailant(s) should have been "covered in blood" because of the visible multiplicity of blood transfers within an area of "close-quarter combat."

Transfer stains were found inside the paper packaging holding what were supposed to be dry blood samples from one of the Bundy blood drops, "bindle #47." According to the State, the swatches had been placed into a test tube the night of June 13, 1994, in the LAPD crime lab; the next morning they were removed and placed onto paper to make up a "bindle." Dr. Lee testified, however, that he found four blood-transfer stains on the paper, leading him to be confused: either all swatches should have been dry, thereby leaving no stains, or if they had been put away wet, there should have been seven stains, not four.

"Something, somebody . . . put the swatch in the [package to] cause such a transfer," Dr. Lee said. "Who did it? What happened? I don't know. Only opinion I can give you under these circumstances: *Something's wrong.*"

❖

THE MOST TELLING comment Henry Lee made from the stand was overlooked by most, but not by the jury:

"I think more than one person know [what happened at the crime]," Dr. Lee said in response to a rhetorical question flung at him somewhat desperately by young Mr. Goldberg.

❖

"WHAT IF ONE guy is in the bushes where Goldman ends up being, and there's another guy in this cubbyhole area by the front door?" Pat McKenna, who spent more hours going over the Bundy scene and poring over its recovered or documented evidence than almost anybody who worked the case, is talking about the two-assailant theory.

"If you look at the gate and you look at her front door, to the left, there's a little alcove in there—a guy could've been hiding there. Nicole could come out the front door. He could come from behind her. After she opens the gate and starts to back up, boom. So you've got a guy that could be hiding up there and a guy that could be hiding down in the bushes. That's what I've always thought happened.

"Because I always felt, shit, there's gotta be two people. I mean, I walked all over that place. I said, Jesus Christ, someone could be right there—because we all talked about it, Johnnie was there, you know, and McNally, we're all standing around saying, What about if you've got a guy here that can see her—she goes out, he comes around following her down, she lets Ron in, and then whammo. The guy downstairs in the bushes is there as backup—you know, maybe two people were gonna whack just one person, but then Goldman shows up. And they take 'em both out. They couldn't have been laying in wait for Goldman. Because nobody knew he was coming. Juditha Brown's glasses getting left and returned was a fluke.

"It had to be two people. Had to be," Pat says with a total conviction unusual for one in his profession.

"Listen to this. Heidstra hears the 'Hey! Hey! Hey!'—which is Goldman getting killed, I think. From there he hears a gate slam. That gate is the *middle* gate. We slammed all three gates, the front gate, the back gate, and the middle gate. The only one that can make that clang is the middle gate. As a matter of fact, I've still got it on tape; we were doing experiments and I had a tape recorder and I was slamming that gate to tape the sound. I played it for Heidstra to see if that was the sound and it was.

"But anyway, Heidstra hears the gate slam and then hears men 'arguing.' Now, I gotta think Goldman ain't arguing anymore. It's gotta be these guys running away. If it's one killer slamming the gate, there would be no more arguing. Who'd be arguing? So what did Heidstra hear? He had to hear the two killers, either arguing or maybe 'What the fuck, there was only supposed to be the woman!' 'Let's get out of here!' Or something like that."

❖

A FTER HANK GOLDBERG'S misguided, unfortunately harsh attempt to discredit Dr. Lee in cross-examination, the world watched as the prosecution brought back FBI Special Agent Bodziak and elicited from this federal employee misleading, inaccurate, brazenly biased testimony in an effort to impeach Dr. Lee. It was Bodziak who tried to tell the jury that it had heard Dr. Lee identify the cement shoe imprint as crime-scene evidence. He heaped scorn upon anything to do with the repeating "parallel lines."

Trial observers, for whom a guilty verdict was the only noble destination of the Trial of the Century, took glee in the effort to diminish "the great Doctor Lee." Apparently, members of the press still hold a grudge against Henry Lee for his testimony in the William Kennedy Smith rape trial; Kennedy bias is surprisingly strong and widespread in the so-called liberal media.

The punditry led members of the defense team to overreact and say that they were probably going to recall Dr. Lee during their case in chief or in surrebuttal. Henry Lee was deeply stung by the negative commentary. As a scientist, as a human being, Dr. Lee is who he is because he has never before had his credibility questioned by anyone, from his days as a police officer in Taiwan to his selection as the man who soon will be releasing to Congress his commissioned report on the death of presidential aide Vincent Foster.

Dr. Lee chose not to answer back in kind. So he would not have to make individual comments to the hundreds of print and broadcast journalists calling the Connecticut State Police Lab, Henry Lee called a press conference. He announced he was not inclined to testify again. That there was no need for it—he had said everything the regimen of science allowed him to say to the jury already. How his findings were interpreted by others was beyond his control.

He also explained that to testify again would only mark him as an advocate—the one thing he teaches criminalists never to be. Science, unlike the criminal justice system it sometimes serves, is not an advocacy process. As a scientist, he is not concerned with guilt or innocence. To tell the scientific truth is his only role. Then he said he "regretted" getting involved with the Simpson case.

❖

DURING THE NOW two years since the murders, I have had any number of conversations with Henry Lee about the case. One of the most informative—and surely the most enjoyable—was this past June in New Orleans. We were up to our elbows in boiled crawfish, crabs, and shrimp at a little soiree in Dr. Lee's honor hosted by Jefferson Parish Sheriff Harry Lee, many months after the verdicts in Los Angeles. Henry wasn't in southeast Louisiana to eat, however; he was there to help solve a 150-year-old murder case in Baton Rouge, which came to light when an almost perfectly preserved victim was unearthed by chance.

While the crime the state of Louisiana had asked him to

resolve is unusual, Dr. Lee being feted by law enforcement is not. He has worked with most of the major law enforcement agencies in Louisiana on cases large and small, and he has taught crime-scene procedures and basic forensic science to almost every detective in the state. As is true in a majority of the other states.

These things have not changed with Dr. Lee's testimony in the Simpson case. He received almost 1,700 letters of support, which he was deeply gratified by, from law enforcement personnel around the country, including FBI personnel superior to Agent Bodziak. (They would continue to need Dr. Lee's help in the future.) He also received seventy-five photos of proven shoe imprints with parallel lines sent to him by criminalists and investigators from across the criminal justice spectrum.

Aside from the personal discomfort his participation in the Simpson case has brought him, there was the enormous cost in time. Many other less celebrated but no less pressing cases of butchered, gassed, poisoned, strangled, bludgeoned, shot, blown-up, mutilated victims remain.

❖

DR. LEE IS perturbed that the Los Angeles District Attorney's Office should have taken his working with the Simpson defense so personally, reacting in the way it did. From the first days on, the prosecution assigned people to follow him to meetings and seminars. They would question people he spoke with, and in the process they would spread out-of-context gossip, smearing his name among the national forensic community.

"They try impeach me before I even come to testify. Why?" Henry asks. "No one ever do before."

Because of the highly visible "battle of the experts" in the Simpson case, Dr. Lee fears the result will be a net loss to the criminal justice system. Dr. Lee, as do many immigrants, holds

American ideals of law and liberty in high esteem, higher than far too many of America's natural-born citizens. "It must be proved beyond reasonable doubt," Henry Lee says with emphasis. "People die for that right!"

❖

A S REGARDS THE crime scene, Dr. Lee notes that the Bundy scene was a "primary crime scene" that was "halfway between" being "an organized scene" and a "not organized scene," which "is very unusual. Things look organized . . . then not look organized. What that mean?" Also that there was a great deal of activity in a small area with two victims, but "two people hard for one person kill like that . . . if two people together when attack."

Knowing who was attacked first would be helpful, Dr. Lee believes but, without other evidence, perhaps not nearly as important as knowing in what sequence and in what fashion Ron Goldman entered the gated crime scene.

It is significant that Nicole was found barefoot. We know the problem with the gate buzzer, and that Nicole had to come outside and manually let visitors in. "She barefoot . . . she just run out house for minute. Don't go someplace barefoot. Plan run out and run back in barefoot. Run out to open gate." The fact that Officer Robert Riske, the first cop on-scene, found Nicole's front door open would fit with Nicole just running out quickly to open the gate for Goldman.

This is consistent with other evidence suggesting that when the attack began Nicole and Ron were together or at the least in sight of each other. The killer was either already there or he followed Goldman in: These would seem the only two ways by which Goldman was to meet his assailant(s). Also, whoever entered last did not close the gate completely, as it was open when Sukru

Boztepe, following the bloody Akita to its home, discovered the crime scene. The Akita would have been unable to get through the gate if it had been pulled shut. Which suggests that some kind of immediate activity intervened so that it was left open.

But Dr. Lee then asks the important question: If Nicole and Ron saw the assailant(s), "how come nobody screaming?"

Dr. Lee does not have a problem with the LA coroner's assessment of the long thin cuts on Ron's neck as control wounds. It would not be unexpected to find such wounds when two victims are dealt with by *two* assailants. This would not be the first crime scene where a victim was intimidated into watching a companion be slaughtered before he was then killed.

❖

B UT THE ISSUE here is this: All of the above questions would have been easy to answer with a properly processed crime scene. Because of the amount of blood, deposited in the fashion it was, the task would have been like connecting the dots: Who did what to whom and in what order.

Problems exist on another level as well, problems regarding the amount of evidence. But not in the way one would think. "How much evidence collected? How much evidence introduced?" is key to the unanswered questions of the trial. "Why nobody ask? Very select introduction of evidence. Much evidence in this case nobody want to introduce, both sides. But defense have to present nothing."

❖

"I ONLY RECENTLY was told that there are close to ten thousand pages more of discovery and statements that they never gave us," Pat McKenna says, echoing Dr. Lee on the selectivity of the evidence the prosecution used or turned over to the defense.

"I've gotta believe that's exculpatory stuff from people that were near Bundy. At least we had some with the courage to come forward and take this thrashing that they took on TV from the government, and then all the subsequent phone messages left on their answer machines by kooks around the country."

❖

A T ROCKINGHAM, DR. LEE is dubious about the notion of anyone jumping O.J.'s back fence. "Nobody can jump fence that way. Fence tall, plant vegetation higher. The gap between wall and fence? Have to jump like helicopter. Straight up, straight down. Not jump over fence, not real person." Nor, Dr. Lee explains, was there evidence of anyone or anything remotely intrusive passing that way. Consequently, the evidence suggests that the Rockingham glove was placed there by someone, not dropped in the activity of climbing and scampering. Common sense says that if the glove was discarded while stumbling through a bed of leaves, the chances of at least part of one solitary leaf being over any part of the glove would be all but a statistical dead cinch, but there isn't anything. No matter how long you stare at the photo, the glove is sitting *atop* everything.

If O.J. left the glove there, then it was a deliberate act; for whatever reason he chose to walk back and place it there. But why? With everything else so cleanly disposed of.

The relative scarcity of blood found in the Bronco poses another problem—all told, less volume than one drop of blood widely scattered. If O.J. was the killer, then he did not drive the Bronco wearing the murder clothes.

❖

THE TESTIMONY OF Allan Park, the limousine driver, is also problematic. Park has always said the Bronco wasn't there when he first arrived but he couldn't remember if it was there when he left. But after his grand-jury testimony and preliminary-hearing testimony, and sometime before his trial testimony many months later, he begins to *think* he might have seen it there when he drove away with O.J. His mother, a lawyer, was allowed to sit with the prosecution during his time in the witness box, and Park would look to her constantly whenever this subject came up. He indicated that his first memory change came during a question-and-answer session with his mother, long after the murders.

Dr. Lee finds this difficult to accept. If the limo driver is positive the Bronco was not there when he'd turned the limo around, how can he not be sure whether or not he saw the Bronco in that spot only minutes later? Particularly since the Bronco should have been dead in his headlights as he steered the long limo out of the gate he'd just turned around in.

If the Bronco wasn't there at either time, or was there the whole time, all bets are off on everything. Of course, the case for accomplices at least is greatly strengthened, if not for another murderer(s) altogether.

❖

ALLAN PARK'S TESTIMONY is problematic as well for Pat McKenna, because Pat believes the Bronco was there all night

"It's Park's first night as a limo driver for a celebrity. He's looking inside the gate, not outside the gate. Not only didn't he see the Bronco, he didn't see Kato's car, which is within three feet of where he's ringing the buzzer. Never ever did he see Kato's car, which was sitting right there.

"Now here's something to think about, too," Pat continues. "Several fellows called me after Park testified at the prelim to say that early on Park was bragging on Catalina Island to six guys that it wasn't a cigarette he was smoking, it was a bowl of reefer.

"O.J. always thought he was fucked up. O.J. used to say, 'This guy was messed up, he missed the 405 [Freeway]!' O.J. was thinking, 'What the hell, how could this guy miss the 405? He drove down the street right next to it, Sepulveda.' O.J. said to him, 'Where ya going?'

"But none of those six guys'll come forward to testify. I tried to get 'em to turn on Park. So Park's a little bit high, shows up, he doesn't see the Bronco, he doesn't see Kato's car—by the way, what kind of a guy is this that when all of a sudden he doesn't know what to do on his job as a limo driver he calls his mother? [When Park didn't get an answer after buzzing at the Rockingham gate, Park called his mother to ask what he should do.]

"His mother would not let us interview him. We took his mother up in the air in a helicopter. Drove over both crime scenes, drove around Bundy, showed her the diagrams where everything was. And we said, 'We don't think your kid is telling lies, we just think he's not paying attention to things he didn't have to pay attention to which were things outside the gate. He was there for what was inside the gate. He was looking for some sign of life inside the gate, when in fact all there was was O.J. upstairs in his bedroom.'"

Allan Park offers no clarification on the matter, as Wendy Park, his mother, would not allow this reporter to interview him either. From her home on Catalina, Ms. Park categorically denies the possibility of her son's smoking pot that night. "Nothing happens on this island that I don't know about. There has never been even a rumor of that. It would disturb him very much."

Exactly what Allan Park saw at Simpson's Rockingham estate is crucial, to say the least. A lot hinged on the whereabouts of the Bronco between 10:15 and 11:00 P.M.

❖❖❖

D R. LEE HAS problems with why police officers and the criminalists, Dennis Fung and Andrea Mazzola, would equivocate over things so inconsequential, yet obvious, as items of evidence being moved during the processing of a crime scene. "Why lie about envelope not move? Jury has eyes. Can see. See police lie when no need to. Things always going to move at crime scene. Not want to, but happen. Most time not big deal. So why lie? Maybe *is* big deal!"

❖❖❖

D R. LEE IS not immune to the sensitivities involved when murders go unresolved by the State. He has put away more murderers than any other single detective or cop in the world. But because he has been at it so long, and understands it so well, he knows that in court "each element of crime must be linked . . . must be complete picture for jury."

But in the Simpson case as investigated, the crime scene leaves too many questions begging to be answered for there not to be reasonable doubt legally and scientifically. But things didn't need to be that way. The answers were there, many may still be there in the photos and reports and physical evidence. But Dr. Lee believes, finally, that the investigators don't really want to know the whole truth in this case. There is a lot of lying going on on all sides, "Too many people lie. . . . Something wrong!"

❖

"VANNATTER GETS THIS phone tip about O.J. buying a knife at Ross Cutlery," Pat McKenna begins his account of what really happened regarding one of the most publicized events from the first weeks of the case. "He goes and talks to Camacho [Jose Camacho, the Ross Cutlery employee who sold O.J. a knife]. Camacho doesn't know which knife O.J. bought. Nobody remembers. They didn't even give him a reciept. Why? Because he paid cash and they probably put the cash in the pocket. Never declared it.

"So Vannatter's asking him, asking him, he doesn't know which one. Vannatter goes to Golden [Dr. Irwin Golden, who did the autopsies of Ron and Nicole] and says 'Look at the wounds. Here's the kind of knives that were in this one tray [at Ross Cutlery] but Camacho couldn't identify which one.' Golden says, 'These wounds would've been caused by this knife or this one.' They were the big knives.

"But guess what O.J. bought? He bought a little tiny knife that can't make these kind of wounds. We had Henry Lee examine it, it still had the price tag on it, it was in pristine condition. But they don't know this yet. So Vannatter goes back and he's muscling Camacho to pick the big knife. Which Camacho does in the prelim, he picks the big knife.

"That's Vannatter—he doesn't care what's true or not. He's muscling it to fit what he thinks is his case. Things like that really pissed me off, because Vannatter, the whole crew was doing shit like that."

12

THE FAMILY BROWN

WHAT EXACTLY WAS Ron and Nicole's relationship going to be that particular night in June if they had lived through it? According to Faye Resnick's book, Nicole had decided to "do" young Mr. Goldman, as it seems these specimens of the rich, famous, and beautiful in Brentwood are wont to call what a lot of other folks call "getting lucky." Judging by the lighted candles Officer Riske found around her drawn bath, which Ms. Resnick has informed us was Nicole's favored ambience for sex, it likely was going to be Ron Goldman's night.

It's not likely he was expecting it, though. He had already borrowed a car to go and meet a friend for a drink after work. The errand of delivering Ms. Juditha Brown's glasses to Nicole was an unforeseen happenstance, surely. To think, even on the level of a tryst, that there was anything more than fate at play in the leaving and returning of the eyeglasses is to swim in conspiratorial waters too much like a mirage for me.

Of course, Nicole could have been planning on having sex with someone *else* that night, the very thing some people say would have to be present for O.J. to lose it and hog-butcher two human beings. And if that someone wasn't plausibly Goldman, or O.J. himself, if Nicole was in fact setting out a shrine to the beast with two backs, then that someone could have been an unidentified person on the scene that night—another spark or another perpetrator?

It's also true that Nicole could have been planning to take a bath alone, with the candles lighted around the tub.

But what has been made clear by this entire case is that these folks, by and large, lived frivolous, perverse lives that do not represent Brentwood, much less Los Angeles, or the nation. Just one incident from the sixteen hours of Kato's tapes with Marc Eliot paints a pretty revealing picture.

Nicole Brown Simpson, at about the same time she asked Kato to provide her with twenty-year-old hunks from the Hollywood factory for her to "do," told him she wanted to experiment with lesbian sex with Faye Resnick. She wanted to try it as a threesome the first time so she would need to "audition" some young males. Yet she drew a strong moral line when it came to having sex with Marcus Allen, O.J.'s devoted protégé. She told Kato she only let Marcus "masturbate on [her] breasts" out of deference to his relationship with her former husband!

In so many ways Nicole and O.J. were two sides of the same coin, and it wasn't a pretty penny. Some have said they deserved each other. That is mean-spirited. It is also presumptuous. It might very well be true.

❖❖

TANYA BROWN, TWENTY-FIVE, is the youngest of Nicole's three surviving sisters. Of the Brown family, she was in court the most often—which was by no means regular or even approaching the daily vigil of the remarkable Goldman family. She is a wholly endearing young woman in many ways. If a beautiful, voluptuous, bright young woman can be likened to any member of the animal world, Tanya Brown would be a St. Bernard puppy. While she shares many of the character traits from the complex Brown family repository, she is surely the most guileless in her quirky comments.

Far and away the most revealing glimpse inside the Brown family psyche, at least in this reporter's thinking, came the day Tanya was trying to explain her relationship with the genuinely fine young man who was her constant, rather gallant courtroom squire to the Authors.

"Oh! He's just wonderful, you know?" she said. "He's so sweet and exciting, and everything. He's tall, and so handsome. I mean, he's just like O.J.!"

It was either Dominick or Joe who picked his jaw up from the ground and got it working soon enough to say, "But, Tanya, O.J.'s on trial for murdering your sister. You believe he did it!"

"Oh," she replied with a bubbling sincerity that was as palpable as it was astonishing, "you don't understand. O.J. is a wonderful guy. He just fucked up."

I know it was Joe who later simply said, "That about sums it up."

❖

I F TRUTH BE truth, and truth be told, as it sometimes should be no matter what, then I must publicly confess to what so many say in private: Unlike with the Goldman family, one has to work hard at being truly sympathetic to Nicole's family.

Let's face it: How many parents, two weeks after their seventeen-year-old daughter has graduated high school, would welcome her moving in with a married man she'd met and slept with for the first time the day before? This has nothing to do with his being black or even being much older; this is not racism or ageism. It has to do with legitimate concerns for the long-term good of one's flesh and blood.

The Browns, however, from all reports, took to the arrangement like white on rice. The family of the retired army sergeant jumped into the fast life as if to the manner born. They now had it all. The sisters got to hobnob at the biggest sporting events, to go on fabulous jaunts and vacations, to have O.J. pay for their tuition—when they actually went to college—to date men they would otherwise never have had the chance to meet.

Lou Brown got a profitable Hertz franchise, and Juditha Brown's travel agency had all the VIP business it could handle. Houses were bought and remodeled and sold. Soon there was a fried-chicken franchise to add to the overall Brown family larder, and then a chain of honey-baked-ham outlets.

No matter where you hail from, there's a word and phrase for the Browns' behavior. It's called pimping, as in "they pimped her out." Now scrape yourself down from the ceiling, put down the poison pen, because there's proof: The pimping did not stop with Nicole's death. Consider the following:

Soon after the murders, Americans being who they are, checks and cash just started showing up in the Browns' mail, marked "for the Simpson children." This money added up quickly. Well into six figures, some pretty good sources say. When word of this windfall came out, certain members of the media did some digging and eventually knew enough to ask where the money had gone. The Browns indicated that it was important to keep Sydney and Justin, the two children of Nicole and O.J., living at the "same level they were accustomed to," and so the money had been spent accordingly. Now that was early fall of 1994, barely three months after the murders, and that kind of money had *already* been spent "for the children."

Lou Brown also dared to say in an interview how tough the added financial burden of the two children was without the $10,000-a-month divorce-prescribed child support from O.J. Well, these journalists did some more digging and found that the checks had arrived like clockwork each month. Even when money was almost too tight to pay for his legal expenses, O.J.

sent that $10,000 check. Lou's answer was he'd forgotten, plus he was misquoted.

Then there was the battered women's organization started by Denise Brown in her sister's name to much publicity. There was a national tour of appearances and fund-raisers for the new charity. Bob Guccione, the publisher of *Penthouse*, publicly handed Denise a large check—and I don't just mean the blown-up version of it for the photo op. A couple of journalists who went digging again discovered that the foundation had never been chartered. There was no trust; there was no paperwork anywhere. Within days of being confronted with this, Denise Brown quickly registered and chartered the organization and trust. Up until that time, some pretty big checks had been endorsed and deposited to the account of Denise Brown.

And what's with this family where the daughters never really marry and leave daddy's house even as they have children?

If the dynamics of Nicole's relationship with O.J. was sick, it may have reflected in some way what she grew up around. O.J. might have controlled and polished off, in his image, the public person Nicole became, but her family shaped her lifelong values and fundamental attitudes.

Yes, it is hard work feeling sympathetic toward the Brown family collectively. Individually is a slightly different matter.

❖

"WHEN DENISE BROWN took the stand, one of the things that troubled me—I mean, my experience of Denise was that she came off as a party person," Dr. Goulston recalls.

"Some would say 'white trash,' except that's racist and mean. Let's say she came off as a party person. As a result, I found myself not wanting to sympathize with her. So I was wondering what might make Denise sympathetic to the jury. Guilt and shame is a big sort of principle that I look for, because I think trying to deny it is an explanation for a lot of our behavior in life: trying to keep guilt from being discovered by others and shame from being discovered by ourselves. We'll use up most of our energy, most of our waking hours, to conceal the guilt from the outside and the shame from the inside.

"And what I said to Chris Darden was 'I don't think she's coming off as that sympathetic and yet I think it's honest. It might be a useful thing to find out. I mean, if I was the big sister of Nicole, and if in retrospect there were cries for help but I didn't hear them, there would be a part of me that felt guilty for not hearing the cries—and maybe shame for not wanting to hear the cries for help—because I like the parties.'

"O.J. was their meal ticket," Dr. Goulston continues after some thought. "He was more than their meal ticket, he was their fame ticket. So she was in denial. So what I said to Chris was 'What might make her more sympathetic is if in retrospect she felt guilty for having denied what she is now aware of. And more than guilty—if she felt ashamed for having maybe sold out her kid sister so the family could have a good time.'

"And Chris asked her some of those questions. 'Did you ever feel guilty or responsible?' And she said, 'I've been in recovery, I've been in a twelve-step program for X amount of months, and if I got into that'—and I thought this was sincere—'if I got into those feelings, I'd be done for.'

"Meaning, as part of my recovery I can't get down on myself. And that is part of twelve-step programs. But with that said, it still might've been a useful thing to at least bring out because if she had said, 'Yes, I'm not just a party person. I have guilt. I have shame. I have to live with that.' That would have made her more sympathetic. *If* she could have admitted to those feelings."

❖

P AT MC KENNA IS harsh on them. "To me they're white-trash hillbillies; they were like gypsies in the night," he says about his client's former in-laws. "They sold everything they could get their hands on, including her memory. I think if they had a videotape of Nicole giving birth, they would've sold that, you know? They would've sold a video of her with her legs up in the air giving birth to Sydney if they had it.

"They all said they quit their jobs because of the trial. What jobs did they quit? The only thing they had, O.J. gave them. They sucked off of this guy like nobody's business. When they saw the well running dry, they jumped ship."

13

THE SOCKS, THE GLOVES, THE BRONCO

WHEN DETECTIVE ALBERTO LUPER asked for the socks found on the rug in O.J.'s bedroom to be collected into evidence in the late afternoon of June 13, he ordered that measurements be taken of their position in relation to the walls. There are, however, according to a former LAPD detective, two conflicting sets of measurements on two reports made at two different times!

According to a very good source, the same day in late September 1994 that Collin Yamauchi packed up the socks to be sent to the California Department of Justice (DOJ) for DNA testing, the Scientific Investigation Division (SID) criminalist also checked out three whole-blood reference samples from the serology lab and brought them into the evidence processing room. These were Ron's, Nicole's, and O.J.'s.

Allegedly, that was the day there was a "vacuum-effect" spillage of blood from O.J.'s reference vial when the stopper cap was removed. Mr. Yamauchi testified the blood got on his gloves. But why? Forget the accident. What purpose, at that point in the investigation, could warrant having reference blood samples and other physical evidence out and exposed at the same time? This is highly irregular, scientifically risky, proce-durally unnecessary, and as yet unexplained.

❖

LARRY RAGLE, THE former director of the crime lab in the Sheriff's Department of Orange County, the rich man's bankrupt county south of Los Angeles, was called to the witness stand to testify about the LAPD's crime-scene work on the Simpson case. His words: "below minimum standards."

Vannatter later refused to shake Ragle's hand, calling him a "traitor."

Bob Blasier, who had directed the defense examination of Mr. Ragle, told the Court that Vannatter's statement and be-havior were emblematic of the "habit or custom" of police of-ficers not testifying against each other.

❖

SERIOUSLY, WHAT *DID* folks expect the jury to think about hanky-panky with evidence when John Maraz, the tow-truck driver who was all over the Bronco at Viertels Tow Yard, said with emphasis: "I didn't see any blood"? He didn't hesitate, he said it definitively, and he was never shaken away from it during a buzzsaw attack by Marcia.

He said he was surprised by the absence of blood because the media was reporting "blood all over" the Bronco. Maraz might be a souvenir thief. The two cleaner's receipts—one for a tuxedo for O.J. and one for a dress for Nicole—which he admits taking from the Bronco but swears he put back in have never turned up. (His swearing he returned them could be self-serving; he has also filed a lawsuit against Viertels for firing him.) But what reason does he have to lie about not seeing blood in the Bronco?

And then LAPD Detective Kelly Mulldorfer of the Legal Affairs Division, who investigated the Maraz towing incident, testified she had "no recollection of seeing blood in the Bronco." What's a juror to think? The most famous four-wheel drive in the world, *the* Bronco? You'd remember whether you saw blood or not.

There are indeed photographs depicting what looks like blood in the Bronco, which the record indicates were taken before either Maraz or Mulldorfer had access to the vehicle. This would seem to settle the matter rationally, but there was a host of contradicting testimony. So much that a jury could easily have reasonable doubt concerning the integrity of the chain of custody of the Bronco evidence. There is no doubt that there was blood in the Bronco the night of the murders. Except these folks' testimony illustrates, graphically, how little blood was in the Bronco, and that it was smeared and swiped so thinly it was hard to see on the beige interior of the car.

❖

WILLIE FORD, AN LAPD photographer, testified that he did not see any socks on the carpet in the middle of O.J.'s bedroom when he videotaped the Rockingham search—a routine procedure to defend against damage lawsuits later from search victims. He said he'd been "told to shoot everything." Johnnie Cochran, with the videotape freeze-framed on the screen, the time and date in the right-hand corner—3:13 P.M. 6/13/1994 (it was agreed that the video-camera timer was one hour off and it should have been 4:13)—asked this unbiased cop witness a question.

"Any socks?"

"No."

Indeed, through direct examination, cross-examination, and

redirect and recross by Johnnie and Chris, Officer Ford answered that question repeatedly enough for Judge Ito to say to counsel, "By my count he's said he didn't see the socks ten times now."

❖

HERB MAC DONELL'S WORK on the socks and his bleed-through explanation were impressive. Particularly the microphotography showing those weird, neat "blood balls" within the fibers of the sock fabric, along with the scientific explanation of what that chemical shape meant: When blood dries on a surface, its structure, seen under a high-powered microscope, consists of perfect little balls. If the blood is deposited on a surface from contact with the dried residue of blood from another surface, then what you see in the microscope are crystalized flakes.

The jury was convinced that a bleed-through process was the most likely occurrence. The who or how of this bleed-through is still open to question. However, since it isn't O.J.'s blood on the socks but Nicole's, the only way O.J. could be responsible for the saturation of this secondary transfer blood-stain of the sock, which had soaked through to the other side of the sock, was if he had taken them off with his fingers dripping in his wife's blood. A bleed-through with a foot and ankle *in* the sock cannot occur.

The police say that O.J. took his socks off in his bedroom at Rockingham. But how could his fingers still be that wet with Nicole's blood? Of course, the State maintains that the half-dollar-sized bloodstain got on the sock at the crime scene by making contact with a direct source of Nicole's blood. Yet how could the blood still be wet enough in O.J.'s bedroom to soak through to the other side, particularly since it was not wet enough to stain the bedroom rug?

❖

"NUMBER ONE, O.J.'S a neatnik, okay?" Pat McKenna says, his Irish ire ratcheting up a notch or two.

"O.J. said, 'Look, when I get cleaned up I throw all my shit in the hamper. There were no socks laying out there. There were no suspenders on the bed. I threw my shit in the hamper. And Gigi [O.J.'s maid] can testify to that.'

"In testimony," McKenna continues, "Lange said, 'Yeah, we went through the hamper.' I mean, these dumb fucks, what they should've done was throw a bunch of shit all over the room. Not just a pair of socks. Those socks had to *fly* from Bundy to Rockingham, because how did they get there bloody with nothing else? No other blood from the crime scene. No blood, no DNA going up the stairs with white carpet, the white walls. No blood except a huge fucking molecular-weight DNA drop of Nicole's blood on a sock right there for the whole world to see it.

"O.J. was going nuts about the socks before it ever became an issue in the case. It was when we were going over pictures that were given to us in discovery. It's early in discovery, the sock hadn't been brought up in court yet. He's going, 'Wait a minute! I never put these socks here!' As a matter of fact, he said, 'See if Gigi took these socks out.' Because, he said, 'I know I throw everything in the hamper. Then, when I took a shower to get ready to go to Chicago—like I always do whenever I travel—the towels that I'm done with, I keep all in one nice little spot and Gigi takes care of it.'

"And sure enough, Gigi said, 'All the time when he's left town he's never left clothes laying around.' Of course, the DA will say, 'He was in a hurry.' That's such a preposterous piece of logic, too. Because if he was in a hurry, how come he only dropped one glove and left socks out? Where is the murder weapon? Where's all the rest of the bloody clothes? I mean, where's all the shit, okay? Bullshit. Total bullshit."

❖❖

M Y EYES STAYED glued to O.J. and the gloves from the moment I realized the prosecution was actually going to be stupid enough to make him try them on.

The look on his face as he suddenly, in a fraction of a heartbeat, realized the gloves were too small, went from great apprehension to great relief. Only then did he begin to overact. But regardless, from a distance of about five feet, to this courtroom observer, the gloves did not fit. Why they did not fit I do not know; but at that moment, those gloves did not fit O. J. Simpson's hand.

❖❖

O UT IN THE hall, shortly after Richard Rubin, the prosecution's faithful glove expert, testified that "fat liquor" is added to the leather for elasticity, Bob Shapiro told me an instant F. Lee Bailey joke: "After Mr. Bailey found out the gloves had liquor in them, he ordered a dozen pair."

14

DNA, LEAKS, EMBARRASSMENT

MARCIA CLARK, Dr. Fredric Reiders, Bob Blasier, and FBI Special Agent Roger Martz battled extensively about EDTA, but the fact of the matter was, there were unusually high levels of the whole-blood preservative in bloodstains on the socks and the back gate at Bundy. Why and how and what it really means is a large question. But it was there. The chemical that police labs routinely use for blood evidence was there in these two items that mysteriously appeared.

Given the EDTA and the fact that the one blood drop on the back gate was not collected until weeks after the murders, what's a juror to think? Is it possible this evidence was tampered with? Is there circumstantial evidence supporting this possibility? If the answer is yes, then that's more reasonable doubt about two major links in the State's "blood trail leading straight to the defendant," as Marcia Clark had characterized her blood evidence.

❖

J OHN GERDES IS a medical scientist and administrator. He is also an advocate of accreditation for forensic laboratories. Because the private DNA lab he operates is primarily a medical facility that matches body fluids and organs for transfusions and transfer to critically ill people, his testimony perhaps carried greater weight. His principal point: the need for law enforcement crime labs, which like medical labs must make precise measurements, to undergo a rigid accreditation process.

With his theme of sloppy, contaminating procedures by the LAPD crime lab, Gerdes cast as much reasonable doubt on the absolute exactitude of DNA inclusion identification as did Dr. Bruce Weir's "I'm embarrassed" error in arithmetic when he testified for the prosecution using inclusion statistics such as "one in fifty-five billion." While I sat and took the best notes I could, I'm too mathematically handicapped to explain the mistake Dr. Weir discovered in his database that caused him to lower his one-out-of-billions inclusion statistics to one-out-of-thousands. But the gist is pretty clear.

All told, the possibility of a mistake by a lab as lacking in scientific peer-review credibility as the SID of the Los Angeles Police Department does loom large. Particularly to a panel of humans who far too often can cite family stories of a bad lab report. The affable, professional Gerdes's testimony was strong enough for Ito to tell Barry Scheck, "I think you have downplayed your effectiveness; you have opened whole new avenues regarding evidence processing."

Gerdes's testimony and Weir's error, taken together, provide enough reasonable doubt in the truly impressive, overwhelming DNA inclusion case the prosecution had at its disposal—but utilized so poorly. Of course, it *should* be hard to find twelve human beings who want to live with the forever-and-ever-amen question of sending another human being to prison for life— certainly if based on folks in white coats testing anything collected or handled by the likes of Dennis Fung, Andrea Mazzola, Collin Yamauchi, Mark Fuhrman, or Phil Vannatter.

❖

OF COURSE, THIS was the wrong jury to hear Dr. Robin Cotton of Cellmark Laboratories, testifying for the prosecution, say that the lab's database, from which the astronomical inclusion statistics for the Simpson case were extrapolated, came from only 240 African Americans in Detroit!

But it got worse. On the sixth day of Dr. Cotton's testimony, Peter Neufeld got her to disclose that some of the data collected by the Red Cross and used for comparisons in the Simpson case included tests on only *two* other blacks.

"And so in your database, the number of people that you have typed like Mr. Simpson across all five loci is just *two* people, isn't that right?" Peter Neufeld asked her.

"Across all five loci, yes," Dr. Cotton said.

The jurors scribbled like mad in their notebooks. After a few double takes.

❖

A MAJOR IRONY OF the Simpson trial is that Dr. Henry Lee was one of the first champions of the use of DNA for forensic purposes. He is largely responsible for its acceptance in Europe and now somewhat in the United States. He stipulates, however, that for DNA evidence to be valid, it *must* be properly collected, stored, and processed—which he felt was not done in the Simpson case. Furthermore, the true error rate of individual labs must necessarily be factored into the inclusion statistics.

❖

"WHEN ROBIN COTTON was on the stand," psychiatrist Mark Goulston recalls, "I said to myself, 'Gee, she's very calm, she's like a nice science teacher. And Peter Neufeld is like a pushy backseat driver.'" And so Dr. Goulston suggested this one tactic to the prosecution, which it used.

"I said, 'I think it might be more useful if Robin Cotton would always put herself between the jury and Peter Neufeld. So that in the foreground you see calmness, in the background you see Peter Neufeld just sort of pacing around.'

"Remember the occasions where she would say to Ito, 'I think I can see it better from down here'? And she'd get up and walk down in front of the jury?"

Yes, I do. Dr. Cotton also always turned away from Peter when she had to stay in the box. She would physically turn one-quarter left toward the jury just beneath her and look back with her eyes at Peter. It was amazing to watch.

The tactic just didn't work, apparently.

❖

TERENCE SPEED, PROFESSOR of statistics and former chairman of the math department at the University of California at Berkeley, in some great courtroom tit-for-tat with prosecutor Woody Clarke, gave what legitimacy was still needed for reasonable doubt in the entire DNA presentation. Professor Speed, an extremely prestigious mathematician who had served with Bruce Weir, the prosecution's expert, on other scientific matters, said flat-out that his colleague Dr. Weir was "scientifically incorrect" in the sum and substance of his mind-boggling testimony. He explained that the issue of the true error rates of genetic labwork was one of the "most important scientific debates of our times." And he went on to say that the bulk of recognized scientists working in the field consider Bruce Weir to be a forensic DNA statistics maverick.

Dr. Speed was not allowed to tell the jury that he and Dr. Henry Lee, in addition to twenty-five top DNA scientists in the United States, had signed a letter protesting Dr. Weir's inclusion theories as published in the journal *Science*.

❖

ON THURSDAY, JULY 6, the prosecution rested its case in chief—after 105 days and 323 hours of testimony from 58 witnesses.

Gerry Spence, commenting on television that night, pointed out what he thought were Marcia & Company's greatest flops: O.J. trying on the gloves; Barry Scheck's cross of Dennis Fung; and Marcia declaring Kato a hostile witness.

Stan Goldman, law professor at Loyola, and a constant presence in the coverage of the trial as an expert commentator, said statistician Bruce Weir's math screwup was the worst—that in the jury's mind it could "negate all DNA" evidence if they were "looking for reasonable doubt."

I remember being in general agreement with both. Having done my share of television commentary during the trial, I probably agreed with Gerry Spence and Stan Goldman more often than I did with most of our other colleagues.

❖

WHEN O.J. LEANED over Joe McGinniss and journalist David Margolick to show the jurors at the gallery end of the box his permanently swollen knuckles, I could see his fingers and hands quivering almost uncontrollably.

❖

I N THE JUNE 1995 issue of *Penthouse*, in an article entitled "Notes from Camp OJ," I wrote the following:

> There has been enough "leaking" out here to sink Camp OJ if it were on a barge—the defense and the prosecution alike. However, both are pikers at it compared to the Los Angeles Police Department. It began last summer with them passing out 911 tapes to journalists as if they were courtesy trinkets welcoming them to town, and reached its nadir with the leaked "DNA sock match" story. Of the latter, this I know: Within two hours of Judge Ito admonishing the police for "reckless disregard" of the truth, the LAPD's worst moment to date, a certain police officer, whose leaks had hitherto been mostly accurate and offered with corroboration, started calling journalists with the story that blood on the socks found in O.J.'s bedroom was a DNA match of Nicole's. This time, however, he offered no corroboration, and became angry and defensive when it was asked for. A number of journalists turned him down. Apparently KNBC did not, and the rest is ugly history for both the press and the Los Angeles Police Department.

I was referring here to a notorious event that occurred in the fall of 1994. On the evening of the day that the LAPD took one of its worst beatings in a courtroom, Tracie Savage, a reporter for KNBC-TV, reported on the nightly news that the DNA results from the socks had come in and they were very bad news for O.J.—Nicole's blood was on them.

The next morning, in open court, the prosecution and the defense agreed no such thing had happened: The socks had not even been sent out for testing yet. Judge Ito blew up at the media in general and Ms. Savage and KNBC in particular. He scolded them from the bench and said he wouldn't stand for any more such reckless reporting.

But that night, not only did KNBC-TV and Tracie Savage stand by their story, they embellished it. Of course, His Honor was even madder the following morning—all kinds of dire threats at the media came slinging from the bench. In the end, Ito huffed and puffed again, but effectively did nothing.

The incident was pretty much forgotten, and I used the story in my article months after the fact to illustrate a point about leaking by both sides during the course of the case. Then on a Friday night in late July 1995, Bob Shapiro, as always, politely returned a phone call I'd made to his office that afternoon. It was one of our usual professional off-the-record chats about the state of the case in general.

At the time, what was happening in the trial was that the defense had subpoenaed Tracie Savage in order to demonstrate that the police had leaked information they didn't yet have. This would serve as circumstantial proof of evidence tampering. In other words, according to the defense's theory, since the report later did come back positive for Nicole's blood, some cop or cops had to have had guilty knowledge that the socks were indeed tampered with.

During this phone conversation, the *Penthouse* article came up, and Bob asked me whether, if I was called to the stand, I would testify to the veracity of that one particular portion of the piece. Having been through this sort of thing before—when I was actually sentenced by a judge to a Louisiana parish prison for refusing to turn over tapes or testify about matters I believed were protected under the First Amendment—I said, of course I would, I had to, the law says I have no choice. But that was all I would testify to, that what I wrote was true. I could not reveal the source or any of the circumstances surrounding my knowledge of the event itself.

Bob said that was fine. He didn't want my source or any other information privileged under the California Reporter's Shield Law. He wasn't sure, he might subpoena me Monday morning, but if he did, he would make out the subpoena and deliver it personally. That way I wouldn't be hassled by its becoming public beforehand. He asked that I not disclose it in case he decided it wasn't necessary. I had no problem with that. There would be fuss enough if he did actually subpoena me, no sense starting it prematurely.

On Monday morning, as we all milled around in the hall waiting for court to start, Bob walked through. He looked at me, we greeted each other as always, but that was it. No special nod, no wink or anything to suggest he was going to serve me. We soon went into court and went through the first morning session. Still no signal from Bob.

All through the break time, out in the hall, nothing. So now I was sure in my mind he'd decided he didn't need me, that calling Tracie Savage to the stand was enough. I was very, very happy. With great relief, I walked back into court last—I was the unofficial doorman at the Trial of the Century, so I was always one of the last to take my seat.

Boom! Right before the little swinging gate where I had to turn right to reach my seat, Bob silently placed an envelope in my hand. My surprise was even greater because I thought I'd dodged a bullet.

I was suddenly very scared. Then, when Bob announced my name as his next witness, and Judge Ito asked me if I needed time to get a lawyer, my head was spinning so much that I actually began telling His Honor that I didn't think so, that I'd been through this kind of thing before and I thought I knew what to do.

Not only was Ito looking at me like I was crazy, but my best friend at the trial, Joe McGinniss, was telling me in no uncertain terms that I was crazy if I went up there without talking to a lawyer.

Finally, with Bob standing there looking at me like "Come on, don't be chicken," Ito waiting with mischievous bemusement at my idiocy, and Joe speaking calmly but forcefully about my absolute lunacy—all of this is happening live on national TV, mind you—something in me latched on to Joe's counsel and I told the judge I'd best talk to an attorney first.

Then began the week of "the Bosco matter," as Ito insisted upon calling the whole DNA-socks-KNBC-news-leak issue, and, it seemed, as often as he possibly could.

❖

WHENEVER I'VE PLAYED the parlor game "What was your most embarrassing experience?" I've always been pretty much at a loss for an answer. Not any longer. Except it is more like humiliation than embarrassment.

The time I spent in that infamous blue chair, I try to keep forever out of mind, which has been made somewhat easier since fear kept me from absorbing much of the experience. For months, I had sat in the courtroom and watched witness after witness take that blue chair and in degrees large or small be lessened by it before stepping back down.

Worse, I'm up there with a broken neck! With this giant steel and leather brace around my neck and up the backside of my head—it hurt to even breathe—I'm feeling very sorry for myself up there with Hank Goldberg cross-examining me and the whole goddamn world watching.

My memory of it is spotty. I do know that I thought Hank was making fun of my sinking-barge metaphor, so I gigged him by asking *him* a question, and neither he nor the judge liked that. Witnesses are supposed to answer questions, not ask them.

Mercifully, it came to an end soon thereafter, and I stepped down from the blue chair, forever diminished, in my mind at least, by the experience. I know I looked and sounded like a barefoot cracker gawking and stuttering in the palace. And infinitely more people saw that than will ever read or hear about anything I write. That is how I will always be remembered. My obituary will no doubt identify me as "the guy who testified in the O. J. Simpson trial with a broken neck"!

❖

PAT MC KENNA ON the predetermined "DNA-sock-match" story: "Tracie Savage, God bless her, she runs the story. Now, she knows where she got that information from. And I'm not asking her to give it up. We know who it was, because he came to us and said, 'Please, guys, I'm a married man. Don't fuck with me.'

"And now he's a commander! [For obvious reasons, this LAPD officer will remain anonymous.] He can look in the mirror in the morning, and he's gotta say to himself, 'Where did I get that information on that sock?' Whoever gave him that information either 'spiked' the sock or knows who did.

"I mean, there's no way that sock can be worn in a double murder of this kind and not have one nanogram of Goldman's DNA on it. There's no way. No soil from Bundy, no Goldman blood, I mean . . . ?"

"So Tracie's reporting it," Pat continues on an issue that makes him angrier than almost any other in the case. "Marcia's standing there saying, 'Judge, it can't possibly be true. We haven't sent them to the lab yet.' I mean, how in the world did Tracie Savage know the exact results of what would be on that sock before the lab knew? The only way she could know is through [that police officer she's sleeping with]. The only way he could know is whoever told him. And the only way anybody could know it's Nicole's blood without it going through a lab is to take it from the reference sample. There's no other way. How would you know whose blood that was? How would you know if it's O.J.'s, Nicole's, or Ron's? How can you know specific results unless you put 'em there?

"When we started fucking around with him, subpoenaing Tracie, putting subpoenas on all of 'em, he went to Johnnie and said, 'Are you guys gonna fuck with me?'

"We heard about [this police officer] and Tracie Savage having an affair in early September. That came to me directly from someone in the police department. And then somebody followed 'em and caught 'em coming out of a hotel together.

"I'm the one that brought it up, in a September meeting at Johnnie Cochran's office. I said, 'You guys aren't gonna believe this.' This was early on, this was before the socks; but Tracie Savage was breaking every story out there first before any other media person. And somebody got pissed off and called. So I took the call, I was the investigator, and it was a female, she sounded like a black female, and she said, 'Look, I'm in the LAPD, and I think you ought to check into the connection between [the police officer] and Tracie Savage.' I said, 'What do you mean?' And she said, 'They're having an affair.' At the time I said, 'Who gives a flying fuck?' You know, I'm not gonna fuck with someone's personal life. What's that got to do with anything?

"But when I brought it up at the meeting—because I'm updating all the lawyers as to my progress, so I just mention this lady calling—Carl Douglas looked at me like I was crazy. He said, 'What are you gonna do?' I said, 'Well, I don't think we need to ruin people's lives. This guy's married with kids. I'm just bringing it up for informational purposes for you guys.' And we never ever thought about fucking with this guy. Not for his benefit, but for his kids' benefit. Fuck him. This motherfucker's out here trashing our client, I would've burned him in a heart-beat. I just felt bad for his kids. To me it wasn't relevant to what our mission was. I mean, it was relevant in terms of 'Hey, stop this leaking by the LAPD to KNBC, especially bullshit.'

"Then the sock thing came out later on. So when we really started pressing on the sock, that's when [the police officer] came to Johnnie. We had a little roundtable discussion. 'Do we burn this guy or what?' We didn't say no to [the guy], we just said, 'We don't know yet.' We kept him on edge. As it turned out later, of course, when we put [Bosco] and Tracie on the stand, Ito ruled it wasn't relevant or material, that it proved nothing, so he didn't let us put you guys on in front of the jury.

"Bullshit! To me it proves that somebody fucked with those socks. That ain't relevant? In this case?"

❖

WHAT MAKES THE above even more relevant—and indicative of exactly what the defense was claiming—is that Tracie Savage and I had different sources! In other words, more than one LAPD officer was shopping this "DNA-sock-match" story around.

15

THE JUDGE'S WIFE, THE JUDGE'S LEANINGS, AND THE LOSS OF A FRIEND

THE DAY JUDGE ITO said, "I love my wife," from the bench and let glisten a tear, he may have had more reason to choke up with emotion than just the promise to love and to cherish.

Captain Margaret "Peggy" York, Ito's wife and the highest ranking female officer in the LAPD, made a declaration under penalty of perjury that she had no "independent recollection" of Mark Fuhrman when he served under her command at the West LA Division. Unfortunately, according to a number of sources, there is reason to doubt this declaration.

In Fuhrman's LAPD personnel file, there is a letter of reprimand from Captain York. It is an incident that Fuhrman recreates, on Laura Hart McKinny's audiotapes, as a one-on-one confrontation: He was in Captain York's office and she was telling him she was recommending he be suspended, that she was also transferring him out of the division. Fuhrman jumped out of his chair, and she yelled, "Sit down!" He said he didn't have to because he didn't respect her. She was "just a woman," not a "real cop," and she wasn't transferring anybody! In Mark Fuhrman's telling, it was a donnybrook, with him winning handily, of course.

A commander is not apt to forget such a confrontation. Particularly when the result is a twenty-two-day suspension of Fuhrman that was upheld on review but later overturned on appeal—all of which generates paperwork that would have begun with Peggy York writing a letter of reprimand.

It is hard, in this reporter's opinion, to conclude anything other than that the commanding officer of LAPD's Internal Affairs Division, the department that, at the order of the court, presided over by her husband, Lance Ito, investigated defense allegations against Mark Fuhrman, *lied under oath*. One can only imagine the pillow talk if and when Peggy came clean with Lance—probably the day Marcia Clark first hit him with the threat of recusal. No one believes that threat was only coincidental to the fact that Judge Ito was about to rule on perhaps the trial's most crucial issue: What portions, if any, of the McKinny tapes would be admissible. There are those among the defense principals who say "it was a guillotine above his neck," that it was flat-out "mind fuck and emotional extortion."

Members of the defense team "debated long and hard on whether" to "push" the apparent "York perjury," but only if it meant "losing Ito *and* still keeping the trial alive." The defense liked their jury and "absolutely did not want a mistrial."

There was no mistrial. The prosecution pulled back just short of the brink. They believed Ito got the message. Everyone knew he wanted to keep judging *his* Trial of the Century at any cost. Besides, they had enough lying cops around.

❖

THERE IS A well-informed, strongly dissenting opinion on this issue. It comes from Burton Katz, an author and former Los Angeles Superior Court judge, who has known His Honor very well over a lot of years.

"How can she *not* have remembered that confrontation? It

indicates . . . well, you know what it indicates," he was sad to conclude concerning the veracity of Captain Peggy York's sworn declaration. "But," he quickly added, "they had two distinct careers. He had the judicial career, he had certain professional obligations, I'm sure some of which prevented him from disclosing to her everything that was going on. And I think she had professional ethics which would probably require her to keep certain things confidential . . . things she could not disclose to him.

"I think they are professional enough *not* to disclose them. I don't think Ito himself would be a participant in a knowing fraud, if that occurred. He's not the type of individual that would do that. Knowing that the level of the LAPD that Captain York is functioning at is one of secrecy—no, it doesn't surprise me that he wouldn't know.

"I just cannot envision that this man, coming from a Japanese-American family, proud of his heritage, proud of what he's accomplished, would be involved in that kind of violation of trust. I think it's the type of thing that were he involved you'd see hara-kiri, I mean, he's a very proud man. You know, that's one of his weaknesses—it's a strength and his weakness." Where lies the truth? Was Captain York, a real cop through and through, standing firm within the Blue Wall and Code of Silence and therefore less than honest about her independent recollection of Mark Fuhrman and keeping it from her husband? Or was she dissembling and did her husband, His Honor, know that she was?

❖

"I T WAS LIKE he pulled up a chair at the prosecution's table" was how a highly placed, longtime deputy DA summed up Judge Ito's consistent rulings in favor of Marcia & Company in "the, uh, Simpson matter," as he constantly referred to the case.

"Let's put it this way," said another Los Angeles deputy DA. "It was no surprise that Ito gave our guys everything but the kitchen sink."

However, one very experienced prosecutor in the downtown office was "quite surprised" by one of Ito's rulings in favor of the State: "He should've let in the stuff on McKinny's tapes about Fuhrman planting evidence. In fact, I was sure that he would. And when he didn't, I believed it was the one sure reversible error he made—moot now, of course. You don't appeal an acquittal.

"But it was Simpson's whole defense—'I was framed. They fucked with the evidence,' " she continued. "And then you have the detective in question bragging on tape about creating probable cause and manipulating evidence? How much more relevant and material does that get in this case? To me, the 'n' word was irrelevant because it only proved Fuhrman lied about a fact not material to the case. The defense ultimately wasn't trying to prove that Fuhrman was a racist. They wanted to prove he had a propensity for planting evidence."

"Can you imagine Johnnie Cochran's frustration?" a well-known Los Angeles defense attorney asked. "He made his mark in this town taking down bad cops of any color. And here, finally, he has a cop talking about being dirty on tape and he can't use it! My God, before, he's had to build meticulous circumstantial cases to bust cops, yet with perhaps the worst of the bunch he gets a smoking gun handed to him as if by divine providence and then it's taken away!"

"Ito could not have done any more to help the DA in this case," Peter Bozanich sums it up. "I mean, I've never seen a defendant 'on rails' with these evidentiary rulings that Ito made; Ito did everything he could to help. A lot of the stuff the defense wanted to present that he would not let in was relevant."

❖❖

E VEN AS PERSISTENTLY pro-prosecution as were Judge Ito's rulings, it is interesting to note that his behavior toward the attorneys personally was consistently more favorable to members of the defense team.

At times it appeared he was allowing the prosecution, particularly Marcia Clark, just enough rope to hang itself, almost gleefully so. But, as often as not, when the prosecution shot itself in the foot, he helped supply the bullets.

It was clear to this daily courtroom reporter, when the body language observed and inflections overheard during the ubiquitous sidebars were placed into context with the transcripts, that Judge Ito aided and abetted Johnnie Cochran's baiting of Chris Darden and Marcia Clark. They were led into making rash judgments that became known as big mistakes, the glove demonstration being only the most celebrated. Ito's words and expressions were often in the tone of "shit or get off the pot."

With Johnnie Cochran, there was no mystery as to the source of the judge's favor. When Johnnie was with the District Attorney's Office, he had been Ito's supervisor and somewhat of a mentor. But then, while he may have his detractors, if one personally observes or interacts with Mr. Cochran over any period of time, it is difficult *not* to be impressed by his skills and to feel a warm sense of friendship and respect for the man behind the silky-smooth charisma.

Judge Ito certainly was peevish enough with Marcia Clark. But then Ms. Clark was so often at her trademark one-note shrill level. That it would come boomeranging back to her from the bench is not surprising.

Ito, however, reserved his greatest wrath for prosecutor Rockne Harmon, the DNA specialist from Alameda County on loan to the Los Angeles District Attorney's Office. When Judge

Ito publicly rebuked him for "reprehensible conduct," Rock, as the feisty, focused, and brilliant but combative former Vietnam gunboat pilot is known, was not pleased. He promised a couple of the Authors that when his part of the case was done with, he was "going to let the little son-of-a-bitch have it full blast— right there in the courtroom, with the world watching!"

With the way the trial fizzled and stumbled to an end, Rock was never presented with the opportunity. But here, he was willing to go on the record: "There's a reason he didn't like me—I think I made his job more difficult. And I think that's my job if I don't think he's doing the right thing. Some of the others would tell me, 'You can't piss off the judge.' And I'd say, 'What do you mean you can't piss him off? If he's wrong, you have to.' What else are you going to do? That's representative of some of the things that happened."

Rock goes on: "He played some strange games," referring to the odd dichotomy in the way Ito favored the prosecution with his rulings on the one hand, but was publicly accommodating to the defense team members and harsh in his dealings with the prosecution on the other. "And I think there's a simple expla- nation for that. If you have an ambitious judge, there's more political influence in the defense bar than there is in the District Attorney's Office. We're not high rollers; we can't do favors for people. Maybe we can try to fix your ticket, or something silly like that, but that's not what counts: 'I need bankrolling for my campaign,' or 'I need a recommendation to the governor for my elevation.'

"Look at Johnnie. . . . Think about the strain that puts on the judge—any judge, but especially this judge—with a guy like Johnnie, who is very influential, whose endorsement can deliver part of the vote that's not typically associated with law enforce- ment.

"One time we were up at the sidebar," Rock continues. "Ito and Johnnie were talking as if I wasn't there. It was something about politics, and Johnnie was teasing him about running for DA. So I smiled, and said 'Gee, I'd heard you were running for governor, and I was hoping that was true so you could recommend me for a judgeship.' And you know me, no way—I'm not judge material. I would never want to be a judge, it's a terrible job. But I was just making fun of something that was very serious between the two of them. I mean, they were kind of schmoozing one another, and I wanted them to know my condescension about the whole idea. But if that happened once, it happened a hundred times. And think about that. Think about how nice he was to them, how deferential, and how curt he was with us."

Judge Ito's "reprehensible conduct" slap-in-the-face of Rock had to do with his alleged "improper" contacting of defense experts, especially Kary Mullis, the controversial Nobel Laureate who developed the much debated "PCR" DNA testing method. Rock's thoughts then and now are: "I'd had it. . . . I just didn't give a fuck about him anymore at that point. And personally I was tired of this bullshit that seemed to imply I had done something wrong, when I'd be more than happy to have a referral to the State Bar, and let somebody else decide, not some little guy who had lost control about ten months before.

"A judge has no obligation to listen to bullshit."

❖

WHILE PETER NEUFELD and Barry Scheck have voiced some strong opinions on the judge, it is not so easy to get the California members of the defense team to criticize Ito—even off the record. "The truth is," begins one member of the Dream Team, "while he didn't do us many favors in the courtroom, he was very, very good to O.J. when it came to special privileges. Particularly allowing Juice to sign autographs and sell things in the jail. That was very important to everyone financially. The truth is Ito is a good man who is just a big law-and-order kind of guy that likes and believes in cops."

❖❖

O NE OF ITO'S most outrageous statements came during the testimony of LAPD Officer Don Thompson, the giant policeman who handcuffed O.J. "within forty-five seconds" of his arrival at Rockingham the morning of June 13. The jury had been sent out because Chris Darden wanted permission from the judge to ask Officer Thompson "what cause he had to handcuff" O.J.

"I could do that in three questions," Ito sniped, almost bragging.

"It would be more dramatic with eight questions," Chris replied.

"We aren't here for drama," Emperor Ito decreed.

❖❖

I T BECAME AN axiom at the Simpson trial that the jury was the most poker-faced panel any of us had ever tried to read. It was maddening at times, the way those folks played it so close to the vest. Dr. Mark Goulston's thoughts about this:

"As we've discussed before, most people spend a fair amount of energy hiding shameful secrets. Because the fear of having a shameful secret exposed is sort of beyond comprehension—a father is exposed as a molester or something. So given the extent that we are experiencing something shameful, or that we were something shameful, we will spend a lot of conscious energy suppressing it. Because what you want to do is insulate yourself from anyone guessing your shameful secret.

"So one way of explaining the impenetrability of the jury is the shameful secret that all of them were carrying is *they were getting off on it*. That they were there to pursue justice, but they were there pinching themselves saying, 'I'm at the Trial of the Century. I'm *in* the Simpson Trial!' So there's the inner shame of really getting off on something and taking delight—'*I'm important. I'm happier than a pig in shit!*'

"What's the guilt? I get to also be away from my screaming kids, my screaming husband or wife. Not only that but I get to be important and get to even tell people afterward to feel sorry for me because I was sequestered—when I got a vacation from all those pains in the neck!

"If you think about it, that had to have been a pervasive thing. Part of their problem is at some level they don't know if they were just, not because it was O.J., but because they got bought off by the seduction of fame. In other words, they don't know how objective they were, not necessarily because it was a racial thing, but because they said, 'I can't believe I'm part of the O.J. jury!' "

❖

I T IS DIFFICULT for me to write about the death of Robin Clark, that gifted wordsmith who covered the trial for the venerable *Philadelphia Inquirer*. That gentle poet from the land of Thomas Wolfe and the Durham Bulls was the first member of the press corps to befriend me when I arrived at early Camp OJ Central, the upstart, unknown, and opinionated *freelancer*—from deepest Dixie, too—wanting a seat at the Trial of the Century. Over the coming weeks, months, year, we became fast and, I thought, forever friends.

On that Friday afternoon in early August 1995 when he, his cousin, and her friend and I parted at the corner of Temple and Broadway after a half-day session at the Trial, they were going to take more home video of the bizarre circus the Criminal

Courts Building and environs had become. Then Robin was going to show the sights of Southern California to his out-of-town guests in his signature vintage VW van. Me, I got in my twenty-year-old Cadillac and went to my apartment for a weekend of sleep, baseball, and no Trial.

I knew that Robin was disappointed in me. He wasn't mad at me; that would've been over and past in a second, because Robin always cut to the quick of every issue, which left little time for anger to build up. No, he was disappointed in me. And that's tough to live with—if you knew Robin.

He believed my not sharing with at least him, Joe, and Dominick the fact that the defense might subpoena me to testify was not right. When I was subpoenaed and it was learned I had some advance warning that I might be, his words were "You sandbagged us, Joe," and he just shook his head.

Things went on as before over those next few days, he did not withhold his friendship, but he and I knew there was this unfinished character issue between us. Then came the phone call that Friday evening; it was a reporter from the *Los Angeles Times* whom I did not know. She had the assignment to report on a very bad car wreck that had tied up the Pacific Coast Highway most of the afternoon, with all three occupants of an old Volkswagen van dead on the scene (of which I knew nothing, not having turned on the TV yet). For whatever reason, she was contacting me before any other member of the Simpson press corps about the death of Robin Clark, wanting an on-the-record reaction. My inadequate remarks were published, but all I remember is screaming to the reporter, over and over again, "You've made a mistake! It *can't* be Robin! I just saw him. I'm telling you, there's been a mistake!"

It was not a mistake. The next few days were a blur of grief, with Joe McGinniss stepping forward to organize the nightmarish details that must be dealt with at such times. Joe and Nancy were of great comfort to Margaret, Robin's love and life-companion, who, though behaving as bravely as Robin would have wanted her to, was devastated by the magnitude of her loss. Robin Clark, an uncommon man, was not replaceable.

There are two things that will always stand out in my mind about those dark days. The first occurred the Monday after the accident, the first day at the Criminal Courts Building without Robin Clark. We asked Jerrianne Hayslett, the court's press officer, to please ask Judge Ito to acknowledge Robin's passing in open court; after all, he'd only been covering that court every day for over a year with some of the purest, sweetest prose any of us had ever read.

Jerrianne immediately agreed. She was as shaken and grieving as we were; she too had grown to admire Robin Clark. His newspaper had been slighted by the judge in the seating assignments perhaps more than other major American newspapers covering the case. Not only was Robin in a rotating pool of several other lesser news organizations, the seat was the absolute worst in the courtroom. It was the last portable chair next to the double exit doors, behind the rows of pews behind the glassed-in booth of the sheriff's deputy; so even when it was his turn to be in court he couldn't see much and could hear less because of the glass barriers.

But Robin never complained. While hundreds of journalists or their bosses were hollering and bitching at Jerrianne endlessly, making her life oftentimes more miserable than her arbitrary orders made ours, Robin always met her in the morning with that little-boy-North-Carolina-aw-shucks smile and a quip to make her, and the rest of us, laugh. Even the sheriff's deputy standing next to Jerrianne with the strongbox holding the all-valuable courtroom badges, which had to be individually handed out and replaced, with the picture ID of the seat holder ensuring its return, enjoyed Robin.

Robin didn't even complain that his workstation was not in the twelfth-floor pressroom, but downstairs across the street in a trailer! In time, as a result of a flap between the Court and a major weekly magazine over the number of cover stories it had or had not run as promised, and the intense lobbying by every news organization that wasn't happy with its seat, there came some seat reassignments. Jerrianne was able to slip Robin into the pool rotating for the few inches of the back-center bench next to her, a seat she had to come and go from with great frequency. It was actually farther back than Robin's other seat, but it was in the dead center of the room, basically looking down the aisle. He could see and he could hear. That Monday morning, the seat was left empty, with Robin's courtroom badge taped to the wall above it.

Jerrianne took our request to His Honor. Nothing. We go through both morning sessions, but not a peep out of the judge about the loss everybody else in the room was feeling. Just before going in after the lunch break, I grabbed Johnnie out in the hall and asked him please to do something. He said he would, and that the reason the defense hadn't done anything so far was that they too were waiting for the judge.

True to his word, we're not back in the courtroom two minutes before Johnnie Cochran is at the podium asking for a moment of reverence for the loss of one of the family. Judge Ito glared at him with more anger than he had focused on Johnnie at any other time. The Emperor had been shown up. He knew it and he was pissed, but he had to do something now. So he pointed out Robin's pass taped to the wall—which he had nothing to do with.

We later found out that the judge had asked "Who?" when Jerrianne made our request. *The Philadelphia Inquirer* wasn't on his to-clip list; it was almost impossible even to get a copy in Los Angeles. So who the hell was this Robin Clark anyway? That's what was coming from His Honor. It was the only time Jerrianne probably ever contemplated mutiny in her life. The judge had disappointed her.

Many of the judge's transgressions I am prepared to forgive. But never will I forgive him for his treatment of the loss of Robin.

❖

THE OTHER THING that stands out in my mind of the days after Robin's death was the most extraordinary memorial service I've ever witnessed. It took place in Joe McGinniss's rented Beverly Hills home.

All told there must have been a hundred of us in the house. It wasn't just the print-press folks; many members of the electronic media came. Truly extraordinary was the fact that O.J.'s sisters and his brother-in-law came. Understand, this was not an invitation sort of thing—one heard about it and showed up.

Bob Shapiro came, and he was totally amazed. We were talking off to the side, watching the gathering, the long table laid out with photographs and copies of some of Robin's best writings, and Bob told me: "I've never seen anything like this. I've been involved with the press for a long time, and never have I seen such a display of total unity. He must have been one hell of a guy to get these many competitors together. I wish I could've gotten to know him better."

It was one of those services without formal structure. At one point, with everybody gathered tightly within the house's L-shaped great room, people who felt moved to speak about Robin just did so, impromptu, unplanned; someone would speak here and then someone over there and then again over there. There was no one emceeing the testimonials; out of the silence following one speaker would come the next. Shirley Baker, O.J.'s sister, was so moved she too spoke out of the thick, together silence.

Jim Willwerth of *Time* then talked not only about the loss of Robin but about the gain of something we had all felt but collectively could not express. Yes, the loss of a loved and unique man had brought us together that night, but he noted that in all his years he had not witnessed as communal a spirit of true goodwill among a gang of press people as was evident with the Simpson press corps that night. In truth, that feeling had been there for months. It wasn't just that we'd been together a long time, he said; in wars he'd covered, press corps had been together for a long time too, but not even the loss of a press colleague in combat had occasioned what Jim saw and felt that night. "We are truly a family," he said, with Robin's greatest gift being that night. It expressed about us what we had been too busy or too cynical to say outloud.

Time has a smart man in Jim Willwerth.

Characteristically, when I spoke, I talked of the loss of an artist, a writer of importance; the loss of one man's distinctive, beautiful use of the language. What I didn't speak about was the unfinished business between Robin and me. I'm sorry I disappointed you, brother. I'll try never to do it again.

16

LIFE WITH MARK AND MARCIA

T HEY FRAMED A GUILTY MAN.

Each of the few people who have heard me privately use this line, given to me by someone who shall remain nameless, has reacted as if it was *the* Eureka to the baffling forensic enigma that is at the core of the Simpson murder case. There are some who say it's the only answer that fits.

This is not to say the ridiculed possibility that O. J. Simpson had nothing to do with the murders will not reveal itself someday to be a fact. In the past few years, my preoccupation with murder, murderers, and the criminal justice game has taught me to never discount the impossible.

As previously discussed, there are real mysteries and nagging incongruities concerning the O.J. crime scenes and time line that beg for serious scrutiny. In almost all complex murder investigations there are certain trails that appear to lead in directions different from where the apparent totality of the evidence suggests. All one knows is there is this odd thing here and then this other odd thing there and that they appear to constitute a physical or circumstantial connection, a trail. In any properly thorough investigation, these trails must be followed. It must be done even though such trails almost always lead to dead ends; they are trails, but they are trails to an exasperating nowhere. Particularly is this true in a case where one finally comes to the certainty that *almost everybody is lying about something!* In this instance, Mr. Simpson, some of his family and friends, as well as the police and prosecution.

However, because Mr. Simpson can never be criminally tried in this case again, it was the State's lying that told the tale that counts.

❖

EARLIER, I WROTE about the conflicting outrages I feel when I dwell on different aspects of the Simpson case. Yet greater than any outrage is my fear.

In the rare instances where spousal-abuse murderers are tried and found not guilty, statistics show they almost never kill again. Very few people are ever at risk. On the other hand, when the State, that monolithic force that is We-the-People, cheats and lies and gets away with it, We-the-People can be in trouble anytime anywhere.

In the matter before us, there is also my very real fear for the Republic—with the naked, gaping schism between white America and black America. And there is my futile, terrible sadness for it.

Consequently, my outrage is reserved for the prosecution in the matter of the *State of California v. Orenthal James Simpson.* Let me put it in these terms: If the man who butchered Nicole Brown Simpson and Ronald Goldman is walking free, and insufferably smug about it—or even if some Mafiosos, Colombians, or Martians did it, and the wrong man was arrested and tried— it is thanks to Marcia Clark.

While there is plenty of blame to spread around, it all starts and ends with America's darling. The woman who was first-chair prosecutor of the Trial of the Century, who was the only one there from beginning to end, deserves America's anger.

This truth is bucking an enormously popular cultural tidal surge. It will be attacked and the message vehemently refuted. But it is the truth. It just might be heard. And perhaps we might even resurrect a venerable, but seemingly forgotten, American secular commandment: *Cheaters never win* (or at least they shouldn't).

❖

I N THE ZEAL to win at any cost, Marcia Clark and other members of the prosecution, at the behest of District Attorney Gil Garcetti, abused almost all of the tenets that are the fabric of their sworn oaths as advocates for the People. And by so doing, not only did they lose their case, they caused to be heard, right now, in courts near and far, a new mantra: "If cops lie, you must acquit." The early returns are that it is effective. A lot of prosecutors everywhere are angry.

Larry Longo, one of the more prominent, and recently controversial, deputy DAs Los Angeles County has, said, "Marcia Clark, by suborning perjury by cops, and there is no doubt she did, has set back the criminal justice system by years."

This is the woman who lost a case with "more good evidence than plenty of other cases combined. Death Row is full of guys convicted on hair and fiber or conventional serology alone!"

This is also the former actress-dancer who now is not coming back to her "life's work" as a Los Angeles prosecutor but, after "writing" her book, is going to become a full-time lecturer and spokesperson for "everything that is wrong with the criminal justice system." These are her words. Folks, our system, now almost eight hundred years refined, for whatever is good or bad about it, deserves far better than Marcia Clark as its champion or savior.

❖

WHY DID THE LAPD turn to Marcia Clark specifically, personally, in the early morning hours of June 13, 1994? They knew for a fact they had a search-warrant problem, plus there were already vague hints of an evidence problem. So according to a source in a position to know, they called a DA who they knew from experience would "tell them how to handle their problems." Which is why we see Marcia Clark and Mark Fuhrman strolling together all over both crime scenes in much of the news video shot that day.

"In my experience, the only things cops call a deputy DA for is help with search warrants, never to go to a crime scene," Lucienne Coleman, the deputy DA who first voiced any question about the State's case to her former best friend, says in her private office on the eighteenth floor of the downtown Criminal Courts Building. "But that does not mean it doesn't happen, just that it's rare. There is procedure for it."

But then Ms. Coleman leans back in her chair and volunteers, with some sadness, "It doesn't surprise me that the police would call Marcia specifically. She's friendly with cops. She would sit and drink with them."

Ms. Coleman remembers a night when she and her husband and Marcia and her second husband were going out for dinner and a movie. A police officer with a search-warrant problem called, and "Marcia stayed on the phone with him so long that the evening's plans were dismissed."

It is widely said throughout the Los Angeles District Attorney's Office that "Marcia had helped cops with evidence prob-

lems on other cases." One prosecutor put it simply, "That's
Marcia; she thinks like a cop, and as a prosecutor she believes
it's her divine right to do anything to win."

Incidentally (or not) the Simpson murders is not the first
case Marcia Clark has worked with Phil Vannatter.

❖

M ARK FUHRMAN. Perhaps he was just too alluring to the
winning-is-everything prosecutor in Marcia Clark. Here
was a police officer witness to lie for: choirboy face, but six foot
three inches tall, square-shouldered, blond, blue-eyed, articulate,
soft-spoken, well-mannered, every mother's favorite son, and
every daughter's heartthrob, the All-American TV Detective.

Too good to be true, of course; but the problem is that
Marcia Clark must have known his slimy history even that first
morning of June 13, 1994, when she went to the crime scene.
"I don't know how she couldn't have known about it, especially
her being so tight with cops," one of Marcia's colleagues said.
The it is the Joseph Britton case.

In 1988, Joseph Britton, an African American, was caught
in the act of an ATM robbery. When he ran, three police officers gave chase. After allegedly tossing a pocketknife on the
run, Britton was cornered in a parking lot. He was shot in the
chest and shoulder six times. Britton says Mark Fuhrman was
the shooter. He also says that as he lay on the pavement, Fuhrman placed a knife beside his hand, and said, "Die, nigger! Why
won't you die?" It was later determined that Fuhrman fired ten
rounds from his 9mm Beretta. At the same time that he pleaded
guilty to the crime, for which he was duly sentenced and began
serving time, Britton sued the city and the police officers.

In late 1993, in a civil trial, a jury, after hearing testimony
supporting Britton's story, came back with a complicated set of
verdicts that, in essence, found that Mark Fuhrman and his part-

ners' conduct was "intentional" but not "unreasonable." The judge ruled the jury's verdict was inconsistent and ordered a new trial. That trial was scheduled to start in early 1995—just before the Simpson jury was to begin sequestration and the hearing of opening statements.

There was no retrial of the Britton case. Only weeks before Fuhrman was scheduled to testify in the Simpson trial, to keep him from having to answer to witnesses' accounts of the Britton shooting and the planting of evidence, the city of Los Angeles settled out of court with an incarcerated repeat offender to the tune of $100,000.

❖

EVEN IF MARCIA CLARK did not know about Fuhrman and the Britton case that first morning of June 13, she certainly was told plenty about the detective within days. That was when Marcia's good friend Lucienne Coleman came to her office and laid out the whole history of racism and misconduct in Mark Fuhrman's career.

Ms. Coleman was close to a Los Angeles police officer named Andy Purdy. When the stories first broke about a racist cop being Bob Shapiro's "incendiary defense," she said to Purdy, "What a bunch of bullshit!"

But Purdy replied, "I wouldn't put it past him."

"What?" Ms. Coleman exclaimed, truly taken aback. "Before the Simpson case, I was so naive; seventeen years in this job, and I still believed cops were always the good guys."

Purdy then told her about a swastika that had been put in his police locker. Purdy's wife is Jewish. He said there was an investigation, "and Fuhrman's fingerprints were all over it." Lucienne distinctly remembers that those were Officer Purdy's exact words.

"He had been caught and warned. He's a Nazi!" Purdy continued to say before two other women in the District Attorney's Office. Fuhrman was known to dress up in Nazi paraphernalia on weekends and would sometimes even wear a swastika lapel pin to work.

But it wasn't until another police officer mentioned that Fuhrman talked about "Nicole's boob job" at a party well before the murders that Lucienne Coleman was moved to act. She thought hard about the ethics of her calling—as well as her career in the District Attorney's Office—and talked it out with her friends. She decided she "had to go to Bill Hodgman—I was leery of Marcia because of her recent behavior toward me. Her blowing up about how guilty O.J. was. But Bill was in Marcia's office so I just went on in. I said my piece. Hodgman's eyes got big and he said something like 'Wow, we need to look into this.' But Marcia screamed, 'That bullshit's coming from the defense!'

"At that moment Cheri Lewis walked in," Ms. Coleman remembers. "She wanted to talk about 'press requests' for Nicole's 911 tape. I wondered why she was handling a matter like that—another deputy usually did that, and Cheri was a bit too qualified for the job.

"But Marcia went ballistic."

With a withering look, Marcia turned to Lucienne and spoke: "Frankly, I'm sick and tired of people in this office trying for self-aggrandizement with *my* case!" Quietly, Lucienne left the room.

About the end of August, Officer Andy Purdy called Lucienne to say he'd been contacted by *Newsweek* and *Time* regarding the Fuhrman Nazi stuff. "What did you tell them?" Lucienne asked.

"I denied it," he said.

When she reported that she had gone to Marcia and Bill with the information, Purdy got angry. It was the "only thing to do," she persisted, and if she "had to take the stand," she "would tell the truth."

"I won't," he replied. "I'll commit perjury."

"I couldn't believe we were having a conversation like that!" Lucienne recalls.

Ms. Coleman's moral predicament was put on hold for several months until it reared its public head on March 7, 1995, when Judge Ito mentioned her name in court concerning a discovery motion by the defense. Immediately she and Purdy talked again: "He said he'd gotten up at three A.M. to burn the log he'd kept on Fuhrman. He did it so it wouldn't get turned over to the defense."

More important, she remembers being "shocked to find out" that Purdy's problems with fellow police officer Mark Fuhrman "were serious enough for him to have kept a log!" Purdy tried to crawfish out of his original "story on the swastika, that it hadn't really been proven that Fuhrman had been the one to put it there. But I said, 'That's not what you told me and two other witnesses.' "

Later Bill Hodgman called Lucienne and "acted as if the conversation in June had never happened."

The hubbub had to do with the defense request for personnel records concerning Purdy and Fuhrman and the swastika incident. In the end, however, upon the ensuing Pitchess motion, a legal maneuver concerning the admissibility of a police witness's official personnel files, and its time-consuming hearing, Judge Ito ruled all of it out.

"One of the biggest surprises of the trial," an experienced downtown prosecutor said to me, echoed later by members of the defense, "was that a cop admitted to Internal Affairs that he'd kept a private log on Fuhrman's misconduct but had burned it as soon as his name came up in court. And Ito didn't blink an eye. I mean, here's proof of just how bad an apple Fuhrman is. This is a cop writing and talking about another *cop!* A real tear in the Blue Wall and Code of Silence."

"To me it never should've been under Pitchess," Lucienne Coleman says emphatically, believing that the "Nazi stuff" was secondary to the revelation of Fuhrman's knowledge of Nicole's anatomy. "It was clearly 'Brady material' "—a legal precedent that compels the State to turn over to the defense any evidence that could tend to be exculpatory to the defendant.

"I mean, an investigating officer with an apparent relationship with a victim? That's why I went to Bill and Marcia way back when," Ms. Coleman says. "To me, the way I've always practiced law, that's clearly 'Brady' and gets turned over as soon as you get it. Automatically."

Ms. Coleman also has strong feelings about Judge Ito throwing out Fuhrman's references on Ms. McKinny's tapes to evidence tampering and bragging of his importance to the case because of "finding" the Rockingham glove. "*Something is wrong there,*" she says.

"And why Ito didn't explore the Purdy statements and log destruction, I'll never understand," Lucienne Coleman continues. "But maybe it was like 'Planting comes in, sure hung jury.' So put judicial ethics on hold and let the appeals court straighten it out—but 'let's try this case to a verdict.' "

❖

ALTHOUGH JUDGE ITO did not allow the jury to hear it, here is some of what Fuhrman had to say to Laura Hart McKinny about evidence tampering and creating probable cause in another incident:

"[After tearing up a motorist's driver's license] I didn't arrest him under anything, just took him to the station, ran him for prints, gave them to the detectives to compare with what they've got in the area. I'll probably arrest a criminal that way . . . I'd be able to correlate exactly what I said into a reasonable probable cause for arrest."

❖

CAPTAIN PEGGY YORK is commander of Internal Affairs. She is the boss of the detectives who came and took Lucienne Coleman's statement in a manner suggesting she was to be discredited rather than interviewed. "They were rude," Ms. Coleman remembers, "and were more interested in tearing down my story than investigating the truth of it. They definitely weren't interested in getting to the truth of the matter."

❖

IN NOVEMBER 1994, Marcia Clark sent an LAPD detective up to Eatonville, Washington, where Mark Fuhrman grew up. There, the detective interviewed people who told him a great deal about how Mark Fuhrman had terrorized one of the few black teenagers in town. They said Mark and his younger brother had been the town's most racist bullies.

Of course, long before November, Ms. Clark knew that Fuhrman had five serious citizen complaints filed against him over his career. That was one fewer than the six needed to be included in the infamous "Christopher Commission one hundred," those police officers officially listed as "problem cops" in the reform atmosphere after the 1992 riots.

And almost from the beginning, Ms. Clark had the records and medical reports of Fuhrman's attempt to leave the police force with a disability pension because job-related stress had left him with a compulsion for brutality and extreme bigotry. He was turned down because, in effect, although the doctors agreed he was a violent bigot with narcissistic tendencies, he was, more important, a liar, and therefore unworthy of medical disability.

In other words, he's a little bit nuts but not too crazy or vicious to be a cop, he's only a liar, and therefore should be put back to work.

The public had a chance to hear his heinous words on Laura Hart McKinny's audiotapes, and bits and pieces of his police files have appeared in the press. But I believe it will make a difference if the public has a chance to know exactly what is said by psychiatrists about Fuhrman's fraudulent attempts to retire from the LAPD with a full pension after only five years of service.

❖

D R. RONALD R. KROEGER, M.D.; report dated November 30, 1982, prepared for Workers' Compensation Division, City of Los Angeles.

Psychiatric Evaluation:
This 30 year old Police officer, employed by the City of Los Angeles, was evaluated at my office on November 16, 1982, and his medical records were reviewed.

Presenting problems: Mr. Fuhrman has been a policeman for the City of Los Angeles since 1975, but has not worked since August 8, 1981. He says that he was placed on medical leave on that date by a psychiatrist, David Gottlieb, M.D., and has been seeing Dr. Gottlieb continuously since then as a patient.

He says Dr. Gottlieb has been treating him for depression and anxiety, as well as an "explosive personality." He felt under a great deal of pressure and . . . was not able to deal with the stress of working. He felt that he might explode and hurt someone.

He has been seeing Dr. Gottlieb for psychotherapy twice weekly, and is "working on violence and depression." He is not taking any medication. He has been going to school at Long Beach State College, majoring in art, however, he says, "School's not working out. I can't stand the classes."

He is preoccupied with violence and this theme frequently entered into his remarks. "If you only knew what it feels like when some guy's doing something, acting cool, thinking no one sees him. And you come and put a shotgun to his head" [laughs].

He traces his feelings about violence to his experiences in the Marines. He was sent to Vietnam and was in Saigon toward the end of the war. "I loved it in the military. You knew what you were supposed to do, and if you did it they rewarded you." From 1970 to 1975 he was in the Marines, and says that he enjoyed it until the last year. Then he says, "There were these Mexicans and niggers, volunteers, and they would tell me they weren't going to do something." . . .

He said he never had any regrets over any damage he did to people (broken limbs, etcetera). He bragged that he never had any second thoughts over what he did in Vietnam, never any "flashbacks." . . .

On March 15, 1980, his [second] wife left him. He says that his wife had been "cheating" on him. "It's better I didn't find out till afterward. I would have killed both of them."

A report from the patient's treating psychiatrist, David Gottlieb, M.D., is dated October 9, 1982. "Mr. Fuhrman is very seriously depressed and anxious, and in no way can he be assigned to duty in any part of the Police Department." He states that the evidence is in the patient's dreams of his violent feelings. He needs to continue psychotherapy on a twice a week basis.

Discussion: In observing and talking to this man, it is hard to conceive that he is being considered for total disability and is applying for a pension from the police force. He is tall and very muscular and speaks well without any anxiety or depression evident. He looks the picture of health from a physical stand point and shows no objective evidence of any mental aberration.

Of course, we all know that it is possible to look healthy and to have significant mental problems. These mental problems would be reflected in his personal relationships, rather than in his appearance. His daily activities would be affected, for example.

What are this man's daily activities? He usually arises between nine and ten o'clock in the morning, has a leisurely breakfast, and then goes to the gym for a two-hour workout with weights (bodybuilding). This happens six days a week. His girl friend is a competitive bodybuilder and also works out.

Two times a week he also plays racquetball. Twice a week he runs. Twice a week he goes to see his psychiatrist. He has a steady girlfriend. Their sex life together is very good.

He also attends some classes at Long Beach City College, where he is an art major, but he is getting bored with that.

He leads a very pleasant and active life, now that he is no longer working as a police officer. The question is, however, whether this is the schedule of a person who is totally disabled from his job.

I don't think so. This man is not significantly psychiatrically disabled, and what disability is present has been there since childhood. He had a bad relationship with his father, whom he never forgave for abandoning his family when the patient was seven. He believes he was over-protected by his mother because of the earlier death of a brother [to leukemia].

His career in the police was similar to his career in the Marines. In both instances he became bored after five years and wanted out. In the Marines, also, he has fond memories of killing and beating up on people without any remorse. This is how he reminisces about his police career, in terms of the suspects he beat up. He brags about his use of excessive force and goes on at great length about how much fun he had breaking the arms and legs of suspects when they gave him a hard time.

Toward the end, no matter what was done for him he was not satisfied. When he tired of the activity and violence of the gangs he was transferred to a foot patrol, but did not like that, either. He complains that he had to deal with too many "assholes."

He was then given an inside assignment, but says that was "like solitary confinement." He was on this assignment when he went off "sick."

His story does not make sense. He complains about the stress of the outside jobs, but brags about how violent he was toward suspects. Then, when he was transferred to more peaceful jobs, he found something wrong with them and said he wanted more "action."

It appeared to me during the evaluation that he was deliberately exaggerating his preoccupation with violence in order to make himself appear unsuitable for police work. The MMPI psychological test given by Dr. Geary also indicated that he was "trying to feign the presence of a severe psychopathology." There was an indication that he was making a "conscious attempt to look bad" on the psychologicals, according to Dr. Geary.

I would agree with the assessment from the psychologicals (Dr. Geary) that this patient is narcissistic, self-indulgent, and somewhat emotionally unstable. These are long-term characteristics, of course. The personality problems pre-date his employment as a police officer. The narcissism and self-indulgence would go along with his preoccupation with violence, and his obsession with bodybuilding.

Just as he is exaggerating his conscious feelings of violence, he is exaggerating the violence in the dreams he presents to Dr. Gottlieb. Even if he were not consciously exaggerating, it is known that patients will actually dream certain dreams in order to meet the expectations of the therapist.

This man has become tired of police work just as he became bored with life as a Marine. He does not want to quit and lose benefits, so he is attempting to get pension and compensation rewards.

There is no work-related psychiatric disability. This man has not changed significantly since his Marine days. He has personality problems, but they are long-standing. He is able to work as a police officer, but doesn't want to do so. If he returns to police work his casual attitude toward violence will have to be evaluated by his su-

periors in terms of assignment, and he might benefit from re-education about the use of violence by the police officer.
    Ronald R. Koegler, M.D.

❖

A LMOST EXACTLY A year earlier, John Hochman, M.D., Psychiatry and Neurology, had conducted an examination and evaluation of medical records of Mark Fuhrman for the City Attorney's Office. The report is dated December 16, 1981. (Underlined phrases are in the original.)

The patient states that he was seen by Dr. Louis Lunsky, a psychiatrist, on August 15, 1981. It is noted that Dr. Lunsky's psychiatric report is not available for review. The patient indicated that he was placed on medical leave by Dr. David Gottlieb, a psychiatrist. Of particular note, Dr. Gottlieb's report and records <u>are not available for review</u>.

He recalls that one time when he was on duty that a man "spit on him." He states he broke the man's elbows and his knees, then reached for his gun. He realized then that he had a problem, and he sought psychiatric help after that.

<u>Psychological Testing</u> (administered by Thomas Geary, Ph.D., 11-18-81)

<u>MMPI</u>:

Profile: The profile suggested in this test is of a person experiencing depression with associated anxiety and agitation, frequently resulting in fear of loss of control. This agitation and depression is sufficient to produce confusion, forgetfulness and difficulties in concentration and attention. Since there is no indication of this in the other tests of the battery and particularly in the behavioral observations of this patient, <u>one is led to the conclusion that the high incidence of psychopathology by the many elevated scales is an exaggeration</u>.

<u>Emotional/Social Functioning</u>:

The pattern suggested by the tests is one of a person who is negativistic and oppositional relative to the tests themselves. There are feelings of hostility and anger. He also seems to have a heightened need to demonstrate virility, which could be suggestive of feelings of inadequacy in this area. There seems to be difficulty in the control of emotions. There is poor emotional and social adjustment suggested. He would tend to be self-centered. He is also highly suspicious and seems to be immature. While Rorschach suggested certain severe pathological responses, the affect connected to these responses was absent and it could be that this was also further indication as suggested by the MMPI that there was some exaggeration of psychopathology.

Family History:

His father worked as a truck driver and a carpenter. The patient describes him as an "insensitive and irresponsible bull shitter," who "doesn't mind hurting people that are close to him." When the patient was 7 years old, his parents divorced. His father moved to Spokane. The patient would see his father once a month, but they did not get along with each other. His father is now 56 years old. The patient has not seen him for nine years.

Childhood and Adolescence:

By the time he was 12 years old, the patient enjoyed hunting and fishing. He was "artistic and articulate" and "a pretty exceptional student." He was in military academy in the fifth and sixth grade.

He wanted to go to art school but went into the Marines instead.

Marital History:

He was 21 years old when he first got married. This marriage ended after 2 years. He says that his wife had financial problems and he did not "communicate" with her after he became a policeman.

Occupational History:

The patient was a machine gunner in the Marines. He was in Saigon when "the war was winding down." He says that he thrives in "a military environment."

He says that he was recruited by the L.A.P.D. Two weeks after leaving the Marines in July 1975, he was in the Police Academy.

He says that he placed Number Two in the academy "without trying hard." . . .

Occupational History:

[As regards an an Internal Affairs investigation into an incident that occurred when he was still working Mexican Gangs and] *what happened to four guys that he and his partner caught: He says that he was "smarter than the people who investigated this incident." He says, "You don't see, you don't remember and it didn't happen. Those are the three things you say and you stick to it."*

In another incident, a man was on PCP and the patient kicked his leg out from under him. Then, he broke the man's elbows. He says that the other policemen were standing around watching him.

In the conclusion of his report, Dr. Hochman wrote:

People with this personality constellation are quite unhappy with life as their personality does tend to make them unpopular, once people get a chance to get to know them better. The patient's emphasis on his "exceptional" nature, this being a <u>lack of self-confidence</u>. . . .

❖

ALL THE FOLKS who still say Mark Fuhrman wasn't smart enough to get away with planting the glove need to reread the above and note how artful, and really quite clever, a cheater Fuhrman is. His attempts at deceiving psychiatrists demonstrate he'd done his homework on psychopathology. He not only knew the right symptoms and current psychobabble buzzwords, he knew enough to fake responses in a Rorschach test to indicate severe pathology, which isn't easy to do. Unless you are a psychopath. Since he did not exhibit any noticeable "affect" to accompany his verbalization, these doctors decided he was just a neurotic bad actor with a personality disorder, a liar who should be forced to return to police duty! One doctor, who saw Fuhrman during his drawn-out disability claim, did suggest in passing that it might be a good idea to keep him away "from guns" when he returned to the force. Good idea, just a little naive. There isn't a position in the LAPD for a regular police officer restricted permanently from carrying a firearm.

❖

IT IS IRONIC, if nothing else, that Fuhrman's saying, "I would have killed both of them," regarding his second wife's infidelity, is not wholly dissimilar to what Fuhrman and his partners are accusing O. J. Simpson of doing.

It is notable that Fuhrman bragged about excessive violence and bigotry in mid-1981, almost four years before he repeated himself to Laura Hart McKinny. When do we start to believe he's not just boasting or exaggerating?

❖

ALL OF THE foregoing Marcia Clark must have known about Mark Fuhrman before she, a sworn officer of the State, a defender of its Constitution, called him to the stand. She sweetly empathized with him over the injury done to his good name by the defense, and then, in the name of the People of California, she vouched for his absolute truthfulness before the Simpson jury and the nation. She put a man who allegedly celebrated Hitler's birthday on the witness stand to commit perjury.

❖

THE SINGLE WORST day of the trial was the day we sat there and listened to Fuhrman vomit his sick lust and ego-driven obscenities to the adoring groupie-like Laura Hart McKinny on her infamous tapes; if that's "interviewing," I'll kiss the south end of a Yankee-bound mule at the foot of Canal Street! The "killing and burning all the niggers" piece of verbal excrement rings in my ears.

When we walked out of our pews at the break, my eyes caught and held those of Carmelita Durio, one of O.J.'s two sisters. When we reached each other in the center aisle, she said to me, "Thank God, finally. You're the only white person who'd look me in the eye."

A few minutes later, I'm on KTLA-TV with my buddy Ron Olsen, the gracious Marta Waller, and the always astute Al LaBlanc *crying* over what I "thought we'd won thirty years ago!" I guess if a Mississippi boy has to make a public fool of himself crying on the new Warner Brothers Television Network, at least it was about an issue as important as it gets.

❖

"I THINK I SHIT in my pants," Dr. Mark Goulston says about the day his name and reputation were suddenly, briefly, thrust into the spotlight of the Trial of the Century. Toward the end of Fuhrman's stay on the witness stand, F. Lee Bailey asked Fuhrman if he'd been prepared for his testimony by a psychiatrist working with the prosecution. Fuhrman denied it. Then Bailey pointed in the direction of Dr. Goulston and asked Fuhrman if he recognized a psychiatrist, Dr. Mark *Gold*ston, mispronouncing the doctor's name. But the point was made. Then there were objections and the matter ended for the day without an answer.

The next day—when Dr. Goulston was *not* present—again Bailey asked Fuhrman if he knew a Mark Goulston, this time getting the name right. Fuhrman said, yes, he'd met a Mark upstairs on the eighteenth floor. But he denied that Dr. Goulston had worked with him in any way to prepare for testimony. He did say the doctor had told him, "You're doing a good job," a day or two earlier. Bailey then let the issue rest.

"In that moment," Dr. Goulston recalls, "the experience was, all the wannabe that I'd ever been in my life, all the anonymity, all the feeling like if I go to a high school reunion people won't even remember I was in their class, and all the ache to be noticed, suddenly turned into the nightmare of being stalked. In that moment, I went from anonymous to 'Jeez, my name was just mentioned across the world' to now the paranoia of being stalked. Now I don't belong to myself. It was an interesting insight, to go from 'nobody knows my name,' like the 'Cheers Bar' song, to really an intense feeling of paranoia."

The defense accused Dr. Goulston of signaling Fuhrman during his testimony. Dr. Goulston, it turns out, had not been privy to any of the preparation sessions for Fuhrman's testimony. His job was to observe performance and effect. He says, "I did give eye-contact support to Fuhrman on the stand, as I did with all the witnesses I was there for, particularly Denise Brown. During sidebars, witnesses sort of look around, and so I tried to be that friendly face.

"It's actually funny," Dr. Goulston says as he begins to relate the only time he met Mark Fuhrman, briefly, just before he testified. "We were in the War Room on the eighteenth floor. And the only thing I asked Fuhrman about, and this was after I saw his notes that were written so meticulously, I said, 'Has anyone ever called you obsessive-compulsive? I mean I hate to use those words.' He chuckled and said, 'My ex-wife said if it was up to me to mow the lawn, I would make every blade of grass the same height.' "

Dr. Goulston was purposely kept in the dark about any of

Fuhrman's psychiatric or disciplinary history. Without further knowledge then, Dr. Goulston found Fuhrman's response revelatory.

"To me, that means in high stakes, where he's being watched, he wouldn't have planted evidence. Because, if he's so geared toward precision—I'm not saying he wouldn't do it in some back alley in his regular thing—but if you're an obsessive-compulsive who needs to have everything that orderly and you come into a complicated crime scene, that's the last place you're going to do anything because of that feeling of scrutiny. Especially with different people. It would militate against [Fuhrman planting the glove] just because of his makeup. It would be my strongest argument why he didn't plant the glove.

"That's the kind of person who wouldn't want to shit on his evidence. He probably wipes nine times a day. Look at him, everything is manicured. Maybe when no one is watching he can be a bully, maybe he can do that. But in the eyes of all these different people, I mean, he ain't gonna do that in this thing. I mean, you don't know a hundred percent. But it just doesn't make sense to me because I know obsessive-compulsive."

Months later, on the day Fuhrman took the Fifth from the stand, Mark Goulston was sequestered under subpoena from the defense. In case Fuhrman testified, they were considering putting Mark on. Indeed, just the day before, Bailey had told the Court that he had reason to believe Mark Fuhrman was not only being coached by a Dr. Mark Goulston but that the doctor might be drugging Fuhrman so he wouldn't erupt on the stand.

That afternoon, not long before Fuhrman climbed into the witness box, Dr. Goulston, with Bill Hodgman at his side, met with F. Lee Bailey and Carl Douglas for questioning. Goulston's answers and calming manner very quickly caused Bailey and Douglas to believe that the psychiatrist had not been involved with coaching or drugging Fuhrman. Dr. Goulston radiates sincerity, truthfulness, and a calm sense that all will be well with the world if we just let it—which is why he is a specialist in suicide work. He has an uncanny ability to talk a suicide into rationality, and most of the work is done with his softly penetrating eyes and his calm, reassuring voice.

Bailey and Douglas were about to leave the room, when Dr. Goulston stopped them: "Mr. Bailey, I have a question," he said. "Yesterday, you implied that I did something improper with Detective Fuhrman, who is probably the most disliked person in America today. Just like you can't un-ring the bell, you can't un-slur a slur. And you slurred me. Any suggestion what I should do about that?"

Bailey looked at the doctor, smiled and said, "I'll trade you a retraction if you tell me what kind of a book you got on me during this session."

Everybody laughed. Perhaps Bailey should be glad Dr. Goulston did not answer what kind of a "book" the psychiatrist had gotten in his eyeball to eyeball with the famed attorney. At one point, while Bailey and Douglas were huddled over further questions to ask, Dr. Goulston leaned over and quietly said to Bill Hodgman, "They know he did it!," with sudden awareness in his voice.

Bill Hodgman, who always got a kick out of the doctor's idealistic naïveté, replied, "Of course they know."

❖

THERE WAS ANOTHER form of racism at play throughout the Simpson case, a racism that no one wants to talk about. From the beginning there was anti-Semitism rampant in the characterizations of Robert Shapiro in the salons, barrooms, elegant eateries, and pool halls throughout both Southern California and America.

And then it got worse. As Barry Scheck and Peter Neufeld became more visibly involved—they'd always been there, predating Johnnie Cochran on the Dream Team—the anti-Semitic rhetoric became even less subtle. In the courtroom, it took the verbal form of "those New York lawyers," referring to Barry Scheck, Peter Neufeld, and Alan Dershowitz.

But in the streets and homes throughout America, different, more ugly words were used. After the verdict it reached epidemic levels. Even months after the jury spoke, Barry Scheck was receiving hate-Jew mail. It was sickening and frightening.

A strange and awesome thing was this Trial of the Century. It managed to bring out almost all that is bad in the American psyche. But only some of the good.

17

AN UNBEARABLE
MISCARRIAGE OF JUSTICE

I HAVE A DISTINCT memory, the first night—Garcetti gets his executive staff together, there's maybe ten of us," Peter Bozanich recounts the very early days of the case.

"Marcia makes a presentation—'This is what the case is.' A couple of interesting things happened that night in retrospect. One, the scenario of facts that Marcia gave that night was exactly the case that we put on. I mean, 'We're going to prove this.' And almost a year later, when the actual trial starts, 'We're still going to prove this,' come hell or high water—even though there were deviations that had taken place where we had some doubts about the quality of the evidence. Whatever it was that first night was what we put on. There was no thinking about how to do this after that, not that I could see.

"Mark Fuhrman's name was never mentioned. There was a diagram there. It was the house, the driveway, and everything else. I said, 'I don't get the glove. What is the glove doing there? It doesn't work.' Everybody said the limo kid was good, and he was good, in retrospect. He tells it a certain way [seeing a large African American entering the estate from the front], but the glove is there. It just doesn't work. I mean, what the hell is the glove doing there? I remember asking whether there was any debris—evidence of somebody coming over the wall? Any evidence of Simpson running down there? What's he going there for? No answer.

"I'm not saying it couldn't happen. I'm just saying I've tried a lot of cases, seen a lot of cases, you seldom get that lucky. That's a huge piece of evidence. And it just didn't fit with what the limo guy was saying. The direction he said O.J. was coming from. Then a couple of weeks later when I read Toobin's piece about Fuhrman [The Incendiary Defense, in *The New Yorker*], I go, 'Oh, Jesus!' You know, if you pick one guy in the LAPD, you could not pick a more demonstrably biased witness. Whether he is or not is a separate issue. But a witness to get murdered—you picked the worst one.

"I thought, 'Gee, that's really a tough break.' But it also could be—maybe it's not a tough break. Maybe this is the worst! And the defense can sell that. They can sell it.

"So the glove troubled me the very first night," Assistant District Attorney Peter Bozanich says.

❖

IT IS OFTEN said by the vast majority of white Americans that even if Mark Fuhrman was a racist rogue cop, there is nothing but rank supposition to suggest he did anything improper at the crime scenes in the Simpson case. Indeed, it is said that it was impossible for Fuhrman to have planted the glove; he was never really inside the Bundy crime scene before seven o'clock that morning, well after he'd "found" and shown the Rockingham glove to Vannatter, Lange, and Phillips. Plus, how could he have picked up the glove at Bundy and hidden it without anyone, other cops, that is, seeing him?

That is all very strange in view of the public testimony of Mark Fuhrman himself and the LAPD crime scene photographer

Rolf Rochar. Since Fuhrman was no longer a credible witness, Mr. Rochar had the most revealing testimony on the issue of the Rockingham glove. It somehow went right past almost all of the press and public—but the jury got it.

Cops were milling around out on the street and sidewalk waiting for the arrival of Lange and Vannatter to begin processing the Bundy crime scene. Mr. Rochar said he was taking the perimeter shots, which procedure allows him to do without the presence of the homicide case officers in charge, when Detective Mark Fuhrman came and got him. Fuhrman brought him into the middle of the crime scene, and told him to take one specific, posed photo—a picture of Fuhrman pointing to the glove. Now, within only inches of that glove are many other pieces of evidence, such as the cap, keys, envelope, etc. But Mark Fuhrman did not ask him to photograph any of those items—only the glove and only with him pointing at it. Mr. Rochar says that no other police officer was inside the crime scene at the time.

A few hours later, as shown on his contact sheets, Rochar did photograph, in sequence, the other items of evidence at Bundy without the assistance of Detective Fuhrman's long pointing arm of the law in center frame. In fact, no other crime-scene photograph was taken with anyone pointing at anything. Only for the glove did someone—Mark Fuhrman—deem that necessary.

Mr. Rochar's testimony to the above, even coming so late in the trial and going without notice by the pundits, remains quite likely the most damning evidence of police misconduct in the Simpson case. The jury apparently concluded that *four* LAPD officers were less than truthful on a material issue. Detectives Vannatter, Lange, Phillips, and Fuhrman have all testified this photo had to have been taken sometime after 7:00 A.M., after the Rockingham glove had been found, and after Fuhrman had returned from that crime scene to Bundy "to determine if it appeared to be a match." While personal knowledge of Tom Lange makes it almost impossible to believe he would be party to conspiracy to manufacture or tamper with evidence, the photo does suggest that, in this one instance, either Lange honestly forgot when that picture was taken or he must be a part of the code of silence that makes police coverups possible.

In his trial testimony, Fuhrman put himself alone inside the crime scene. He testified that, by himself, well before Lange and Vannatter arrived, he entered the yard of the residence on the north side of Nicole's condo and walked up to the fence where Ron struggled and died, to "get a look at the wounds" to Goldman's back.

Of course, the prosecution immediately put on Lieutenant Frank Spangler to impeach, without announcing it, this part of Fuhrman's testimony. Lieutenant Spangler indicated that he followed Fuhrman to the other side of the fence to get a better view through the foliage of Ron Goldman's back wounds. Fuhrman was never out of his sight, he testified. Question is raised, why would a ranking officer have cause to watch the activities of *one* detective at an exciting crime scene? Does this denote *cause* to watch Fuhrman? If so, the reports of police on-scene whisperings about "an evidence problem" take on deeper dimensions.

But if Lieutenant Spangler is conveniently misremembering in the State's favor, then it is a further example of the Blue Wall. Either way, the veracity of the LAPD witnesses took another hard hit in front of the jury.

❖❖

REASONABLY, THE LOCATION of a second glove at Bundy need not be alongside its mate. Things physically separate that become dislodged within bursts of activity are likely to be found separate, even distant, in their deposition within the crime scene. So the fact that a dozen cops say they saw only the one glove under the broad leaves next to the blue watch cap doesn't in any way preclude another cop—Fuhrman—from stumbling upon something several feet distant.

Yet, what is more than just puzzling about the Rockingham glove and the theory that it was dropped by O.J. when he climbed over the fence and banged into the air conditioner, is why wouldn't O.J. have used his easy *secret* entrance to the Rockingham property? Kato Kaelin informed anybody who read Marc Eliot's book of the secret trail that leads from the pool area, past the tennis court, and eventually into the neighbor's backyard. Everyone who lived at Rockingham knew of it and used it on occasion. Indeed, after the crime, this entrance was used regularly by people who wanted to avoid the mob out front.

❖

TWO MORE OBSERVATIONS regarding the question of Fuhrman planting the Rockingham glove with or without the knowledge and complicity of any other police officer:

Leather gloves are pulled off at the fingertips; you pull straight back in an unsheathing action. You can't peel them off as you would a surgeon's plastic gloves, by yanking from the wrist. Consequently, it is difficult to accept the prosecution's theory that O.J.'s blood was found in only one spot on the glove, at the indented hem at the wrist flap of the Rockingham glove, because he was pulling it off with fingers bloodied from his cuts. Of course, why there isn't any of O.J.'s blood anywhere else on the gloves—inside or out—isn't included in the State's theory.

A plausible reason is offered by the defense, however. They say it's entirely possible that the staining happened the day Collin Yamauchi admits there was spillage of Simpson's reference sample blood onto Yamauchi's plastic gloves, the same time the leather glove was allegedly out and exposed in the evidence processing room.

The State maintains that the glove at Rockingham had to have been dropped upon the bed of leaves not long before 11:00 P.M., and that Fuhrman found the glove some seven hours later. Yet there is not a single leaf over or above the glove. In fact, there is no debris of any kind on the glove, not even a single breeze-blown particle of dirt or vegetation. Fuhrman testified that when he found the glove, it appeared to still be wet, even after all that time, without any debris.

The notion that Fuhrman didn't know if O.J. had an alibi so he would not have risked planting any evidence does not hold water. There is scant chance of that. It is an axiom of detective work that almost always the husband is guilty when a woman is murdered under these kinds of circumstances.

So follow along with this scenario: If it turns out that everything is square at Rockingham, that O.J. is clean and in no way a suspect, Fuhrman doesn't plant the glove. He returns it to the scene at Bundy or, more likely, just discards it. Preposterous that a cop could remove or replace evidence at a crime scene without its being widely noticed? You need only remember all of the things that were *not* discovered at the crime scenes or in the Bronco for weeks and months—what the State conceded was simple human error and omission.

❖

WHY DIDN'T FUHRMAN document his interview with Rosa Lopez, the maid at the estate adjacent to Rockingham, that early morning? Did he only want to find out what could be seen of the path behind Kato's and Arnelle's rooms from the neighbor's vantage point?

"Where does Fuhrman go?" asks Pat McKenna. "He goes

next door to Rosa's. I mean, if he's gonna go door knocking that morning when the sun comes up, why does he only go to one place? Why doesn't he go across the street? Why doesn't he go to the house behind O.J.'s? Why doesn't he go across the street on Ashford there, where that house is? I mean, O.J.'s house is surrounded by homes, and where does he go? To Rosa Lopez.

"He never ever makes a report, he never writes a note about Rosa. Here's a guy that takes copious notes at Bundy. Anybody that knows him as a detective knows he takes very good detailed notes, he's a thinking detective. Why did he go interview Rosa? To eliminate the possibility that she saw him take that glove out of the Bronco at six o'clock in the morning, because it's light out, not dark like he claimed."

❖

HERE IS ANOTHER intriguing circumstantial fact that is not public knowledge: Of the dozens of cops of all ranks who have been identified and documented as having been present in some capacity at the Bundy crime scene, even as looky-loos, one who definitely was there does not appear in any report. That police officer was Detective Brad Roberts, Mark Fuhrman's long-time former partner.

"Roberts is all over that crime scene, and he's never ever brought into the case," Pat McKenna says. "And not only is he not brought into the case, there are no reports by Roberts anywhere. He's a detective, he didn't write one word? Give me a fucking break."

❖

ACCORDING TO A former cop who knows all the parties involved, even before the arrest of O. J. Simpson a "detective close to Fuhrman" went to a shop in West Hollywood and placed an order for baseball caps emblazoned with the international "no" symbol of a circle and diagonal bar superimposed over the number "32." Beneath it, the legend LAPD JUICE BUSTERS. "32," of course, was Simpson's old football jersey number.

❖

P AT MC KENNA, WHO was responsible for the defense locating Laura Hart McKinny and her audiotapes, did a great deal of work on the Fuhrman issue. His theory of Fuhrman, the planting of evidence, and the actions and motives of some members of the LAPD in the Simpson case, which follows here, will pique interest as well as controversy:

"When Lange and Vannatter first arrived on-scene at Bundy, Fuhrman had to be saying, 'Hey, here's the story.' I believe they are telling the truth when they say they didn't know Fuhrman. Because if they did know him, they would know he's a crazy racist bastard that plants evidence.

"I think Fuhrman convinced them. Now mind you, there's two hours between the time Fuhrman is on the scene and Vannatter and Lange show up. That gave Fuhrman plenty of time to make a couple of trips up to Rockingham for Rosa Lopez to hear him going up and down the driveway."

Not only does Pat KcKenna believe that Fuhrman left Bundy and went to Rockingham before Lange and Vannatter arrived at the murder scene, he believes that Detective Brad Roberts was with him: "I swear that's who went up to Rockingham with Fuhrman, because Rosa hears voices, men's voices, plural. Now, it's either Fuhrman and Phillips or Fuhrman and Roberts. And I've gotta believe it was Roberts who ran up there with him because Phillips was hanging around Bundy.

"I always felt he stuck it in the Bronco," Pat continues. "Every cop has a slim jim—but O.J. never said the Bronco was locked. He didn't even know if he locked the goddamn thing. He says he almost never locks it. It could've been wide open when Fuhrman first got there.

"If you notice, whenever Fuhrman disappears from the other three musketeers, evidence appears. When he left them over at the Ashford gate to go strolling around, he comes and brings them all over to the Bronco and says, 'Look, there's a spot of blood on the door handle.' Whenever he's alone, shit happens; evidence appears or disappears.

"I believe in my heart of hearts that the glove he pocketed was found on the other side of the fence at Bundy—you know, it got there from a struggle—when he said he was going around to the north side of the fence to look at Goldman's back wounds. That's the glove he can grab with no one seeing him. It's outside the crime scene; he sees a perfect opportunity. Which fits with his psyche of planting evidence.

"I think he stuck it in the Bronco first trip up. Which would make him come back and point at the glove before the second trip back."

To prove McKenna's theory, the defense asked for the records of the flurry of cell-phone activity among Phillips, Roberts, and Fuhrman during the time in question.

"What we finally got were sanitized telephone records. We wanted to know what all those blacked-out calls were. Who else were they calling? We wanna know. We weren't going to disclose those things. See, that's the line of bullshit you get from the DA, like, we're gonna dump 'em to the media. We didn't give a fuck who they were calling unless there was some kind of shit that didn't jibe with what they were testifying to. And why are they hiding 'em from us? What was in those cell-phone records that we shouldn't know? Could we have jeopordized someone's life? No. It's total bullshit why we couldn't look at those cell-phone records."

A question comes to mind: If Fuhrman and Phillips and Roberts are together at Bundy, why would there be any telephone communication among them at that time?

On the logic of Fuhrman planting the glove, McKenna says, "I've thought a lot about this. It matches with his personnel records, where the one supervisor said he's always trying to make the big case. I don't think he was acting, at least on a conscious level, on his racial animus. I think he was acting on 'This guy's a wife beater, I'm gonna catch him.' He made the leap that O.J. murdered 'em, and he said, 'I'm just gonna sweeten the pot'; you know, cops do this all the time, just wanna sweeten the pot a little bit. 'I know he did it. He's such a cunning murderer, killer, et cetera, I'm just gonna help the case a little bit.'

"I think that's what happened in the lab. It wasn't so much of a police conspiracy. You had a rogue cop over at Bundy and Rockingham. And then the socks: Somebody just said, 'Hey, these guys wanna say we planted a glove, let 'em explain this sock!' Except they weren't thinking the sock through enough, because they should've put Goldman's blood on it."

McKenna, who is known and respected by cops wherever he's been in his eventful career, on the involvement of Tom Lange and other cops in a broad conspiracy to frame Simpson: "They're not thinking like we're a bunch of racist guys and we'll finally get that bastard. I think they're thinking, 'Hey, we're good cops, this bastard did it, we've gotta catch him.' I think Tom Lange is a straight-shooting guy; he's an honest, decent guy trying to do the best job he possibly can. And I think, you know, hey, if he thinks O.J. did it he's certainly not going to go way overboard and be the Boy Scout of all time and tell the complete truth if it fucks up one of his guys. If in his mind he feels, hey, I'm not really sure so I'll go along with the group, then, 'Yeah, we all did send Fuhrman back to see if the glove matched.'

"Maybe they did ask Fuhrman to go back and see if it matched. That's good. Because I don't think those guys saw two

gloves when they were at Bundy before they went to Rockingham. There was only one glove and a hat when they were there.
The other glove is long gone up there by Rockingham. Fuhrman
stashed it for the time being in the Bronco.

"An interesting thing happened early in the case. One of
the cops who was at the scene that night shared an apartment
with his brother. They also shared a car together. Well, the cop
brother was supposed to be home off his midnight shift at eight
in the morning and drop the car off. He didn't get home with
the car until eleven in the morning and told his brother all
about the O.J. case. He said: 'We've been running all over trying
to get evidence on O. J. Simpson!'

"The brother told the mother that story, and the mother
used to call me up all the time and say, 'Look, there's something
real funny going on. I don't think my son believes O.J. did it,
and he was on the scene. But I'm never going to be able to give
you my name.' At one point she started crying and hung up.

"I had so many anonymous calls. I had a guy saying he
worked at the lab. He wanted to come forward but he was not
only afraid for his job but his life."

❖

WHILE FUHRMAN'S KNOWLEDGE of Nicole's "boob job" is
public record, the fact that for at least two years before
the murders, Fuhrman referred to himself around the West LA
Division as "Nicole's private cop" is not. But it is true.

❖

ACTUALLY, IT IS difficult to believe that—considering his
known psychiatric history, his extreme narcissism and
amoral compulsion to score big, and the fact he had just been
removed from a murder case, the scenario of which must have

been the stuff of his fondest fantasy—Fuhrman would *not* have thought about planting evidence. Doesn't he boast to McKinny and her tape recorder only weeks after the murders: "I am the most important witness in the Trial of the Century. If I go down, their case goes bye-bye"?

In fact, he was working his pat routine—according to his words on McKinny's tapes—of "creating probable cause" in case he needed it in his questioning of Kato. Lange, Vannatter, and Phillips had moved on to Arnelle's room and then to the main house at Rockingham. But Fuhrman stayed and gave an "under-the-influence" eye-reflex field test to Kato with his pen before searching the room and questioning him. There is no law against being intoxicated in your own apartment. Fuhrman didn't have a search warrant. Yet he's searching Kato's room. Probable cause is *I don't know if this dude even belongs on the property and he's stoned to the gills. So I bust him, and straighten the shit out later.*

Everything surrounding Fuhrman seems rather pat: A murder case where the perpetrator somehow successfully disposes of his bloody clothes and murder weapon yet is such a bungler that he leaves one of a pair of gloves at *each* crime scene—perfect bookends for a library of murder clues that Fuhrman manages to retrieve. Fuhrman popping up in Nicole's life at moments of crisis: the undocumented domestic violence call at Rockingham in 1985; Fuhrman being asked to write a report from "indelible" memory in 1989 of the events of the 1985 incident that would play a large role in O.J. agreeing to plead no contest to spouse-abuse charges; Fuhrman bragging to other cops about his personal relationship with Nicole; Fuhrman being one of the two detectives who arrived first at the Bundy murder scene; Fuhrman volunteering to go with Lange and Vannatter to Rockingham because he "knew the way" after the two detectives from the elite Robbery/Homicide unit had "taken his case away"; Fuhrman leaving his higher-rank colleagues futilely ringing the gate buzzer while he wandered off around the corner by himself only to find blood on the exterior of the Bronco, giving "probable cause" to enter the property without a search warrant; Fuhrman being the officer to go over the wall first and then walk around to the gate and let the others in.

Interesting, isn't it, that Detective Mark Fuhrman appears all over the latter years of the obviously sick relationship between O.J. and Nicole: two *other* narcissistic, totally self-absorbed, promiscuous, manipulative liars and emotional cheats who perpetually chose to live life in the passing lane of a *two*-lane highway. This was a bloody "no accident" waiting to happen.

❖

M Y THIRD WORST moment of the trial, and my second most embarrassing, came one afternoon not long after I'd broken my neck. I'm sitting in my pew with my neck brace on and I sneeze. Not just once, but three times quickly, and it hurt like hell. Now, when you break your neck, one of the things you have to get used to is everybody around you behaving as if you're an eggshell with a bomb inside. I mean, folks try to give you a wide berth; they're really quite sweet, when you think about it. It's genuine concern and not shunning.

But not with 30 million people watching! Sure enough, after my string of sneezes, Judge Ito interrupted the proceedings and said, "Be careful, Mr. Bosco. You might hurt yourself."

My reply: "I believe I already have, Your Honor."

❖

E VERY TIME MARCIA CLARK stood up and told the jury that the prosecution represented the victims, that she and her crew were the advocates, indeed the voices, of the murdered pair crying out for justice, and every time Marcia Clark claimed they represented the victims' loved ones, the grief-debilitated families sitting there a few feet away from the jury, my innards roiled and boiled.

Sorry, folks, but HORSEFUCKINGSHIT!!!

At a time when crime victims' (and their familys') rights are all the polite rage, it might be politically very incorrect to ask, but when did the bedrock of our American way of justice get reversed without Congress, the president of the United States, the United States Supreme Court, and We-the-People knowing about it? As a paid and sworn advocate of We-the-People, and thereby the State, a public prosecutor is in the courtroom, by law and statute, *to seek truth, wherever or whatever it might be.* That's it in one small nutshell. By its very definition, truth can have no agenda, no side to be on; truth is what it is, even when it's only a legal abstraction.

As a public prosecutor, you look for it as well and as rigorously as you can; then you present what you find of it to a jury. You do this as effectively as you can, as dramatically and strategically as you can. You do this because the State's position is that it has enough evidence to prove *beyond a reasonable doubt* that the defendant before the bar is guilty of the crime for which he is accused and should therefore be, one, isolated from society for society's protection, and two, meted out prescribed, appropriate punishment as a deterrent. That's it.

You isolate, punish, or exonerate in the name of the People, in *our* name collectively—but you most definitely do not do it as legal representative of the victims or their families seeking vengeance. If that were the case, then each side would have hired the best private firms possible from the beginning and proceeded right on to the civil trial.

In criminal court, the papers don't read The Goldman Family or The Brown Family versus O. J. Simpson. They read:

PEOPLE OF THE STATE OF CALIFORNIA, Plaintiff, v. ORENTHAL JAMES SIMPSON, Defendant. Case No. BA097211.

There truly is an important distinction here.

18

IN THE KITCHEN WITH ROSA

THE SIMPSON JURY did not hear Rosa Lopez testify, so the El Salvadoran maid of Simpson's neighbor had no effect on the verdict. But the world saw Rosa's testimony, and what she got was scorn and ridicule. Ms. Lopez may have been the most tragic victim of the blue chair. Not surprisingly, there is far more to the story of Rosa Lopez than hit the media eye.

"I spent eight days with her, not to mention all the previous interviews," Pat McKenna begins the true story of Rosa Lopez. "I interviewed her first with John McNally, after hearing from Bill Pavelic [a very prominent PI in Los Angeles, a former detective with the LAPD and Robert Shapiro's favored investigator in the Simpson case; he played a major role until he got caught on national TV, in the courtroom, with a tape of an interview he'd conducted with Rosa Lopez that the defense had not given to the State] she had all this information, you know, that she saw the Bronco at ten-fifteen. We went and interviewed her; she doesn't say ten-fifteen. Now, we don't put words in her mouth, we're just interviewing her.

"We go back to Pavelic, 'Hey, Bill, she's a little hinky on

this ten-fifteen thing. It's more like ten o'clock, or she wasn't sure. . . .'

"Anyway, I go back to see Rosa a second time, because John and I had problems with what she was saying, you know, according to what Bill said. But what she was saying, as I evaluated it, was fine with me.

"She spent the early evening with Sylvia [Guerra, a maid who worked in a house not far away]. At Rosa's, they're eating tamales. They take the dog out. Rosa says they see the Bronco at eight-thirty at night. Rosa said she commented to Sylvia that it was parked out in the street funny. Now, she didn't say that to me, okay? I never heard that. And I thought that was Bill putting that in her mouth to make it fit with what the cops were saying that it was parked funny.

"See, I don't do my thing that way. I don't give a fuck who thinks it's parked funny. If I'm interviewing a witness, if they tell me it's parked funny, okay, that's their perception, that's their recollection, but because someone else says it's parked funny—that is, the cops—I'm not going to try to get a witness to say, 'The car's parked funny.' If they say it, that's great if it fits with what the cops are saying. But I never thought the car was parked funny. I don't see how anybody in the world could say it's parked funny. The ass end of it ain't out that much. Total bullshit, that was to fit with O.J. arriving home in a hurry and banging on the air conditioner and dropping a glove. That was all DA bullshit.

"O.J. remembers backing the Bronco out after golf that day. Because he came home, it was inside, he backed it up and put it outside on the street, seven or eight in the evening, before he went to McDonald's, because he took the Bentley to McDonald's. It's too bad he didn't take the freakin' Bronco to McDonald's.

"I always interviewed Rosa with the Salingers [the people Rosa worked for] present. The Salingers always told me this woman is wonderful, she doesn't lie, we trust her, she's honest. The more we got to talking, the more we got the sense that it was around ten o'clock when she saw the Bronco. And I always thought that was cool. That was fine with me. It never bothered me that she saw it at ten and then saw it in the same place at eight in the morning. That was perfect for me. That was wonderful, because what she also said—which was the most important—was about those *footsteps* all night long.

"We were in the house, I was in her bedroom up near that window. We've been there at ten o'clock at night, we've been there at one o'clock in the morning. All different times. That was the most important thing to me—these men's voices, and what she called hard footsteps, in other words, dress shoes. That's what I always felt was Fuhrman and Roberts, or Fuhrman and somebody.

"She claims she heard it throughout the night; well, it was probably two times. She probably heard it the first time they were up there, which was probably shortly after two in the morning when they figured they'd grab O.J. right, you know, leaving the murder scene. They didn't see any sign of life in the place. Then they ran back to Bundy. That's when he points at the glove with Rochar. He'd already seen that the Bronco was there. He stuck it in the Bronco the first trip up.

"What happened with Rosa then was, Johnnie does his opening argument. Johnnie's opening argument says ten-fifteen. Well, I now know after talking to Rosa that she's told her family, she's told Sylvia, she's even told Robert Heidstra what she heard and saw. Did you know that Heidstra was also the car detailer for the Salingers? Oh, yeah.

"So they had conversed about what each of them had seen and heard. Okay? Rosa is this devout little Catholic person. All the people, when they heard opening arguments saying that Rosa says ten-fifteen, well . . . I think her daughter went ballistic, figuring that her mother was going to lie under oath. Because her mother obviously had never told the daughter ten-fifteen. She told the daughter what she told me, probably what she told Sylvia, what she told Heidstra, what she told everybody: It was around ten!

"If you listen to what Pavelic did with her—even Bill finally admitted it was a major mistake. But Bill says, in his interview, what she did was make a cup of tea, okay? Bill gives that five minutes, for boiling the water and everything else. Then she puts a collar on the dog; Bill gives that five minutes. And then she takes the dog out to pee, and he gives that five minutes. Thereby pushing ten o'clock to ten-fifteen.

"I sat with her. I said, 'Rosa, let me see where your teapot is.' She didn't make it in a teapot. She put a fucking cup of water in the microwave. You know how long it takes to make tea? Forty-five seconds. While the tea is in the microwave doing the forty-five seconds, she's putting the collar on the dog. I watched her put the collar on the dog; she could put a collar on the dog in thirty seconds! The collar on the dog, and the tea are both done simultaneously, thereby still before ten o'clock. She takes the dog out to pee. You can do that in under a minute. The dog's out there, it piddles, and you're back inside your house *before* ten o'clock.

"And O.J. goes out to make that cell-phone call at ten-three. So she's back in her house at ten, when she'd probably noticed the Bronco there. You know, she could see it.

"That's what caused her to freak out, caused her daughter to say I'm leaving, caused her all sorts of personal anguish.

"When I went out there, the media was all over. Number one, she absolutely—if she saw the Bronco out there at ten-fifteen—exploded the prosecution's case. So therefore, the media went nuts—'This is the most important witness'—they just went crazy over there.

"She in her own mind is thinking, 'Wait a minute. I never

said ten-fifteen.' So she's all perplexed as to how she is going to get out of this situation. And I was talking with her. I used to say, 'Rosa, you don't have to say ten-fifteen.'

"I finally went back to Bill—actually I went to Johnnie—before we put Rosa on. There was a bunch of the lawyers in the room, and I said, 'Guess what, guys? We're going to have to eat something here. Because I've been spending a lot of time with Rosa. She didn't say ten-fifteen, she said ten o'clock.'

"Johnnie felt a little bad because he'd already committed to ten-fifteen. He's feeling like he's going to look like a fool. But as for me, I just wanted her to say what the truth was. Because I kept saying, 'Hey, we can live with ten o'clock. Because here is what else is important: the footsteps. Fuhrman coming to talk to her in the morning. Fuhrman never making a report of their interview.'

"I thought this was all tremendous stuff. But because it became such a nightmare personally, she wanted to blow; therefore we had to put her on in the middle of the DA's case. Which exposed her to like this whole attack by Darden.

"And so when she's on the stand, they make her out to be even more of a liar, when in fact we're getting all kinds of people calling in saying the interpreter in the courtroom is misinterpreting the entire context of what this woman is saying. We kept getting call after call. So we went to the judge, and of course this is the judge's favorite little interpreter. She got bent out of shape. But we're saying, 'Wait a minute.'

"For example, Darden said, 'Did you have reservations to go?' Rosa said, 'Yeah.' Well, according to the travel agent, she hadn't completed the reservation because it hadn't been paid for yet. But she had called them, asked about plans to leave, et cetera, et cetera. In her dialect, what a linguist told me was that in her mind, making the plans and all that stuff, that is consistent. When Darden said, 'Do you have reservations to go?' Darden's figuring he's going to catch her in a lie because he knows she doesn't have actual plane reservations, because what did they do? They checked with an airline. But they didn't check with the travel agent.

"In Rosa's mind, she's leaving. The plans are made. And in her language that meant reservations, 'Yes, I did have reservations to go.' But it's not really reservations like you or I would know them. Therefore the interpreter is answering back—they were calling and saying Rosa says something and the interpreter says it back in English, which is not what Rosa's saying.

"So Rosa became like this complete plant by the defense, according to the media. But if you ever spent time with Rosa you would know that this was a devout Catholic. You know, her whole mission in life was to save up enough money to bury her son in the family plot—he was a war hero down in El Salvador.

"To me, Rosa was the best witness we had—one of the best in the whole case. It just got mishandled.

"It's okay for you to clean my house, as long as you keep your mouth shut and you don't take it outside of these doors," Pat continues the Rosa Lopez story. "Because that was the thing, I thought, that made Sylvia upset." (While never putting Sylvia Guerra on the stand, the State had her ready. They had leaked to the press that Sylvia would impeach Rosa's testimony; they even brought her into the courtroom once, as a visible deterrence.)

"Sylvia had immigration problems. These people that come over here with immigration problems, but work in some of these fancy homes, know that the unwritten code is 'You keep everything inside these walls.' And therefore Rosa had even violated that. The testimony was coming out that she and Sylvia had tamales together. So I think Sylvia was pissed off for two reasons: One, Rosa never told her ten-fifteen, and two, Rosa gave up her name. Thereby causing flak for Sylvia. We always heard the government went to her and said, 'We'll take care of your immigration problem; we need you to go against Rosa.'"

19

SMARM OVER STUPIDITY

T
HE STATE DIDN'T lose only because it cheated and got caught at it. Marcia and her troops were also incredibly stupid, inexcusably arrogant, almost daily unprepared, and totally leaderless.

Bob, Johnnie, and Barry didn't steal a win through smarm, obfuscation, and deception. They outlawyered Marcia and her troops at every turn of the screw. They worked harder and more efficiently, they were always better prepared, and most important, they told a better story.

❖

"I
DON'T THINK THERE was any kind of a real strategy to the case," Peter Bozanich sums up. "It was just to put on all the evidence without any thought of making a presentation to the jury as to the scenario of what happened, just put on everything. And the jury simply cannot absorb it.

"The jury has to bond with a prosecutor; there was no bonding. Marcia went almost three months without handling a witness in front of the jury.

"The evidence was overwhelming, just staggering amounts

of evidence, but there was no editing. It's kind of like there wasn't a director in charge. Nothing was left on the cutting-room floor. I'm sure that when a director makes a movie he probably has twenty, thirty, fifty hours of film that he has to make a coherent presentation out of. This was not a coherent presentation. It was a director who didn't know what he was doing.

"You can only hold a jury's interest for so long. Once you get that much evidence in front of a jury, they don't know what's important and what's not."

❖❖

IT WAS MORE than revealing, it was jaw dropping, to learn from Rock Harmon and Woody Clarke, the two DNA prosecutors on loan from Alameda County and San Diego respectively, that the only time the prosecution players ever had a meeting together during the trial was one night during rebuttal! They waited until the closing moments, when the campaign was all but lost, to call a full team meeting! But then Rock and Woody, who for months carried the State's ball with valor, were always treated as outsiders not to be completely trusted by Marcia & Company. (Truly talented litigators, with contrasting styles, Harmon and Clarke were by far the best trial lawyers on the prosecution team.)

To be sure, the unusual wall of secrecy surrounding anything to do with the Simpson case was an insult to many of the other nine hundred deputy DAs in the office. "Never seen anything like it. Everybody and everything was zipped up tighter than a drum. Hodgman was the only one who would even give the time of day to people those folks worked with for years," one deputy DA said. It was a sentiment widely expressed among the prosecution team's colleagues.

But what was the secret?

❖

"BY THEN IT was almost a bunker mentality," Peter Bozanich says. "It was a very closed circle. They would take no advice from anybody. No input. The case is going south in front of everybody's eyes. And they would listen to nobody. They almost fed off each other. I was still downtown until just before the verdict. I mean, all of us were just walking around the halls saying, 'This is nuts, the way this case is being tried.' But there it was, day after day after day.

"Because of this bunker mentality they just got sidetracked and there was nobody there to bring them back. But then, Garcetti doesn't listen anyway. He wants things said that he wants to hear. He doesn't want to hear what he doesn't want to hear. And anybody who tells him things he doesn't want to hear is excised. That's what I'm doing here. That's what very, very capable people are doing countywide. He just excises people he doesn't want to hear from.

"I was on his executive staff there for a couple or three years when he first formed it, and I sat in the room and looked around and said, 'What am I doing with these people?' It was unbelievable. Nobody ever would argue with him; no one would tell him you can't do that. So I think he gets very bad advice. Because people have a sense of what he wants and that's what they say."

❖

YES, IT IS true that the trial on the ninth floor was micro-managed from the big suite on the eighteenth floor with a bank of TV sets tuned to each television station carrying live coverage. For over a year we in Department 103 sat and watched Marcia jump up and run to the wall phone by the clerk's cubicle whenever her silent pager gave a vibrating jolt. But to argue, even in theory, that Gil Garcetti, a politician born and skewed, with little or no trial-court experience, provided real leadership is embarking on one very slippery slope. The prosecution was, in practice if not theory, totally leaderless.

When commands came down to Marcia from on high, more often than not those commands originated with Suzanne Childs, Garcetti's press officer. This—disturbing and improbable as it seems, which is why it has gone unreported in the national press—was in keeping with Garcetti's view of the trial as public relations. Ms. Childs, the former Mrs. Michael Crichton, is also Garcetti's longtime extra-marital companion.

"I think a lot of it is Suzanne Childs—she was the brains behind all this. She ran Gil and that just kind of like percolates on down," Peter Bozanich says, having no compunction about coming out and saying what he knows to be the case.

❖

As the trial wore on, a process of leader du jour developed, with Marcia always the house whip and field commander. By the end of the trial, she had convinced Childs and Garcetti that Brian "The Genius" Kelberg was the savior. It was Kelberg who, against the strong advice of Bill Hodgman—"the only truly talented trial lawyer of the bunch," say Larry Longo and others—ordered Chris Darden to go after Laura Hart McKinny in a meaningless, mean-spirited cross-examination, even though her credibility had nothing to do with the tapes. Of course, it was "brilliant Brian," again against the strong counsel of Hodgman, who ordered the insanity: "We must destroy Henry Lee!"

❖

T WO EXAMPLES OF trial lawyering:
   Detective Tom Lange had been on the stand for several days. Johnnie Cochran had methodically (well, as methodically as it is possible for Johnnie to do anything) grilled his unflappable old friend and occasional professional adversary almost beyond endurance.

During a mid-morning break, Tom and Johnnie find themselves in the ninth floor men's room with only a couple of book authors around. Tom says to Johnnie: "You looking at that jury?"

"Yeah," Johnnie groans.

"We've lost 'em," Tom says.

"I know it, they're gone," Johnnie agrees.

"They're no longer listening," Tom says.

"Think we oughta shut it down?" Johnnie asks.

"Yeah. We're not doing anybody any good now," Tom answers.

"All right, let's go back in there and shut it down," Johnnie says.

Then they go back in and do just that.

Almost four months later, we're into the second week of Dr. Sathyavagiswaran's testimony. Brian Kelberg and I are in the same men's room. We have the place to ourselves.

I say, "Brian, you looking at the jury?"

"No. What are they doing?" he asks.

"They've shut down. They're not listening. Christ, I caught Ito dozing off once, and I've been nodding out and in for days."

"I don't care, I'm going to get my points in."

Kelberg actually says this.

Which is exactly what he goes back in and does. Pity the jury's not listening.

❖

"If you're a deputy DA in Los Angeles, there are lots of cases," Peter Bozanich says. "I understand this was a very important case—but you put it on. It is what it is. You can't force a case to be what you want it to be—you can't force it to be two execution murders if you don't have the evidence to show that's exactly what it was. You can't just be blind to the glitches in your evidence, to the weaknesses of your witnesses. You've got to work with what it is. And I think one of the problems in this case was they tried to force the case to be a certain way."

❖

It was tactically stupid of Marcia Clark to use her child-care problems as a pretext to keep from putting Rosa Lopez in front of the jury in a special night session. Ms. Lopez, after a long, emotional day on the stand out of the presence of the jury, was ready to break down. Marcia could have seriously wounded the defense. But no.

Even the next morning, the prosecution was still terrified to let Rosa go before the jury. Marcia argued to Ito that it would "rip the fabric of the State's case."

Then Johnnie reminded the court that Darden had said he "welcomed the opportunity to put her before the jury."

❖

In seat B-13, I was almost always sitting just behind and to the immediate right of Fred Goldman, father of the murdered Ron Goldman. From a distance less than twenty-four inches, I observed this man and his family—his second wife, Patti, and his daughter, Kimberly, every day for sixteen months.

I watched the outward manifestation of his grief, his bottomless anger and hatred, but I could not even imagine how horrible he must really have felt inside even though my only son is the same age Ron would have been. I saw the stoic tears, I heard the repeated, low, hard mutterings, "You murderer! You murderer!" I saw his jaw muscles clinch. I heard the sometimes quick intake of breath, and the sometimes slow, emptying exhale. I saw him reach endlessly to touch, to strengthen, to comfort Patti and Kim, his right hand and arm or shoulder for one, and the left hand and arm or shoulder for the other.

At least twice, my hand almost went out to stop him from going over the rail and straight at O.J., but always he had the self-control to stop himself. We knew for months he was going to explode.

It is with some measure of sadness then that I have to report this: When Fred Goldman finally did explode—that day he went down to the first floor press-conference area and poured out his rage at racism taking over the trial of the man he believed murdered his son, that day he cried out, "How dare they!"—on that day I sat there just before the break and watched Marcia Clark get his attention and nod a very purposeful *yes*.

Immediately, Fred Goldman made a beeline to the first floor and held that forever memorable press conference. And then it happened again; the next time he let his raw pain come screaming out on camera, Marcia, minutes before, had gotten his attention and given him the same nod as before.

I am not implying that Fred's words and emotions were any less than what he absolutely felt—he has felt that way since the moment he learned his son had been murdered. What I am saying is that the timing was orchestrated by Marcia Clark for a purpose.

It is part of the lawyering craft that you sometimes want a witness to become emotionally overwrought in front of a jury. It was actually brilliant, for example, the way Marcia kept one eye on the clock and the other on Denise Brown until a minute

or two before 5:00 P.M. on a Friday, waiting to ask the question
she knew Denise would bawl the most over. A crying sister of
the victim in the minds of the jury for the weekend? That's
good lawyering—one of Marcia's best moments.

But what audience was Marcia & Company playing for with
Fred Goldman emptying his gut and soul into every living room
in America with increasing frequency as we drew closer and
closer to an ending? An ending that was defeat in the courtroom?

❖

T HE DEFENSE HAD on its side Dr. Jo-Ellan Dimitrius, a jury
consultant. She came with an impressive list of wins, among
which were the McMartin Preschool case, the first Rodney King
trial, the Reginald Denny trial. Exceedingly bright, she stands
at the forefront of her field, and her input served the defense
team well at every turn of the case. She focused on the nuances
of the only audience of the trial that mattered in the end—the
jury.

The prosecution had on its side Suzanne "Bubbles" Childs,
who focused on the public watching the trial on television—a
jury that had no vote. She also paid attention to visiting celebrities in Department 103.

❖

" T HE CASE WAS presented not for the twelve in the jury box,
but for the national television audience," Peter Bozanich
says. "It was a P.R. campaign by Garcetti more than anything
else.

"And he actually got away with it." Bozanich shakes his
head. "Because the media has not attacked him. It's a sexy story
that blacks and whites don't get along. 'Payback.' The Howard

University cheering section and stuff like that. It set back race relations in America a long way, I think. People are probably going to vote to get rid of affirmative action because they're so mad at the O. J. Simpson case.

"And nobody has called Garcetti to task. I'm just stunned. When he said this was an 'emotional verdict'—you're saying this was a racial verdict. And I don't buy it's a racial verdict. I mean, the jury was lost. I mean, this was *not* an unreasonable verdict.

"I'm convinced Simpson did it. I don't know *what* he did. It may be a voluntary and a second, a voluntary and a first, and like that, I don't know. But the DA wanted two firsts and that's all the DA wanted. There wasn't any inquiry into what was going on."

20

GIVE ME THAT OLD-TIME RELIGION AND TEAMWORK

AWHOLE LOT of folks got upset over Johnnie's closing argument. Most especially the comparison of the racism of Mark Fuhrman to the racism of Adolf Hitler, who went from being a small-time thug in a Munich beer hall brawl in 1923 to the architect of the Holocaust twenty years later.

Folks demand to know: How can you compare one half-baked, scorned artist-turned-foot soldier who wanted to destroy whole races of people and then burn their remains, removing them entirely from the circle of life, to Hitler?

Oh.

Yes. Remember, before joining the Marines and going to Vietnam, Mark Fuhrman, the town bully, wanted to be an artist; he couldn't make a living at it so he went off to a bad war and came back an even meaner hater. He led a club of other haters and picked out an easy first target for his uniformed cohorts to terrorize—female cops. They called the "club" M.A.W., Men Against Women. In truth, though, Fuhrman and his troopers were equal opportunity haters; they hated everyone except themselves. This is an important distinction. Perhaps too much emphasis has been placed on Fuhrman's racist attitudes toward blacks and Hispanics and Jews, because Fuhrman distrusted and hated everybody who wasn't a male cop with an attitude.

Fuhrman was investigated and suspended for his M.A.W. activities (the work of Captain Margaret "Peggy" York). But he came back and made it all the way up to detective. He even left an account of his life and thoughts on Ms. McKinny's audiotapes.

Any of this sound familiar? The parallels with the first decades of Adolf Hitler's adult life are uncanny. There was a time when Hitler was just a thug in a uniform with a handful of nasty friends. Would that somebody had ridiculed and shut him down then. Perhaps he too might have slunk off to the outback somewhere and "retired."

I have never looked into the eyes of Adolf Hitler. But I have, on numerous occasions, looked into the eyes of David Duke, the Nazi from New Orleans who left the Ku Klux Klan to form the National Association for the Advancement of White People, NAAWP. For some twenty years I've been fighting David Duke with a personal fervor. Why that particular hate merchant? Because the first time I looked into his eyes was the first time I believed there could be such a thing as the devil, some form of evil incarnate.

I'm not much on organized religion, and I don't spend much time on the concepts of a heaven or hell, angels or devils. But this I know: David Duke's cosmic evil is so palpable, it oozes out of his boyishly handsome face, with his blue eyes and that well-groomed blond hair and perfectly modulated intelligent-seeming words from warped white-speak lips.

I now know that David Duke is not alone. I have seen the devil for the second time in my admittedly worldly life. I saw the evil incarnate in the eyes of Mark Fuhrman in Department 103 for six days. What must always be remembered about monsters of the likes of Hitler, Duke, and Fuhrman is that what makes them dangerous is also the thing that most often causes people to underestimate their effectiveness. They are first and foremost cowards, weak in character and self-esteem, pitiful when caught in the light alone. To ask how such men can be taken seriously is perhaps the most dangerous question of all.

❖

ACTUALLY, JOHNNIE COCHRAN didn't write the part of his final argument about Hitler. A Jew did. A Jew who lost his whole family in Hitler's death camps. His name is Chuck Lindner, one of the most respected defense attorneys in Los Angeles. A bit of a quixotic iconoclast, Chuck is known for his literary acumen as well as his windmill jousting and courtroom skills.

Chuck had been a consultant to the Simpson defense team at different times throughout the case, but at the end, when Johnnie believed he and Barry needed to hit the long ball with their closing arguments to win decisively, to avoid the dreaded hung jury and mistrial, Chuck Lindner was brought back in.

"The judge wouldn't let the jury hear just how bad this really evil man is," Chuck remembers. "From his own mouth, no less. So I wanted to find a way for Johnnie, with word pictures, to fill in the visceral gaps the jury had with Fuhrman. How do you paint complete evil, the kind of evil that says it wished it could kill every black person in America and then burn them—just what he said on the tapes—how do you make a jury understand the level of hatred and evil we're talking about with Fuhrman?

"I thought about what absolute evil was in my life, in my world. There's no question. It was Hitler and the Holocaust. Then I saw the parallel between the two. So I wrote it that way. Johnnie did the rest."

❖

J OHNNIE'S CLOSING ARGUMENT—was it jury nullification? Coming from a place where jury nullification was basically the law of the land from the end of Reconstruction to the end of Jim Crow, I have something to say on that question. For almost ninety years, jury nullification was an all-white criminal justice system reinforced by an all-white jury pool. Prosecutors didn't need to ask jurors to send a "message" in certain cases—that is, race cases. The message was the method, and it got sent every day in every way. That's why it took twenty-nine years and another generation to right the wrong of the rubber-stamped all-white verdict of acquittal for the *known*, bragging murderer of Medgar Evers.

Also, way back then, just a few miles from my house, a young man not much older than myself was nullified long before a jury could do it. For looking the wrong way at a white lady, he was tortured and murdered and his weighted-down remains dumped into the river. It was *officially* said, "The dumb nigger, he stole more chains than he could swim with."

But then two wrongs can't make anything right. The sins of the father can never be repaid by his sons, and society can't work if it keeps forever trying to. Jury nullification, however, is not just a race thing, despite what many pundits would have us believe. The send-a-message closing argument formula is one that is taught in law schools across this nation. In my experience, I've heard the send-a-message jury oration most often from prosecutors, usually in cases involving current hot-button issues. "Send the message that we're sick and tired of (*fill-in-blank*) in our neighborhoods, in our streets," et cetera, et cetera.

Having said all this, I must now say that the closing argument I heard and saw Johnnie deliver in Department 103 was *not* jury nullification. Yes, Johnnie's sermon was a version of the send-a-message form of closing argument, but the message was to send it in *this* case. Particularly with his gestures, it was clear to me that Johnnie was saying send Phil Vannatter, Mark Fuhrman, and Marcia Clark & Company the message that they can't do what they did with the evidence against O. J. Simpson and expect a jury to convict.

I grew up hearing Southern Baptist revival preachers, and Johnnie Cochran is pretty damn good—forget what that posturing Yankee Bugliosi says; he wouldn't know a downhome covered-dish revival from a crawfish boil. Revival preaching is an art form meant to move and shake you into either falling on your knees or rushing toward the pulpit begging to be saved. You're overcome with the spirit of the Holy Ghost. This is an art form most of the best trial lawyers emulate to one degree or another, defense attorneys and prosecutors alike. They damn sure want to move a jury to an apotheosis of righteousness that they hope will carry over into deliberation.

Fact is, Chris Darden used a somewhat more modern variety of stump preaching during *his* closing argument. He just wasn't quite as effective as Johnnie. Perhaps the difference is best explained by an old Mississippi joke: The difference between a Northern Baptist and a Southern Baptist is that a Northern Baptist says, "There ain't no Hell," and a Southern Baptist says, "Th' hell they ain't!"

Perhaps Chris has gotten just too much Yankee in him since his family left the South a generation ago. Regardless, Johnnie Cochran, whose family also migrated west from Louisiana, same as Chris's, to this courtroom observer, was not guilty of jury nullification, just some damn fine *preaching*. A little long, perhaps; but I was always more interested in the doughnuts at revivals, not the sermons.

❖

TWO MONTHS BEFORE closing arguments, Dr. Mark Goulston told Marcia Clark, "You should end with playing the 911 tapes. You want to haunt the jurors. And what's going to haunt the jurors? They've heard enough of your voices. They've seen enough DNA. What would be more haunting than the 911 tapes, Nicole's voice saying, 'It's O. J. Simpson, I think *you know who he is. . . .* ' "

Of course Marcia used it. That closing montage of the two 911 tapes edited together, playing in otherwise dead silence while the horrific, ugly, and sometimes poignant visuals slowly flicked by on the screen, was the only really effective part of Marcia's closing. It had all of us close to tears. I remember thinking maybe that alone could alter whatever verdict was forthcoming. Naturally, Marcia took full credit for the idea.

❖

THERE WAS NO question among a small number of us from the beginning that the letter accusing juror Francine Florio-Bunten's husband of contacting a Los Angeles literary agency about a book deal while she was sequestered was a fake. We also knew it came from the direction of the defense camp.

I cannot identify with journalistic certainty the individual I believe responsible for the letter. I can only say that shortly before it popped onto Ito's lap, a Simpson hanger-on and erstwhile journalist with a bogus press pass, whom folks tolerated because he seemed harmless enough, handed me another one of his badly typed "news releases." This one was about a juror looking for a book deal; that juror was Francine Florio-Bunten.

I can say with journalistic certainty, however, that the defense attorneys themselves had no knowledge of it. I can also say with the same certainty that the person most often mentioned as the culprit, Pat McKenna, did not do it.

It is, to be sure, a very serious matter. And not just because Ms. Florio-Bunten—who was dismissed by Ito without any inquiry—after the trial was over said she would have held out for a conviction. Whether it affected the outcome of the trial or

not, the fake letter was a crime almost immeasurable in its potential danger if such behavior is widespread in the system. I do
not believe it is widespread, if only because so few defendants
have the money to pay for such malfeasance, or as is almost
surely the case here, the fame to have it done for free.

However, the question of jury tampering in the Simpson
trial goes far beyond Francine Florio-Bunten. Indeed, one of the
real reasons she was bounced was because Ito lost count of his
chits in the tit-for-tat lopping off of ten jurors in one case!

On more than one occasion bouncing jurors, Ito would after
the fact realize he'd made a wrong call out of haste. Then, like
a bad baseball umpire who tries to compensate for a bad call by
making another one, he would trade off with the defense and
prosecution. In this case, it was one Florio-Bunten for Willie
Craven and Jeannette Harris, with Farron Chavarria the player
to be named (dismissed, that is) later—and she was.

But the more basic problem was the concept of investigating
sitting jurors to begin with. Because of the Simpson trial, most folks
in America probably think it happens all the time. It does not. In
the relatively rare occasion where jurors are dismissed for misconduct, it is usually something that comes up spontaneously and is
then looked into and dealt with. In the Simpson case, within hours
of the swearing in of the first twelve jurors, investigators for both
sides were actively initiating investigations into the most minute
details of each juror's life. People have gotten U.S. government
top-secret security clearances from the FBI with less digging into
their private life than the Simpson jurors were subjected to. And as
far as the digging went, it was the prosecution that delivered the
first punch in the ten-round fight to the finish.

If one looks at the record, the score on jurors whacked is:
Prosecution 5, Defense 4, Court 1. (Of the ten jurors dismissed,
one was a no-brainer for everybody—the young lady in question
was having a nervous breakdown right in front of our eyes.)

It could be said that this fooling around with jurors, this

affront to the system, cut both ways. Both sides must be con-
demned for it. Ito no less, perhaps more, for allowing it to continue for so long.

Ito is, I will dare to say, also guilty of another form of jury
tampering, of the prior-restraint kind. He immediately bounced
for cause virtually everyone who admitted regularly reading a
newspaper or a news magazine, or watching real news programs
on TV. By doing so, he effectively banished before the fact
jurors who, one would think, would have the diversity of life
experiences and general knowledge desirable in jurors in a first-
degree double-murder trial.

The thing that made all the jury skulduggery in the Simpson
case possible was the fact of sequestration itself.

At the beginning of the case, I believed that full sequestration was the proper choice; if any case called for sequestration,
then the Simpson trial surely did. I am no longer of such a mind.
I now believe sequestration must almost never be used, and then
only for short, albeit intense, trials. Sequestration is an unnat-
ural existence. At the end of long sequestrations, the jurors are
not the same people they were when they were selected to serve.
A group or team or unity mentality sets in and in the end is an
obstacle to debate: Who wants to argue with someone they've
come to feel as close a bond with as men do in long stretches
of combat?

No. Let jurors live and sleep and read and watch TV at
home. I truly believe now that abstract legal guilt and common-
sense justice will be at least as well served by it—as well as a
whole lot cheaper and less tempting to tamper with.

❖

I'M OFTEN ASKED what I think about Bob Shapiro's immediately distancing himself from the rest of the defense team
upon the end of the trial. In fact, he had set the process in

motion earlier, committing to a Barbara Walters interview to be taped immediately after the reading of the verdicts.

My answer is not as short as I would've liked it to be. I got to know Bob Shapiro earlier than I did Johnnie Cochran and the other principal players on the defense team. I first spoke to Bob not long after O.J.'s arraignment. Because of my relationship with Dr. Lee, and the subject matter of my book *Blood Will Tell*, Bob and I had cause to talk on the telephone regarding a television show Dr. Lee and I were asked to appear on.

Along with dispensing some basic information on the case, he said the most important thing, that he liked my book and talked as if he'd actually read it! After that I was hooked. The master schmoozer had a friend. And it stayed that way—even to this day. We spoke on the phone recently; he was returning my call, calling from Cleveland where he was doing a signing on his book tour.

It stayed that way even as I got to know Johnnie better and then Barry and Peter—*as well as* members of the prosecution team. It stayed that way during the time when Bob was the lonesome man out—actually at times walking down the ninth-floor hallway by himself, when before he would have been mobbed by reporters right on into the john.

Of my professional and personal relationship with Bob during these now two years since the murders, the moment I'll remember always was the night he sadly told me they'd finally had to tell O.J. they did not think they could win. They weren't going to lose, the hung jury was always there. But it did not look like they could win outright. This conversation took place during the opening weeks of the defense's case in chief, when they stumbled badly coming out of the box. They had taken serious hits to their case, but also to their jury. Willie Craven was gone. In the defense camp, he had been referred to as "the Enforcer." Someone they believed would either dig in or lead a charge as need be in deliberations. And Jeannette Harris was gone. Jo-Ellan Dimitrius had been right on her, too; she was solidly defense but she was gone.

"We can't win it, Joe," Bob had said with fatigue in his voice. "We had to tell him. He didn't like it, of course. But right now I see it nine to three for acquittal and no budge. How do you see it?"

I said, "Eight to four for acquittal."

"Yeah. . . ." Bob was tired, he was very down, and we didn't talk long that night.

But the defense came charging back.

When the verdict came in, they had won a hard fight, victory that was total and complete. An incredible come-from-behind win that in the end wasn't even close. A team of otherwise lone wolves had come together, worked and played and fought through good and bad times, and won in the Trial of the Century.

But something was wrong with the picture. The team captain wasn't there. He was off by himself at a press conference of one, disavowing the whole team's effort.

I'm sorry. I have played and coached football and baseball too long not to believe you win and you lose as a team. In moments of victory or defeat, the team is a unit. There will come the passing of time and one's views can become known later if necessary. But one man does not upstage the team in its moment.

The point is moot, anyway. Bob Shapiro put together that team and set the overall strategy for victory from the beginning. He did his job superbly. He even proved he could handle himself as a trial lawyer. If he feels the need to distance himself from his role in history, I can understand it; giving in to it I cannot.

21

CLOSING ARGUMENTS

I CAN ONLY ASSUME that most white folks went to make a ham sandwich when Judge Ito read the jury its instructions. Particularly when he told the jury what they may do with testimony they believe came from a witness who had been proven to lie about a material fact from the witness stand: "False in one . . . false in all."

If the Simpson jury determined that the four principal investigating LAPD detectives lied to them, isn't that almost by definition reasonable doubt?

❖

THERE IS AN aspect of the trial and verdict that many people may not be aware of. In a totally circumstantial-evidence case, as the Simpson murder trial was—no eyewitness, no confession, no murder weapon, no direct evidence (DNA, unlike fingerprints, is not considered direct evidence in a number of states, California being one)—the standard of proof the State must meet is *not* just beyond a reasonable doubt.

While each state uses varying legalese to express the concept, it can be commonly expressed thus: Not only must the

State prove each and every legally prescribed element of the crime beyond a reasonable doubt, the State's case must also *exclude all reasonable hypotheses of innocence.* In other words, if there is even *one* theory or scenario, presented by the defense and supported by evidence from the witness stand, under which the crime could have been committed that reasonably tends to exculpate the defendant, then the benefit of doubt *must* accrue to the accused. A verdict of not guilty must be returned. That's it.

Police officers, being professional witnesses, understand this concept all too well, and they hate it. For a police officer to try to bolster a case he or she believes in with "reinforced evidence" is not, therefore, all that infrequent in police departments everywhere.

❖

DR. MARK GOULSTON, like many other learned folks, is now beginning to question if the words "beyond a reasonable doubt" are indeed appropriate in today's courtrooms.

"One of the problems is that we are all prone to doubt in our current society. You're foolish to *not* doubt. And so it takes very little to create doubt in reasonable minds. You can manufacture doubt because people are so suggestible today.

"This was one of my faxes. It said,

For instance, you can say to people:
Is the sun going to rise tomorrow?
Oh, yeah.
Oh, so you're saying you can predict the future?
I didn't say I could predict the future.
No. But you're certain the sun will rise tomorrow?
Yeah.
So you're saying you predict the future?

No, no. I never said that.

So how do you know absolutely for certain it's going to rise tomorrow if you can't predict the future?

Well, because it rose yesterday.

I understand that. But how do you know it's going to rise to-morrow?

Well, I guess I don't.

"So I am saying you can create and manufacture doubt in people. Because there's nothing we believe in. You can't believe in marriage, people get divorced. You can't believe in church, the priests molest kids. You can't believe in the government, you've got Watergate. Everything today is geared toward not believing. We look for reasons to not believe. We look for rea-sons to distrust so that we don't get taken advantage of. We don't look for reasons to trust anymore."

❖

"IT'S SUCH A dangerous thing that Garcetti has done with the polarization, with the spinning, and everything," Peter Boz-anich is saying in his assistant DA's office in Compton. I am with him as his younger deputy DAs bring in problem cases and he dispenses advice and often quick justice for cases that never go before a jury.

"As an experienced lawyer, who's tried a lot of cases, I see it was a reasonable-doubt case. But the media, I think, decided it's more of a story to polarize the races than to say the DA dropped the ball. That's a more sexy sort of story. And that's real unfortunate. People take up the spin from what they see in the media. Simpson is accurate when he says the media has been biased against him. There is no question of that. Oh, there is no question of that. Maybe they should be; I'm not saying that they should not be. But they sure should criticize Garcetti. And they sure should criticize some of the efforts put forth by the prosecution team. But they don't.

"In the final analysis," Bozanich continues quietly, "I think Simpson killed these people. But because he was acquitted doesn't mean the system failed. Both sides got a fair crack at bat, put on the evidence, and the jury decided to find him to be acquitted. Does that mean that justice wasn't done? I'm unclear, *because that's the system that we have.* There are people that are acquitted every single day. Like here in this particular courthouse it happens more often than I'd like to accept—but that's the system. So do you alter the system because of the O. J. Simpson case? I think some alteration will take place because of it, because people can't accept that you have to prove guilt to such a high, high standard. Maybe the public cannot accept that now that they know it. They probably didn't know it before.

"It says a lot about America as far as what do we have to do with the system. Because if you want it to change because of this case, I think that's a mistake. But if we have such a things as guilt beyond a reasonable doubt to twelve purportedly impartial people, if that's the system that we have in place, that's what happened here. Those twelve people heard the evidence, followed the law, and acquitted him. And I think to accuse this jury of being kneejerk racists getting even is just a mistake. That's not what happened here. What happened here, the case was so poorly presented that the jury had to follow the instructions and acquit.

"Clearly most of us believe there's some amount of guilt involved with Simpson: Is it murder? Manslaughter? I don't know what happened, but he is the culprit; he may not be a murderer, but he's the perpetrator here. Yet if you have the system where you've got to prove it beyond a reasonable doubt, and it wasn't done, well that's what the justice system calls for. And then to criticize the jury for following the evidence and the law? The jurors didn't do anything wrong. It's really unfair."

❖

"I 'LL TELL YOU, I felt a little hurt at the end when I wasn't one of the people acknowledged when Garcetti thanked everyone," Mark Goulston tells me. He says this without rancor.

"Yet I understood it because the public's going to say, 'They have a *psychiatrist*, so there is *manipulation* going on.' And I can understand that, because there is that view."

❖

"NO ONE WILL ever know for sure unless we find two killers," Pat McKenna says. "I in my heart of hearts believe he did not do it. And I've been trying to trap this guy with little mis-statements, or see if he'd step into a little trap here and there from the first day I started talking to him. And it just gets stronger and stronger in my belief that he didn't have anything to do with it. So I've gotta go with what I find.

"For O.J. to have murdered two people, and then comport himself the way he did, just defies him being a murderer. Because, if anything, if he was that cool, calm, and collected, he would have checked behind him and in front of him. He wouldn't have left such obvious evidence. He would've got on the plane. He would've gone to Chicago; when he got there he probably would've checked in at the hotel to see if he's got any messages. He probably would've called back home under the pretense of seeing if Arnelle got home from the movies okay. He would've wanted to know how close they were be-hind him."

❖

To ME IT is beyond interesting—it's incomprehensible—that more national hatred is reserved for O. J. Simpson than for McVeigh and Nichols who blew up the Oklahoma City Federal Building, shredding 168 men, women, and children. Those rabid animals' names aren't attached to the obscenity-laced vitriol heard in conversations in every corner or crag of this land anywhere nearly as often as O.J.'s is. Still. Even now as it approaches a year since the verdict. The vituperative volume of noise spit out in Simpson's name is, like everything else connected with the case, unprecedented.

Perhaps I'm missing something here, but don't folks know that guilty dangerous felons go scot-free every day in America? Many victims get no vengeance or what we imagine to be justice. There are too many grieving loved ones of murder victims who have to live with the knowledge that the murderer of their flesh and blood will never be punished. And these killers are usually multiple offenders, socially lost elements of hardcore criminality who will prey upon society until they are caught and put away. But folks are not screaming about them. No, they're screaming at a rare decibel level about O. J. Simpson. Why?

Thousands of murdered Bosnians can't get more than an afterthought in America's daily discourse, but O. J. Simpson smiling on the golf course can start and end almost all conversation. Why? Even if he *is* the double murderer in this crime of passion, O. J. Simpson is no more of a danger to society now than any other John Q. Citizen—the chances of his ever killing anyone else are statistically all but nonexistent. So why?

Two genocidal monsters in Bosnia thumb their noses at justice and most folks in America can't pronounce or spell their names. But "O.J."? Those two letters spell fighting words if you're in the wrong company. Try "Johnnie Cochran." Best know the lay of the crowd before using those syllables. I have the physical scars to prove it. Tell me why?

Perhaps that's the most important—and some would say the only—mystery of the Simpson murder case. That mystery *must* be solved.

❖

IT HAS OCCURRED to me that if the Los Angeles Police Department and the District Attorney's Office are so absolutely certain the verdict in the Simpson trial was a miscarriage of justice and that O.J. is the double murderer, there is something they can do about it.

Forget the civil case. That's about money. If you want justice, and you believe O. J. Simpson got away with murder, then investigate and prosecute whoever helped him. If you know this case, you know that, realistically, *if* O. J. Simpson is the killer he had help. Period. Somebody, somewhere knows about missing bloody clothes and a murder weapon. Somebody is a loathsome human being. Somebody *else* is guilty of some kind of murder.

Depending on the state and the circumstances, that person can be guilty of being a principal to murder, an accomplice to murder, an accessory after the fact to murder, aiding and abetting a murder, and a number of other charges. These crimes carry sentences from ten or twenty years to life in prison.

These are substantial crimes with heavy consequences. If you really believe what you say, Gil Garcetti, indict and prosecute whoever helped O.J. Send *that* message.

Or shut up.

ACKNOWLEDGMENTS

SINCE VERY FEW things about the Trial of the Century were succinct, it should be no surprise that thanking all of the people who helped make this work possible is not a small task. One caveat, please: If I leave anyone out who should be here, it is almost surely because I either do not remember a last name or know how to spell it. We will go by categories, and the individuals are listed in no particular order.

From the Los Angeles District Attorney's Office and the Simpson prosecution team I wish to thank: Rockne Harmon, George "Woody" Clarke, Peter Bozanich, Lucienne Coleman, Hank Goldberg, Bill Hodgman, Mike Montagna, Jim Grodin, Larry Longo, Dr. Mark Goulston, and all the others who requested anonymity.

From the Simpson defense team I wish to thank: Johnnie Cochran, Robert Shapiro, Barry Scheck, Peter Neufeld, Carl Douglas, Robert Blasier, Dean Gerald Uelmen, Sean Chapman, Jo-Ellan Dimitrius, Larry Schiller, Bill Pavelic, and expert witnesses Dr. Michael Baden and Herbert MacDonell.

From the Superior Court of Los Angeles I wish to thank Jerrianne Hayslett, Deidre Robertson, and Judge Lance A. Ito.

From the private legal sector I wish to thank attorneys Chuck Lindner, Donald Wager, Burton Katz, Kelli Sager, Doug Mirell, Stan Goldman, Al LeBlanc, Luke McKissack, Laurie Levenson, Manny Medrano, and all the others who requested anonymity.

From the Los Angeles Sheriff's Office I wish to thank Fidel Gonzalez and John Castro.

From the Los Angeles Police Department I wish to thank

Detective Tom Lange and all the others who requested anonymity.

The media. In an event such as the O.J. Simpson trial, there is a fluid mass of knowledge that is constantly added to by every journalist who works the story firsthand, even if briefly or sporadically; the informed questions and answers from national correspondents and news superstars were appreciated. I'd like to thank Stone Phillips, Diane Sawyer, Barbara Walters, Katie Couric, Geraldo Rivera, Art Harris, Charles Feldman, Kathleen Sullivan, Gil Gross, Erin Moriarty, Gerry Grant, Wally Kennedy, and Jerry Bowen.

Then there were the full-time residents of Camp OJ, a small city of television, print, and radio personnel who reported every facet of the Trial of the Century to America and to the world every day for almost a year and a half—the permanent Simpson press corps, the family we became. I cannot mention even most; Camp OJ consisted of hundreds of people at different times in the trial. The following are only some of the wonderful people with whom I daily shared knowledge, gossip, tedium, excitement, and occasional burnout: Bill Whitaker, Fred Graham, Dana Adams, Sandra Hughes, Myra Ming, Jim Moret, Courtney Bullock, David Goldstein, Marta Waller, Kathy Braidhill, Gregg Jarrett, Jeff Anton, Laura Mecoy, James Zoltak, Jessica Seigel, Sally Ann Stewart, Ron Olsen, John North, Bill Robles, Joan Adams, Chris Bancroft, Dan Abrahamson, Haywood Galbreath, Barbara Pierce, Harvey Levin, Ken Noble, Elaine Lafferty, Kristin Jeanette-Myers, Tim Rutten, Joan Adams, Michael Fleeman, Matt Krasnowski, Bridget Baiss, Shoreen Maghame, Furnell Chapman, Jackie Markham, Carlota Espinosa, Chris Cahan, Ann Toler, and Dennis Schotzman.

Within the family there are people for whom thank you can never be adequate, but it's a start: Michelle Caruso, Joe McGinniss, Dominick Dunne, Bill Boyarski, Gerry Spence, Joe Demma, Henry Weinstein, David Margolick, Dan Whitcomb,

Janet Gilmore, James Willwerth, Michael Harris, Linda Deutsch, Cynthia McFadden, Andrea Ford, Shirley Perlman, Jose Ubaldo, and Rebecca Liss.

Then there are those whose contributions transcend this one book. Dr. Henry Lee, Peter Bloch, Liza Dawson, Elmer Luke, Giulia Melucci, Pat McKenna, Nancy Trichter, Sid Cotlar, Les Abel, Mike Sullivan, Roger Friedman, Grace McQuade, Suzanne Oaks, David Feldman, Jack Olsen, Janet Tegley, Ron Calamia, Patrick Weathers, David Sheffield, Cynthia Walker, Joey Adams, Cabot Laroux, Buddy Sheffield, M. C. Gainey, Elvin and Samara Whitesides, Ken Gaines, Mary Turner, Eddie Baytos, Michael Simmons, Edie McClurg, Laddy Sartin, Richie Montgomery, Sandy Dugas, Sal Marquez, Diane Behrens, Pearl Bosco, Sylvia Bosco, Wilma Bosco . . . and of course, now and forever, my son, Joe, and my wife, Linda, *thank you*.